Praise for *Making Hope Happen*

"In *Making Hope Happen*, Shane Lopez shares inspiring and compelling stories of real people—parents, educators, entrepreneurs, youth and seniors, citizens and leaders—whose lives are transformed through hope, and how this transforms the lives of others."

—Deepak Chopra, coauthor of *Super Brain*

"The world's leading expert on the psychology of hope shows us people who have succeeded because they had hope, and how we can create hope in our own lives to help ourselves and our world."

—Ed Diener, author of *Happiness: Unlocking the Mysteries of Psychological Wealth*

Create the Future You Want
for Yourself and Others

———————

MAKING
HOPE
HAPPEN

———————

Shane J. Lopez, Ph.D.

ATRIA BOOKS

New York London Toronto Sydney New Delhi

ATRIA BOOKS

A Division of Simon & Schuster, Inc.
1230 Avenue of the Americas
New York, NY 10020

First Atria Books hardcover edition March 2013

ATRIA BOOKS and colophon are trademarks of Simon & Schuster, Inc.

For information about special discounts for bulk purchases, please contact Simon
& Schuster Special Sales at 1-866-506-1949 or business@simonandschuster.com.

The Simon & Schuster Speakers Bureau can bring authors to your live event.
For more information or to book an event contact the Simon & Schuster Speakers
Bureau at 1-866-248-3049 or visit our website at www.simonspeakers.com.

Book design by Ellen R. Sasahara

Manufactured in the United States of America

10   9   8   7   6   5   4   3   2   1

Library of Congress Cataloging-in-Publication Data

Lopez, Shane J.
Making hope happen : create the future you want for yourself and others /
Shane J. Lopez.
p. cm.
Includes bibliographical references and index.
1. Hope. 2. Positive psychology. 3. Well-being. I. Title.
BF204.6.L67 2013
158—dc23
2012037272

ISBN 978-1-4516-6622-9
ISBN 978-1-4516-6627-4 (ebook)

To the woman who makes my life beautiful.
Alli, you say you were my first hope student,
but I think I was yours.

In memory of Rick.
I interpreted your promise of a lifetime
of mentoring to mean my lifetime.

A Note from the Author

All of the stories in this book are true. Names, personal characteristics, and settings have been changed to protect the privacy of clients, students, friends, family members, acquaintances. (When first and last names are used, identities have not been altered.) Any resulting resemblance to other persons, living or dead, is coincidental and unintentional.

Contents

Contents

CREATING A NETWORK OF HOPE

THINKING ABOUT THE FUTURE

Chapter 1

What the Man with No Future
Taught Me About Hope

I T WAS the fall of 1997 and I was starting my final year of clinical
training at the Eisenhower VA Medical Center in Leavenworth,
Kansas, trying to get good at using psychotherapy to treat depression
in veterans of all ages. My primary rotation was in the Mental Health
Clinic.

The clinic itself was cast in the image of its director, an old-school
military psychiatrist named Dr. Theodore McNutt. McNutt's white
coat was a bit yellowed, but perfectly pressed with lots of starch, and
he walked with a posture that suggested his clothes could crack at any
moment. During my time in the clinic, Dr. McNutt had thrown me several softballs. Most of the veterans he had sent my way had needed little
more than someone to talk to plus a few new techniques for managing
sadness and stress. McNutt had a way of making me feel like a part of
the treatment team without overwhelming me.

One morning, I heard McNutt's black wingtips coming purposefully down the corridor. He walked right into my office, looking very

serious and dispensing with his typical formalities, and sat in the chair reserved for patients.

"There's a man in the lobby who just got some bad news. He needs someone to talk to." So far, it was a typical McNutt referral—a guy needing some support and a little bit of cognitive therapy. "There's more. He is acutely suicidal. He said he'll shoot himself as soon as he gets home. I'd rather not hospitalize him. It's just not a good option for this veteran. The inpatient psychiatric ward would scare the hell out of him—you know what inpatient is like—and probably make him more desperate. So he has to go home today, but he can't be a threat to himself. I will go get him."

Go get him? What? Now? Wait! Dr. McNutt had no time for questions and had already turned on his heels and was double-timing it to his office.

The vet who had just received the bad news was John, a full-bodied sixty-three-year-old veteran of the Korean War who had spent his life both before and after his years of military service in the cornfields of Kansas. Dr. McNutt escorted him and Paula, John's wife, a short, sturdy woman with tired eyes, into my office. John sat silent and stared at the floor while the three of us quickly recapped the day's events. Pragmatic from his silver flattop to his brown cowboy boots, John had never before seen a psychiatrist or a psychologist; he had never needed to.

But early that morning, John had come to the hospital complaining of fatigue and high blood pressure. He'd seen the physician, taken a bunch of tests, and then waited for the results, thinking he would just have to up his blood pressure medication. He merely wanted the new script and his discharge papers. He was ready to go back to work.

After reviewing John's test results, however, the young VA doc had an unexpected diagnosis that he had to give John. He tried the "bad news, good news" approach: "John, the bad news is that your kidneys are failing. The good news is that you can live a relatively normal life with the help of dialysis."

Paula said that John had handled this revelation well, initially—

until the physician had described the treatment regimen. "The closest dialysis center is about an hour and a half away from you. You will need to go there three times a week. Plan on being there mid-morning. You can be done by lunch, and you'll have the afternoon to rest."

That's when John started to lose it, Paula said. His first question was "Doc, how will I run my farm?" The doctor groped for an answer and came back with his own question: "Can someone else do it for you?"

To John, the diagnosis plus dialysis equaled a death sentence . . . for his farm. The internist made it clear that John could not run the farm while on dialysis, so that treatment option did not make sense. But not getting treated would also leave him too sick to work his fields.

So John was trapped:

Get kidney treatment, lose the farm.

Don't get treatment, lose the farm.

John saw himself as a man with no future.

When John said the word *suicide* out loud, the internist sent him and Paula straight to the Mental Health Clinic. By the time they were shuttled over, John had mapped out a plan. He was going home to shoot himself. "I want to die. I will kill myself," he said. And we all believed that he would.

A strong John Wayne type, he seemed like someone who would never give up. In fact, there was nothing in John's past that suggested he would react this way. He was a survivor—he had already made it through a war, a big recession that hit his farm hard, and the summer floods of 1993, which turned his fields into a giant lake. For decades, nothing could knock this man down. But now, as he faced the idea of losing his beloved farm and the future he had worked for his entire life, John had given up on living.

When the full story was told in my office, Dr. McNutt said, "John, you are going home tonight. Shane here will see that you are safe." McNutt patted me on the back extra hard and walked out of the room.

Fortunately, after a few hours, a few of my clinical techniques did work enough to stabilize John on that first day, and he got to the point where he was no longer a danger to himself. Though still entertaining suicidal thoughts, he shook hands with me on a deal that he would not act on those thoughts. We made sure that he had a safe home to return to and plenty of support once he got there. With the help of his family and friends, recruited by Paula with just a few phone calls, all of his guns were removed from their home. Paula, an amazingly strong woman, took responsibility for seeing that John made it through the night.

But after they left, I was confronted by my own sense of helplessness. None of my training had prepared me for this situation. How could I help a person who was so utterly hopeless? In a just a few hours' time, the strongest of men—a battle-hardened Marine—had simply given up on the future and on his life. Could something that broken be fixed?

I had no answers. Once home, I grabbed a beer and then started trying to think of a plan. After an hour or two, I reached for another beer and a book, *The Psychology of Hope,* written by one of my graduate school professors, Rick Snyder. Rick talked about hope as a life-sustaining force that is rooted in our relationship with the future. He wrote, "Just as our ancestors did, today we think about getting from where we are now, let's call it Point A, to where we want to be, say Point B."

John had lost his way, his Point B. He needed new strategies for getting to his old goals, or he needed a new Point B.

The next day, John returned to the clinic with less intense suicidal thoughts and with a question: "So, Doc, what's my story?" After fumbling a bit, I realized what he was asking. John needed a way to explain his illness to the "boys at the coffee shop" (his fellow farmers), to his family, and, most of all, to himself. He wanted to know how to talk about being sick, going to treatment, and getting better or getting worse. He was looking for a quick, go-to response to the simple question that now seemed difficult to answer: "How are you doing?"

We spent the next two hours talking about his future. Somehow, I had to convince John that hope had helped him through hard times in the past and hope is what would help him deal with his diagnosis and treatment. All of John's thoughts about the future focused on his farm. All of his goals were wrapped up in his land. He was clear about what the farm meant to him: "Everything." He had leveraged his whole life to keep it going. Like many farmers, he owed hundreds of thousands of dollars on farm machinery. Over the previous year, the stress had gotten the better of him, and he believed that he had to work harder than ever, every day, or he would lose the equipment, the land, the house, all of it. His eighty-hour workweeks, though doable for most of his life, had worn him out.

I asked John about people who could help him out of a jam. Paula was doing everything she could, as were his friends, local farmers who were, as John described, "up to their ears with their own corn crops." Then he admitted that he had one more possibility. "Well," he said hesitantly, "there is my son, Carl." It was clearly difficult for John to discuss his relationship with Carl, which was strained. Two decades before, father and son had worked side by side, planning the farm's future. But they had stopped speaking. John couldn't remember why, but he did not see that changing, even though his life plan had always been to pass down the family farm to Carl.

That night, John went home, again under Paula's supervision. He was no longer suicidal, but he still had no Point B, no story about his future.

The following day, at the beginning of our next session, John announced, "I got it, Doc. 'I am working on it.' How about that? When people ask me how I'm doing, I tell them, 'I am working on it.'" For John, those words would help him save face in front of his friends. For me, they meant that John once again saw himself as an active participant in his own life.

"John, what's the next big job on the farm?" I asked.

"Gotta get the corn in."

Timing is everything when harvesting corn. After fifty years in the fields, John knew exactly what to do to get a good yield, weather permitting. The harvest typically involved two weeks of eighteen-hour days. But as he talked, I realized John still did not have a clear understanding of his kidney failure and his need for dialysis. The clincher came when he told me, "If I get the corn in, and the price is right, then I can take some time off for that kidney treatment."

John thought of kidney failure as a virus that could be knocked out by a course of antibiotics rather than a chronic ailment that required a lifetime of care. Nevertheless, after John and I consulted with his physicians, we all agreed that John could postpone dialysis until after he got the corn in. With the support of his docs and some cooperation from the weather, John started his one-man harvest. During that time, he occasionally visited with me in person or over the phone during his lunch breaks. And four weeks after threatening to shoot himself, John finished his harvest and sold his corn at a good price.

True to his word, John scheduled an appointment with his primary physician to begin preparing for treatment. He took a new battery of tests, and the results surprised us all. His GFR (glomerular filtration rate) was slightly improved; even though he hadn't undergone any treatment at all, his kidneys were somehow functioning *better* than they had a month before.

Feeling feisty, John tried to strike a new deal with his doctor: "How about you give me two more weeks, so that I can do some custom baling?" John was excited about his new Point B. If he could finish the hay-baling jobs around the county, he could save some money for the long winter.

Meanwhile, Paula had identified a Point B of her own—she would reconnect her husband and son. Her plan was simple. John would go out early in the morning, as always, to start baling a large field. But once he got started, he would look across the field to see another baler coming toward him from the opposite side. Although John didn't know it was going to happen, Carl showed up to do what his mother asked—to take the first step—and the two men met in the middle, in more ways than one. A father and a son reconciled, and both the family farm and the family itself were much more stable after that day.

Those sessions with John were the highlight of my training. He would breeze into the clinic, wave hello to Dr. McNutt, sit down in my office, start eating his sandwich, and tell me all the things he had done around the farm. His eyes would sparkle as he envisioned the next big thing he wanted to accomplish before he went on dialysis. Winter passed, and so did the spring. Together, father and son knocked down one big goal after another. And, somehow, contrary to all reasonable medical expectations, every month, even without treatment, John's kidney functioning either stayed the same or improved.

By the time my rotation ended, John and Carl had a long list of goals to tackle together. And John had made peace with a future that included kidney treatment (which he finally understood to be a lifetime course). He conceded, "Carl will run our farm while I get treatment." A few months later, before I left the VA at the end of my internship, I pulled up John's records one last time. The most recent note read, "Dialysis postponed again due to improved kidney functioning."

I am not telling John's story to claim that hope can cure chronic disease—although in this case his health improved along with his hope. His story challenged a tale I had been telling myself—the one about what helps people have a good life. Until then, I thought you could smart your way into a good life and out of a bad one. Turns out, smart is not enough. I was just another academic putting too much stock in passive analytical intelligence—book smarts—and too little in what makes us believe that the future will be better than the present and that we can make that future our own.

Through my work with John, I realized that how we think about the future—*how we hope*—determines how well we live our lives. John's transformations, from thriving to suffering and back to thriving, were simple and compelling. When he had clear hopes for the future, his life was good. When John had a sudden break with his future, he felt his life was not worth living. As John reconnected to a meaningful future, his life became good again, and he was excited by it. And his health mysteriously stabilized.

Since the day I met John, I have studied hope, both in my clinical work and in my research. Every client that followed John benefited from what he taught me—that our relationship with the future determines how well we live today. I asked my clients new and different questions, starting with "How hopeful are you about your future?" I changed the way I opened my first session with them. "How can I help you today?" became "If therapy is successful now, what will your life look like in five years?" I didn't see clients as broken in the way I once had; I wasn't trying to fix them anymore. I was doing everything I could to help them be better students, partners, or patients so that they could realize bigger goals in their lives.

The very week I met John, I stopped doing research on human intelligence. For a few years, I had been cranking out papers that demonstrated that IQ could be reliably measured and that it mattered and affected, somewhat, how well we did in school and at work. Until John came around, I had never really questioned the value of that research. Journal editors liked it. Other researchers cited it. It would get me tenure at a good university. So why stop? Well, John's IQ didn't—and couldn't—help him bounce back. For all his intelligence, he didn't have a clue about how to cope with the threat of losing life's meaning—his reason to get up every morning. And nothing I'd learned from my research on intelligence could actually help John—or my other clients or anyone else I knew—when he needed help the most. So I decided that intelligence is overrated. It is much discussed and celebrated, and it is somewhat important at school and in the workplace, but a high IQ is not essential to a good life. However, hope is like oxygen. As I saw then and continue to see every day, we can't live without hope.

What Lies Ahead

Since my experience at the VA clinic, I've met thousands of hopeful people around the world and followed up with some of them for years. Through my own research and Gallup polls, I have studied the hope of millions of people, including students of all ages and workers in many types of jobs. Recently, I began identifying the most hopeful individuals in schools and businesses and determining what sets them apart from others.

Although some people still believe that hope is too "soft" to study scientifically, other researchers and I have convincing evidence that hopeful thoughts and behavior propel everyone toward well-being and success; that hope underlies purpose-driven action, from showing up for school to leading organizations and communities; that it correlates positively with health and even longevity; and that it does not depend on income level or IQ. In addition, while only half the population measures high in hope, hope can be learned, and the hopeful among us play a powerful role in spreading hope to others.

Now my mission is to make hope contagious. In order to address the problems that face us, both as individuals and as a society, we need to create hope. Everywhere I go to spread this hope contagion, people are eager to learn how they can create a better future for themselves, their families, and their communities. I've presented the "hows of hope" to audiences of parents and teachers, bankers, health professionals, mayors, corporate executives, and to the toughest judges of all— middle school students. Their questions, concerns, and stories helped me shape each part of this book.

The first part of this book ("Thinking About the Future") explores the thoughts and feelings that create the unique energy of hope. Hopeful people share four key beliefs that underlie their approach to any challenge. These beliefs have a power that distinguishes hope from optimism, wishing, and other ways of viewing the future. They're also crucial to our present behavior, with immediate effects on our well-being and productivity. I'll introduce you to some of my superheroes of hope and you'll be able to take a simple test to measure your own levels of hope. I'll also take you back millions of years to explain why we humans are the only animals who hope.

The second part ("Choosing a Better Tomorrow") tests hope in tough, real-world situations and against the personal limitations most people have. You will meet mothers who took on an entrenched bureaucracy to create a better school for their children; a woman who overcame poverty, illiteracy, and abuse to realize her dream of an education; and a tech hardware start-up that flourished during the recession. I'll also explore the three core competencies—goals, agency, and pathways—that help you move beyond past and present limits and build strength and confidence for the future. And I'll take on the destructive cultural messages that undermine hope.

The third part ("Practicing the Three Hope Strategies") is a practical toolkit for building hope in your everyday life. It is also a guide for teaching the skills and habits of hope to those you care for or lead. I'll lay out step by step everything I've learned (much of it from extraordinary individuals) about how hopeful people set effective goals, plan for and deal with the obstacles in their way, and sustain motivation and progress despite setbacks and the passage of time. You'll see why the hopeful almost never "go it alone," but instead become masters at recruiting support and resources.

The final part of this book ("Creating a Network of Hope") addresses the big questions for our society. How can we help our children acquire the beliefs and skills of hope so that hope becomes a default setting in their lives—a strength they call on automatically? What effect does a hopeful leader have on his or her followers or employees, and how do organizations gain or lose hope? How can individuals, businesses, and public agencies plant the seeds of hope in their communities? My hopeful vision at the end of this book is that you will join me in creating what Robert Kennedy called "ripples of hope"—currents of change that improve not only our own lives, but those of everyone around us.

My message seems simple to me now, but it took me more than a decade to figure out:

* Hope matters.
* Hope is a choice.
* Hope can be learned.
* Hope can be shared with others.

Chapter 2

❀

Looking for Hope

I USED TO think hope was just a warm, vague feeling. It was that sense of excitement that I got before Christmas when I was a child. It lingered a while and then disappeared.

Working with John changed the way I thought about hope. When he saw himself as a man with no future, he was at best paralyzed with fear and at worst suicidal. But when he was doggedly pursuing something that mattered to him, he was full of life. That got my attention. I wanted to know more about how our thoughts about the future could affect us today.

So I became my own guinea pig. I made up some simple thought experiments to test my future thinking. For example, I tried to *not* think about the future. Go ahead. Try that for a bit. Unless you are in a deep meditative state, totally focused on a task, or sleeping, your mind goes to the future within minutes, maybe even seconds. I discovered that my mind jumps to the future even before my feet hit the floor in the morning.

I then tried to recall the first time I understood that the present and the future were connected through my behavior. As a little kid, I went to the bank with my mom every Friday to put money in our family's Christmas Club savings account. It surprised me that she was thinking about the holidays even during hot and humid Louisiana summer days.

I noticed that, like my mom with her Christmas Club, good parents invest in the future on behalf of their children. Parents purposefully or inadvertently teach their children how to think about what's coming up. They calm a child's fears by describing what happens at a doctor's appointment—and talk about the treat the child will get afterward. They take their preschooler to kindergarten roundup to foster excitement and reduce anxiety about starting school. Or they preview travel destinations through books and brochures to build anticipation for a family trip.

Sometimes parents use pointed questions to spark future thinking. "What will your grade be in physics?" one friend asked her daughter. That question got the girl talking about what was possible for her in a very challenging class. It led to a long conversation about the grade she hoped for, the steps needed to achieve it, and the role of her own effort in getting the desired outcome.

After tracking my future thinking back to my past, I started another thought experiment: I tracked advertisements that play on our tendency to think about the future. Suddenly I was noticing how marketers make every effort to associate their products and services with tangible future outcomes. Bankers, insurance agents, and money managers promise to shield us from disaster and assure us a golden retirement at a beach house or golf course.

Tracking my future thinking and those "plan for your future" media messages led to two important realizations. First, we think about the future a lot—both because it gives us an emotional boost and because other people (parents, teachers, marketers) encourage us to do so. Second, not all thoughts about the future are created equal. I wanted to examine this discovery a little more closely, so I did what I often ask my clients to do: I recorded my thoughts.

Every day for a week, in fifteen-minute stretches, I wrote down my thoughts about the future. This gave me a snapshot of my future thinking, which fell into three categories. Sometimes I was *fantasizing*: I had big thoughts that were pure fun and entertainment about a fast convertible, next summer's vacation, or retirement on the beach. These gave me a quick high—sometimes followed by a bit of a low. At other times I was *dwelling*: I hyperfocused my future thoughts on the bad things that might happen, such as struggling to get a job, taking thirty years to pay off my student loans, or never being able to retire. These made me anxious. And sometimes my thoughts balanced fantasizing and dwelling, which were exciting thoughts about my future even while I acknowledged the challenges before me. That's when I was *hoping*.

Hoping felt different than the other types of future thinking. When hoping, I felt compelled to act. Hope came along with a whole rush of plans for moving toward that future. To understand why hope had this effect on me and to learn more about *how* people hope, I called my grad school professor, Rick Snyder. A master in the classroom, Rick was at his best when talking about his favorite subject—hope. But when we met for our first one-on-one chat, I had to admit that I hadn't really bought into hope until I worked with John. This didn't faze Rick, who said, "Our clients teach us so much."

John had shown me that hope was active, not passive. And that it took hard work. Rick listened intently to my account of John's therapy sessions and then chimed in with a simple observation: "John realized that he could get there from here."

Potent Thinking About the Future

"You can get there from here." That favorite saying of Rick's has become one of mine, too. It's shorthand for a potent way of thinking about the future. "Here" is the present, which is in some way less desirable than our imagined future. "There" is the target of our longing. And "you" are the one moving yourself from here to there. We expect something from the future, and also from ourselves.

In our minds, our beliefs firm up links between ourselves and the future, priming people for hope. People do this by setting high expectations about the future (somewhat tempered by reality) and then acting on them.

The hopeful share core beliefs that set them apart from others. Two of them are:

* The future will be better than the present.
* I have the power to make it so.

The first belief comes naturally to us. The Gallup World Poll shows that the vast majority of people on the planet think their lives will be better in time. Regardless of age, most people have an optimistic bias, generally believing that tomorrow holds some promise, and that things can change for the better.

The second belief, "I have the power to make the future better than the present," requires us to see ourselves as lead actors in our life own story: we have some say in how our time on earth unfolds. This belief is learned, usually in early childhood. (Toddlers are trying it out when they insist, "Me do," and even when they say "No" to almost everything.) We hold on to this belief if we have some wins in life where we can see the link between our actions and good outcomes in school, sports, creativity, and work.

This way of thinking about the future differs from its weak cousins, such as wishing and the various kinds of unrealistic "positive thinking" that are touted in popular culture. They share a positive vision of the future, but wishing and thinking like Pollyanna don't connect us personally to that future *through our own efforts.*

Two more core beliefs that underlie hope require some mental flexibility, which comes from experience. As Rick emphasized, the way from the present to the future is seldom a straight line, and almost never a single line. We need to do some cognitive work to get from where we are now (Point A) to where we want to be (Point B). Hopeful people believe:

* There are many paths to my goals.
* None of them is free of obstacles.

The excitement we experience while pursuing our goals primes us to find pathways or routes around obstacles that stand in our way. We reinforce our capacity for hope each time we experiment with problem-solving strategies and persist until one works.

People who develop these hopeful beliefs are resourceful. They identify multiple strategies for moving toward their goals. They are realistic because they anticipate and plan for difficulties, setbacks, and disappointments. They are resilient because they know that, if one path is closed, another can be cleared.

This type of thinking about the future gives us momentum and staying power. The sustained energy we devote to our most important goals represents another crucial way in which hope parts company with plain old positive thinking.

These four core beliefs are prerequisites for hope and they prepare us to craft and pursue goals that matter to us most.

Thinking and Feeling Hopeful

Along with my thought experiments and conversations with Rick, I wanted to know what nonacademics—the people I met and worked with daily—meant when they talked about hope. I began asking friends, family, and clients. I polled the students in my psychology classes. I'd try to draw out audience members whenever I gave a talk. That's how the Head-Heart-Holy test came into being. In its current form, it goes like this:

Today we will talk about hope in your lives. Before I get started, I need to know how you make sense of this thing called hope. Here is what we are going to do. I'd like you to raise both hands, and then, on the count of three, please point to where *your* hope comes from. Given your background and all of your life experiences, where do you think hope originates . . . in your head [I point to my head]—that thinking part of you . . . in your heart [I point to my heart]—the feelings that move you . . . or from the holy [my hand makes circles above my head]—whatever you find sacred? Maybe all three, but since you only have two hands, you'll have to choose your top two. Or you can point to one place with both hands. So, on three, . . . one . . . two . . . three.

What have I learned over the years from this (admittedly unscientific) exercise? First, people don't hesitate—they each have a working theory of hope based on their experiences. And second, they inevitably look around for the people who share their brand of hope.

"Heart" almost always gets the most votes. Most people see hope primarily as an uplifting feeling that makes brief visits to our lives. But many others consider it a gift of the mind that builds on information while putting emotions on the back burner. And "holy" evokes a range of responses, from churchgoers who immediately point straight up, to those who wave their hands around a bit and speak of a higher power, of faith, of the sacred, of nature, of whatever most gives meaning and purpose to their lives.

Which way do you lean? The truth is, wherever your hands land, you can probably expand your sense of hope. As I'll try to show, feelings of hope may be ephemeral, but they strongly influence our actions. Hope also requires complex cognitive operations that incorporate emotions, not dismiss them. And hope almost always involves a leap of faith, as we move toward a future that even our best efforts can't guarantee.

We often think of hope as a sunny feeling, but it actually calls on the full range of our emotions. Hope encompasses awe, interest, joy, excitement, and even euphoria (like the hope we take away from weddings, births, spiritual awakenings, and even college basketball championships). Hope inspires us to transcend ourselves. We dream a little bigger, we aim a little higher. But the cognitive, reality-testing side of hope reminds us not to take euphoria with us when we're shopping for a home or trying to solve a serious problem. We may be lifted emotionally by a goal, but our vision may need to be tweaked many times on its way to being fulfilled.

Hope also walks hand in hand with fear, one of the most universal and most painful emotions. When fear is working for us, it reminds us of realistic limits or alerts us when we're straying from our path to a meaningful future. But fear can also hijack us. Fear gives us only three behavioral options: fight, flight, or freeze.

I sometimes describe hope as the golden mean between euphoria and fear. It is the feeling where transcendence meets reason and caution meets passion. This interplay between hopeful thoughts and feelings is dance-like. Thoughts react to feelings and feelings respond to thoughts. As I'll describe in chapter 3, we use our big brains to integrate our thoughts and feelings about the future with the experiences of a lifetime. We draw on our memories of the most hopeful people we know, of our own hopeful pursuits, and of our successes at getting out of tight spots in the past. These thoughts and feelings may help us see pathways where others see brick walls. We persevere when others give up; we work harder when it would be easier to quit. And the whole time, we are carried along on a current of energy to a better place in the future.

I'm going to pull these ideas together with a story you probably remember from childhood. It's Aesop's fable about an ant and a grasshopper sharing a corner of the wilderness. This is the version I like to read to my son, Parrish:

While lounging on a floating lily a carefree grasshopper puffed on a tiny harmonica. After playing a jaunty tune, he hollered to a colony of bustling ants as they filed by. "Fellas, fellas, slow down. You're working way too hard." Each ant toiled with a grain he carried from a nearby field to an underground storage room. "Come on, guys, it's a beautiful summer afternoon. Take a load off. Come dangle your busy little tootsies in the pool—or better yet, grab a partner and sashay on over. I'm just getting warmed up! Besides, all your marching is messing up my rhythm!"

One serious little ant stepped out of line. "We are gathering food for winter, sir, and if you don't mind a little friendly advice, I suggest you do the same." And, without another word, he balanced a kernel on his head and shuffled back to the procession.

You may recall how the standard version works out: the pleasure-loving grasshopper starves to death and the prudent, hardworking ant survives, snug in his winter nest. But here is the revised ending I read to Parrish, starting with a proposal from the grasshopper:

"Well, little fella, how about we work together? I will play some more tunes to lighten the mood and make your work go faster. Any talented musicians in your crew?"

Throughout the day, music played and insects worked. The grasshopper soloed while the ant worked hard with his friends and then a five-ant band played while the grasshopper followed his serious little ant buddies in collecting food for winter.

When we're hopeful, our ideas and feelings about the future work together. Our thoughts look ahead and tell us what we need to do today to get where we want to go. Our feelings lift us up and give us the energy to sustain our effort. Hope is the work of the heart and the head. Hope happens when our rational selves meet our emotional selves.

That's the moral of the story I want to tell, and it's also the secret of the most hopeful people in the world.

Choosing Hope

Jerome Groopman, M.D. lived through a nightmare of chronic pain. A running injury followed by failed back surgery led to nineteen years of severe disability, to the point where Groopman monitored every movement to avoid "the electrified fence" of searing pain. And as he says in his book *The Anatomy of Hope,* "Along with unpredictable pain came its companion, a sense of prevailing fear."

Everything Groopman tried made things worse, until a colleague referred him to a specialist who made a startling claim: his pain was not from permanent injury but rather from lack of use. An intensive program of physical therapy could restore his mobility, the doctor explained. He could live a normal life again. But it would require months of pushing through the pain he would experience when his atrophied muscles were forced to move.

As Groopman faced this choice, he realized that he had "completely abandoned" hope. He had no assurance other than his doctor's confidence in the program. (Past doctors, with equal reputations and equal confidence, had made his condition worse.) But this doctor had ignited a sense of possibility.

Groopman had to decide whether to take the risk. On the one hand was the promise of improvement—maybe even of regaining a "normal life." On the other was the reality of more pain and the chance of another crushing disappointment. He was up against a natural human tendency: we often fear loss even more than we desire gain.

In the face of doubt and uncertainty, Groopman thought of a future that was compelling enough to help him overcome his fears. He summoned up what he called "a dreamy vision of the future: walking hand in hand with my daughter to a pond some two miles from our home to feed ducks and search for frogs; emerging from an airplane feeling strong and ready to explore a new city; dancing a traditional Eastern European circle dance at a family wedding."

He carried this vision into his physical therapy, using it to keep going despite the pain, imagining how every small improvement brought him closer to his psychological and physical destination. Whenever he brought these special scenes to life in his mind, he felt "a current of warm, soft energy" that seemed to suffuse and soothe his body. And a little over a year later, he reports, "I awoke in the morning unafraid. . . . I felt reborn."

Consider how thoughts and feelings—the cognitive and emotional parts of hope—are intertwined in Groopman's account. He deliberately chose and crafted the images of the future that would support him most. These detailed visions were rich with emotional content—his love for his daughter, the excitement of travel, the joy of a family wedding. His hopeful thoughts shaped his decision-making, but they were more than dry, rational goals. They were aims that excited him, that were worthy of his longing.

Hope is created moment by moment through our deliberate choices. It happens when we use our thoughts and feelings to temper our aversion to loss and actively pursue what is possible. When we choose hope, we define what matters to us most.

The Hope Cycle

To attain hope, you need to create momentum. It's helpful to name the core beliefs that support the how of hope, but it's even more important to know how they work together. So I'd like to offer another way, first proposed by Rick Snyder, to understand hope in action. It combines the beliefs into a three-part process that carries us to a better future. It also describes each element of the process as a set of learnable skills. Here are the three parts:

Goals: We seek out and identify an idea of where we want to go, what we want to accomplish, who we want to be—whether tomorrow or over a lifetime. Some goals are vague or fleeting and quickly forgotten. Others are actively shaped and modified over time. Hope is built from the goals that matter most to us, that we come back to again and again, and that fill our minds with pictures of the future.

Agency: The word *agency* is shorthand for our perceived ability to shape our lives day to day. As "agents," we know we can make things happen (or stop them from happening), and we take responsibility for moving toward our goals. Over time, we develop our ability to motivate ourselves; we build our capacity for persistence and long-term effort. Agency makes us the authors of our lives.

Pathways: We seek out and identify multiple pathways to our goals, pick the most appropriate routes for our situation, and monitor our progress over time. These are the plans that carry us forward, but we're aware that obstacles can arise at any time. So we remain curious and open to finding better paths to our desired future.

For now, I just want you to visualize these elements as a continuous feedback loop. Each element can set the others in motion. Each interacts with the others in ways that can reinforce, modify, or diminish them. When each is strong, together they form a cycle that enhances hope. When even one is weak, hope diminishes until we intervene to strengthen the element that is undeveloped or faltering.

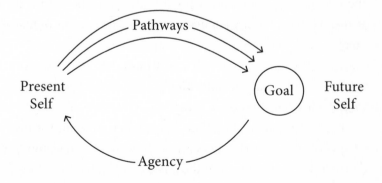

The Hope Cycle

This simple model works whatever your goals, age, or circumstances, whether you're most concerned about your family, your business, your community, or your personal development. Every example and story in this book builds on this model. But the stories also remind us that life is anything but simple, that hope has many faces, and that it flourishes in unexpected places. They also remind us about one of the most striking qualities of hope: hopeful people spread hope to almost everyone they meet.

Finding Hope in Our Lives

I can't go a day without finding hope. Maybe I cast a wider net than I used to, looking everywhere now for people in hot pursuit of what's next. Or maybe I surround myself with hopeful people, spending time around folks who are excited about the future.

Where do you find hope? Who is the most hopeful person in your life? Answering these questions and talking to the most hopeful person you know will help you firm up your own ideas about hope.

I find hope in abundance when I join my son Parrish at the playground. Watching the children play tells me a lot about hope. A child's vision transforms a series of obstacles (tall ladders, hard-to-reach monkey bars, wobbly wooden bridges) into limitless opportunities and challenges. Goals become clear ("I am going to swing across all the monkey bars"), the plan develops ("I am going to climb the ladder, grab the bar, and swing from the first one to the second one"), excitement carries them forward, though sometimes they need support ("Can you help me up?"), and all the while confidence grows ("I think I can . . . Yeah, I did it!").

But I learn most about hope as I watch hopeful people hold on to what matters in the darkest of times, and when they have major obstacles in their way. Rose Naughtin does this better than anyone I know. That's why she wins my "Most Hopeful Person" award.

The daughter of one of my former coworkers at the University of

Kansas, Rose walked into my life when she was nine years old. My wife, Alli, and Rose's mother became close friends, so I heard more and more about the beautiful little girl with the soulful blue eyes who would visit our offices and play with the toys on our desks.

Already famous in our town, Rose had undergone a heart transplant when she was only four years old. The community had rallied around her and her family, hosting fund-raisers for her treatment and checking in on her recovery. She had grown into a gentle, beloved child, with a special quality that even strangers felt. When you meet Rose, you can feel that she's an old soul.

Rose's family lived only two blocks from our house, and she enjoyed coming over to play with our miniature dachshund or just to hang out. At some point, Alli decided that Rose was her unofficial little sister. The spring before Rose was to begin junior high, she announced that she wanted her bedroom to feel more grown-up, and the two of them pored over paint chips on our dining room table, happily dreaming about Rose's teenaged room.

A few months later on a class field trip, Rose became dizzy walking up a steep hill, sat down on a curb to rest, and fainted. One of her friends, who knew about the transplant, insisted that someone call her mother, who immediately took Rose to her cardiologist. A heart monitor turned up nothing wrong, but a biopsy told a different story: Rose's heart tissues were inflamed. Rose's transplant—the second heart of her twelve-year-old life—was failing.

That beautiful late spring was a scary time. A lot of us spent weeks fearing the worst, talking around possibilities that were too frightening to discuss head-on. Rose missed the end of the school year, her parents drove her everywhere, even to our house, and her energy went downhill fast. Finally, her family got the call that a heart was available, and within minutes they were in a medevac hospital, speeding toward Children's Hospital in St. Louis.

Think of the difference between having a heart transplant at age four and again at age twelve. This time, family and the doctors prepared

Rose by explaining the procedure and giving her positive but realistic information about the future. When Rose was rolled into the operating room, she knew what she was in for and the risks involved. With the awareness of adolescence she felt both numbing fear and the strong pull of hope.

Fortunately, the surgery went fine, and Rose returned home to friends, family, and the room of her dreams—completely redecorated, and featuring a poster of her then-favorite band, the Ramones, autographed by Johnny Ramone himself. But despite another outpouring of community support, and the exhilaration of simply having survived, Rose became overwhelmed by the reality of the hard work ahead of her. The medications she needed to take in order to recover—heavy-duty painkillers and steroids—triggered serious side effects, including depression, mood swings, and weight gain. For the first time, Rose allowed herself to really cry. She now looks back on this period as "the emotionally darkest part of the experience."

For solace, Rose looked to the future. She spent hours imagining how it would be to rejoin her friends, to walk down the halls of her junior high talking about normal things, tackling the new subjects she'd signed up for. But once she got back to school, another reality hit. Some of her old friends just didn't know how to respond, and she felt separate from the other kids because nobody could understand what she'd been through.

"I was upset about a lot of things, but even then I knew it could be a lot worse," Rose now says. "Being in the ICU of a children's hospital, I'd seen people around me who were a lot worse off—sick kids, dying babies, and scared and sad families. It made me feel that my worldview was so different from other people my age—I had faced that something really bad can happen. How could I be the same after that?"

As her third heart gave her back her glow and vitality, Rose's life returned to normal, but she still felt separated from other kids, because she was on a life course of immunosuppressant medication to ensure that her body wouldn't reject her new heart.

For me, this is where the evidence of Rose's hope really shines. Rose has to take this medicine three times a day. At first, her mother monitored her meds closely. But when Rose reached high school, her mother stopped reminding her to take them. This is an especially dangerous time for teens on life-sustaining medication of any kind. They want and need independence, but their anger about being different can lead them to "blow off" the long-term consequences of noncompliance.

Rose never took her future or her health for granted. "I initially used clocks to help me remember," she recalls. "But now I don't even need them any more. And in an eight-and a-half-year period, I've probably missed only four doses." (By my calculations, that's four out of more than *nine thousand* doses.) She's also changed her perspective on her meds. "I no longer think of transplants when I take them," she told me. "I look at things in terms of health."

Today, Rose is going to college studying Hindi and working in the bakery of our town's popular food co-op. She continues to be an active collaborator with her doctors and nurses. She is vegetarian. She walks everywhere. She is in charge of her life. She is also an advocate for Midwest Transplant Network, which raises money to support organ transplants, and for Gift of Life, which takes her to high schools to share her story and encourage students to discuss organ donation with their families.

When she looks into her future, Rose sees herself married with a family, living in a new city and working in some sort of public service. "I'm still not sure exactly what I'm going to do, but I know I like to make things happen," she told me. And when she looks back at her second transplant, she says she still feels bad for that scared twelve-year-old she once was. "I want to comfort my past self and say, 'Look ahead! Everything is going to be fine.'"

Rose Naughtin and the Elements of Hope

Goals, agency, and pathways are the elements of hope that worked together for Rose in her pursuit of a healthy life.

Goals: Rose knows that she must take her medication as prescribed for her health. She links her goal of "taking medication four times a day" to her bigger goals that matter to her most. These include leading a healthy lifestyle to prevent future heart problems and having a happy family of her own.

Agency: Rose has been the beneficiary of support and love from her entire community. This support has generated a wellspring of energy and confidence that Rose puts to good use at home, school, and work. Rose likes "to make things happen" and she aims this energy at her most important goals, which keep her healthy.

Pathways: In middle school, Rose borrowed hope from her mom, who would hand-deliver her meds and remind Rose of the dose schedule each time she left the house. In her teen years, Rose set alarms to prompt her to take her pills. As a college student, she takes her medication with her wherever she goes and imagines where she will be when she needs to takes her next dose.

Putting Hope to the Test

Rose puts her hope to the test every day to keep her health in check. What about you? Do you hope at will? I constructed a brief scale to measure your current level of hope. After you complete the hope scale as directed, either on this page or at www.makinghopehappennow.com, you can go online for help understanding your scores.

Directions: Read each item carefully. Using the scale next to each item, ranging from Strongly Disagree (SD) to Strongly Agree (SA), please circle the number that best describes you.

		SD				SA
1.	My future will be better than the present.	1	2	3	4	5
2.	I have the power to make my future better.	1	2	3	4	5
3.	I am excited about at least one thing in my future.	1	2	3	4	5
4.	I see many paths to my goals.	1	2	3	4	5
5.	The paths to my important goals are free of obstacles.	1	2	3	4	5
6.	My present life circumstances are the only determinants of my future.	1	2	3	4	5
7.	My past accomplishments are the only determinants of my future.	1	2	3	4	5
8.	I make others feel excited about the future.	1	2	3	4	5
9.	I spread hope through modeling or support of others.	1	2	3	4	5
10.	I spread hope through the way I live my life.	1	2	3	4	5

Scoring

Questions 1–5: On a range from 5 to 25, where did you score? This is your Hope score. If it is below 15, it will take hard work and much practice to raise that score. If you scored 16 to 20, your hope is an asset to you every day, but there are many strategies that can help you increase it. If you scored 21 or above, you are a high-hope person whose thinking about the future is an asset.

Questions 6–7: This is your Readiness to Hope score, ranging from 2 to 10. The higher your score, the more you believe that your future is dominated by your past and present circumstances, and the less room you have for hope. Learn to expand your sense of personal freedom without denying the realistic constraints we all face. Take more control of the future.

Questions 8–10: This is your Hope Contagion score, ranging from 3 from 15. If you scored above 12, you are a model for others and consciously boost the hope of those around you. A low score suggests that you would benefit greatly from seeking out the support and companionship of high-hope people in your daily life.

Chapter 3

Nexting and Prospecting

O N OUR morning walks to his elementary school, my son Parrish and I do lots of *nexting*. We talk about his next basketball game, the next movie we'll watch, our next family trip. Nexting comes naturally to kids. It seems to pique their curiosity and give them little boosts of joy.

Nexting is my way of practicing hope with Parrish, a seven-year-old. By encouraging him to talk about the future, I find out what he is excited about. I learn about his plots and plans, and I help him come up with lots of ideas for how to make things happen. We explore his "wonderfully horrible ideas," discuss why some of his strategies may not be appropriate, and then pivot to another idea.

Talking about the next important event in Parrish's life also lets me gauge whether he is confident, nervous, joyful, fearful, or downright giddy. When he is feeling positive, his mom, Alli, and I do our best to "fluff him up" even more. We know the emotional lift helps him think about ways to make his performance better, the best it can be. When we see that he is nervous or fearful, we try to figure out why, and whether we need to intervene or let him work it out. In all this, Alli and I avoid automatic cheerleading and easy reassurances. If we see obstacles and pitfalls, we address them together, and sometimes we work with him to *regoal.*

On a good day of nexting, Parrish and I talk about his dreams, plans, and feelings, and we both enjoy practicing the how of hope. He gets better at thinking about the future, and I get more excited about what lies ahead for our family.

Hope is a miracle of the human mind, a miracle we all share. In this chapter, I want to tell you about our mind's unique capacity to think about the future, the complex language that helps us craft an evolving life story, our deep awareness that we will one day die, and the neurobiology of prospecting, all of which makes hope possible.

Hope Comes to Mind

When I was a little kid, I had two superpowers (at least I thought I did). Every morning I climbed our bathroom wall, just like Spider-Man on TV. I'd get a running start, jump as high as I could, and then try to stick to the wall. I'd frantically flail and slap against the wall to propel myself toward the ceiling. Every now and again, I got close, but never all the way up. I finally quit throwing myself against the wall when I was about ten.

My other superpower was time travel. Mentally, I traveled into the future and saw my friends and myself as older kids—riding bigger bikes, playing baseball (instead of tee-ball), and talking to girls. These images were so vivid that they helped me learn how to be a big kid. As I grew a bit older, I started imagining that I was a teenager—driving to school, competing on a bigger field, and kissing girls. This time travel superpower never let me down and got stronger as I got older.

For years, I thought I was the only person on the planet who could travel into the future. Was I wrong! *Everyone* can do it. But I don't think that makes the power any less super, because we are the only animals who think about the future in a very complex way and who act on those

34

thoughts. To understand how we got this way, we need to take a trip back in time . . .

Time Travel

The story begins 1.6 million years ago, when one of our human ancestors, *Homo erectus,* first made a simple distinction between what he needed in the present and what he needed in the future. *Standing man,* by dissociating a bit, basically uncoupled the present from the future in his mind. This cognitive leap led our kin to fashion a pear-shaped hand ax that was beautiful and effective in its symmetry and a vast improvement over the one-sided rock scrapers of old. This invention suggests that early humans saw into the future and realized that they would need tools for many jobs over time—so they invested time and energy into crafting a tool that would last. That investment paid off every time they used a hand ax to skin a mammoth or to fashion another tool.

Fast-forward 1.5 million plus years. Somewhere around one hundred thousand years ago, our cousins, *Homo neanderthalensis,* started practicing burial rituals. They dedicated a special site for the burial and seemed to carefully position the bodies. In some cases, they adorned the dead or prepared them for future battles by placing antlers or other objects, such as panther paws, in the graves. According to some archeologists, an offering of flowers was placed next to some of the corpses. These practices are an early sign that a bipedal primate thought about a future that went beyond life on earth. Future thinking transcended the earthly body, and this vision of an afterlife became a foundational belief for many of the religions that guide our behavior today.

About thirty-five thousand years ago, Neanderthals began to die out and a new animal appeared on the scene, *Homo sapiens.* With big brains characterized by frontal lobes that had grown sixfold in a short evolutionary span, *knowing man* developed imagination, the ability to symbolically represent thoughts and experiences. Later, he was able to link imagination with an increasingly refined sense of time. Eventually, we *Homo sapiens* labeled natural phenomena with minutes, hours, days, weeks, years, and decades. This combination of imagination and time sensitivity gives all humans the power of mental time travel, the capacity to think of ourselves experiencing any and all instants of the past and future.

Imagination and time sensitivity also gave us a unique evolutionary advantage, setting us apart from all other animals. According to psychology's Bischof-Köhler hypothesis, only humans can put the needs and demands of the present aside, anticipate future needs, and take action to secure them. Our hominid ancestors looked ahead and crafted new, improved, long-lasting tools. Today we stock the freezer during a sale, accrue vacation days to spend all at once, and set aside money for college and retirement. So whenever someone poses the question "What's unique about humans?" feel free to skip the traditional answers about opposable thumbs, tool use, and language, and instead answer, "Hope."

The Power of Stories

In December 1994, during a hike in the hills of southern France, Jean-Marie Chauvet noticed a draft of air coming from a cleft in the rocks. He recruited two friends and, with their help, moved heavy rock and opened a small tunnel that led into a series of chambers. With their flashlights, they saw what is now believed to be one of the first cave drawings ever made, a red ochre mammoth painted on a rock hanging from the ceiling. Subsequent trips into the caves revealed more art depicting horses galloping, rhinos battling, and hundreds of other paintings and engravings.

The thirty-thousand-year-old art in Chauvet Cave is now preserved by the French Ministry of Culture. The walls of the cave "talk" to us through humanity's oldest known drawings. All but one of the images is of animals. The exception is a Venus-like human figure, a woman swollen with fertility. On the floor are bones of all types. In one part of the cave, a cave bear skull is placed precisely in the center of a large stone, possibly serving as an altar for rituals. These scenes were created by storytellers documenting their lives and possibly their futures.

Like our French cave-painting ancestors, modern-day humans are compelled to tell stories. With the help of our complex language, we have gotten quite good at it. I learned the art of storytelling growing up in south Louisiana, where Cajun stories are a social currency and people get richer by the day. Most of the stories that my parents and their friends told at crawfish boils and family barbecues were about the good old days. Yet the stories that may be even more captivating are the ones we have only imagined.

You don't need to be a novelist or screenwriter to craft fantastic tales. We all seem to share the need to embellish day-to-day reality. Neuroscientist Tali Sharot of University College London discovered this in the course of exploring what she calls the "optimism bias," the inherent tendency of the human brain to see things in a positive light. Her study focused on the brain function of people who were asked to imagine future events in their everyday lives. She presented the most innocuous of prompts to her participants: your next haircut, a trip on public transportation, a plane ride. But her subjects made the mundane magical. A haircut became an opportunity to donate hair to Locks of Love, an organization that creates hairpieces for young people who have lost their hair to cancer treatment. A ride on a ferry became a setting for romance. The flight was the beginning of a great adventure.

Even more surprising is how creative we are about our past. "You're constantly rearranging the narrative of your life," says Antonio Damasio, a professor of neuroscience at the University of Southern California. "And you're rearranging as a function of the experiences that you have had and as what you imagine your experiences in the future ought to be." Each time we retrieve a memory, we tend to revise or edit it, adding some new elements to the story and taking away others. In time, we decide that certain stories are representative of who we are and who we want to become. We rehearse them and we may share them with others. And we look to these stories for emotional guidance.

Little by little, we choose to make our stories less hopeful or more so. Hopeful narratives steeped with meaning provide survival tools for the storyteller and for the audience gathered around the campfire. The most hopeful stories trigger positive emotions in others, making them feel lifted up, joyful, or curious, and ultimately drawing them closer to us. These positive emotions also inspire others to think more expansively about their own life stories.

Reliving previous experiences through hopeful stories also makes it likely that we will *prelive* a future experience with a hopeful bent. Right now, I am thinking about a speech I have to give to a large group of youth development experts in Omaha, Nebraska. I am preliving the event in vivid detail . . . and it is stressing me out. So I decide to relive one of my best public-speaking performances—March 2011 in Fairfax, Virginia. The story starts with my friend, Nance, telling me that I had done a great job and thanking me. She was so kind and generous in her praise; I can still see her bright smile. Then I see mental snapshots of me sharing ideas, playing a video that made the audience cry (in a good way), and giving folks a good laugh. Phew! Now I am less stressed and more positive about my yet-to-be talk in Omaha.

Reliving and preliving help shape our lives. The stories of our past don't predict the future, but they do help us find paths to where we want to go. By focusing on the what, when, and where of our experience, we can learn how to exercise the modicum of control we have over our future.

Sensing an End to the Journey

Our capacity to look over the horizon has a downside—a big one. I alluded to it when I described Neanderthal funeral rituals. Our special awareness of the future gives us the unsettling knowledge that we will one day die. I will die. You will die.

Why am I emphasizing this in a book about hope? Because genuine hope incorporates *an unvarnished assessment of all of life's limits*, including the limits of life itself. And because we can't understand hope without understanding our quest for purpose and meaning—a quest fueled by our awareness that one day our lives will end.

The promise of death was made real to me when my first and best friend, Jared, died. At six years old we had been friends for a lifetime, playing cowboys, chasing after a football, and watching cartoons. My recollections of the first day he did not feel well enough to play are sharp. My mother and I drove over to Jared's house. His mom answered the door and I bounced into the living room looking for my buddy. The moms sat down and started talking in low voices. I walked over to Jared's room and found a closed door. His mom told me he was too tired to come out. Even at six, I knew that was bad and sat quietly in a corner with Jared's toys. After a short while, my mom hugged Jared's mom and we left. I never got to play with Jared again.

My understanding of Jared's illness and death was limited, but his passing told me that I might not necessarily live to be an old man. For a while, I lost my superpower to see into the future. Why bother visiting the future if I was going to die? But weeks or months later—I can't remember how long—something shifted, and those thoughts of big-kid fun began to draw me again. And I began to chase them a little faster, just in case I was running out of time.

As our time horizons shrink, most people become increasingly selective about the goals they pursue. Dinners with close friends replace late nights at the office. Vacation with the grandchildren takes priority over a business conference. My patient John certainly knew he was mortal, but he faced his mortality only when his kidneys began to fail. When he learned that treatment could mean losing his farm, he was ready to foreclose on his future, but when he realized that he had some life left to spend, he rebuilt his relationship with his son, and the farm became a legacy they could share. When we perceive that time is short, we invest in people and in our most meaningful goals.

Facing death seems to bring us more to life.

This Is Your Brain on Hope

Before I give you a glimpse of how your brain on hope works, I'd like you to try a thought experiment: I want you to hope for something. Specifically, I want you to think of the really good job you will have about a year from now. (If you like your current job, make the new one even better—your dream job.) What would be the best way to spend your time during the week? Picture where you would be and what you would be doing. Now add details. Who is working with you? How do you feel at the beginning of the day? At the end? Give yourself a minute or two to make that image as vivid as possible. (Need help? Go to the makinghopehappennow.com website for a guided imagery that walks you through this exercise.)

I have no way of knowing what story you told yourself about your dream job, but I do know that you drew on your past experiences to imagine your future. Repeatedly and rapidly, you compared and combined pieces of your past to create something better. You pictured likable people around you (leaving behind the jerks at your old job). You thought about the resources that would make the job better (for most people, these include more pay, more freedom, and a greater sense of meaning).

You no doubt felt positive emotions when you saw yourself in your new role: maybe excitement and pride, serenity and joy, or a feeling of security. These emotions aren't just a feel-good by-product. They actually work as cognitive guides that lead you to invest in certain lines of thought and to avoid others. They help you convert general information about "good jobs" into an image of the job that would be the best fit for you. And they begin to arouse the motivation you'll need to make your dream job real.

I know all this about your thought processes, because, like all other card-carrying psychologists, I studied natural experiments of sorts that revealed how the brain worked. For example, accounts of the injuries and complicated recovery of a patient known as "KC" taught us much about how prospection, the act of looking forward, works. KC became an amnesiac after a motorcycle crash. Deprived of his past, he remained stuck in time, unable to mentally travel into the future.

Today, neuroscientists go well beyond their own observations to give us a real-time report on what is going on inside our skulls. Using technologies like functional magnetic resonance imaging (fMRI) and electroencephalography (EEG), they monitor blood flow, oxygen consumption, and electrical activity in precise areas of the brain. With that information, they can track a hopeful thought, such as landing a good job in the next year, along what I like to call the *prospection pipeline*. This is the path we take from thinking about the future to developing and executing the plans that make that future a reality. It's a trip through the unique and shared functions of relatively old and relatively new parts of our brains, all working together in incredibly complex ways.

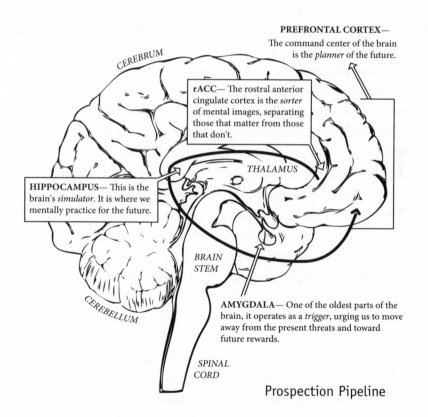

Prospection Pipeline

PREFRONTAL CORTEX— The command center of the brain is the *planner* of the future.

rACC— The rostral anterior cingulate cortex is the *sorter* of mental images, separating those that matter from those that don't.

HIPPOCAMPUS— This is the brain's *simulator*. It is where we mentally practice for the future.

AMYGDALA— One of the oldest parts of the brain, it operates as a *trigger*, urging us to move away from the present threats and toward future rewards.

CEREBRUM

THALAMUS

BRAIN STEM

CEREBELLUM

SPINAL CORD

Remembering the Past, Simulating the Future

As I discussed previously, we build our hopes from memories. To imagine a good job in the future, we can use a past job for contrast. For example, when I conducted my own "dream job" thought experiment, I didn't have to go in on Saturdays and Sundays, because I drew on the seven years of my high school and college life when I worked almost every weekend. I had a flash memory of driving to my old job on a quiet Saturday morning and used that to prospect a different future.

This work is done in a brain area called the hippocampus, two tiny seahorse-shaped structures that face each other between your temples. We take snapshots of our experiences and then move them around as needed. The most meaningful episodes, both good and bad, tend to be the ones that stick, and we gradually tie them together into an ongoing story of our lives called "autobiographical memory."

But these memories are not only our personal résumé—they also help to create the next story. You could not have formed the detailed images of your dream job or felt the emotions connected with it without images from your past. Your ability to imagine depends on your ability to remember. In some cases, we can also remember things we *imagined* in the past as vividly as actual events.

This "prospecting" function of the hippocampus is so important that some researchers now think its primary evolutionary role may have been to anticipate the future by creating simulations of what an animal might encounter. For prehistoric humans, a good memory for past dangers increased their chances of surviving similar situations in the future—and getting enough to eat by remembering where the sweetest fruits grew.

In a typical study using brain scans, research participants are asked to either recall a past event or imagine an event to occur in the next year. Once they have this image vividly in mind, they alert the researcher by pressing a button. Whether they are remembering the past or preliving the future, the hippocampus lights up. When we anticipate a new situation or are faced with a challenge, we automatically scan our memory for guidelines, and then we mentally practice how we would deal with the threats and challenges. Training in our brain's simulator is less risky than going into novel situations unprepared.

Sorting Through Images and Emotions

Okay, the dream job exercise activated your hippocampus (meaning that blood surged to bring it more oxygen and its electrical charge increased). The image of your new job expanded and became more vivid, and you essentially created a new memory, one of the future. Now the prospection pipeline leads to another brain structure, the rostral anterior cingulate cortex (or rACC). The rACC sits about an inch behind the center of your forehead, and it works with the amygdala, one of the oldest parts of the brain, a center that triggers reactions to emotions. The amygdala is best known for spurring us to act when we are threatened, but it also triggers us to act on the feelings and drives that energize our vision.

Your rACC tracks how important and meaningful each of your mental images and goals are—how much they matter to you at the moment. It helps you let go of goals that don't matter anymore or aren't in your best interests and links you to goals that warrant your resources. It pushes you to make smart choices.

This is the part of my brain that nudged me toward reality and helped me recognize that I wasn't young or talented enough to pursue one version of my dream job—shortstop for the Boston Red Sox. The rACC was also at work when Jerome Groopman was trying to figure out whether he should experiment with more treatment for the back injury that caused him so much pain. Groopman had to sort through the best- and worst-case scenarios for the future and align these scenarios with his feelings, his years-long emotional battle with pain. Only then could he choose hope.

Planning Your Next Steps

The final key station along the brain's prospection pipeline is the youngest part, the prefrontal cortex. It lights up when college students are asked to think about the courses and credits they need to graduate, when CEOs are challenged to develop and execute a vision for their company, and when you are asked to think about how you will search for that dream job. The prefrontal cortex functions as the brain's command center, carrying out the executive functions needed to convert vision to reality. It gathers and coordinates information from many other parts of the brain, develops strategies for reaching a goal, and executes the plan. It moderates the constant interplay between our emotions and our cognitive functions, and it also processes social cues from the world around us. All this is necessary for us to be able to develop and follow a course of action to the outcome we desire.

One recent study of prefrontal cortex functioning stands out for the way it reinforces the importance of hope. Suzanne Peterson, business professor at Arizona State University, used EEG technology to tap into the minds of fifty-five business and community leaders as they created visions for their organizations' future. The leaders were first given a hope test and then asked specifically to think about how their organizations would grow, how growth would align with their core values, and how they would better serve clients. The electrical activity of their brains was mapped as each individual envisioned the future; then all the maps were compared. Every executive showed prefrontal activity, but those who had previously tested low in hope showed more activity on the right side—the side associated with negative outlooks and behaviors. Those who came up with the most positive plans for the future showed more activity on the left prefrontal cortex, where prospection, our hopeful vision, becomes pathways—hope in action. Take your index finger and point to the middle of your left eyebrow. Now move your finger up about an inch. There you are.

In the prefrontal cortex, we attach ourselves to the future through a goal that matters to us. Our hopeful brain then helps us marshal and manage information that is relevant to the desired event (including recognizing any obstacles to this goal) and it produces an elevated feeling that firms up our commitment to the future and attracts others to us. Ultimately, the hopeful brain tells us to reach out for more resources and support.

Spreading Hope to Others

Hope is not just a personal resource. It's one of the most important ways we create our families, our communities, and our society. Thanks to our big frontal lobes, we humans outstrip every other species in the size and complexity of our social networks. And from the moment we're born (in some cases, even before), our brains and minds are shaped by the bonds we form with those closest to us.

Emotions are as contagious as the common cold. We often feel someone's anger or sadness or indifference even before they say a word, and our own mood shifts in response. But when we're "in sync," our motions and gestures start to mirror those of other people. Our breathing becomes coordinated and physical markers like heart rate align. We feel engaged, safe, *good*. We're attracted to hopeful people because being around them makes us more energized and hopeful ourselves.

Brain scientists can now tell us why this happens. They've begun to map systems of "mirror neurons" that appear throughout our brains. These neurons are precise mimics; they fire whenever we see someone making a movement just as if we were making the same movement ourselves. From the slightest clues, they pick up others' intentions and emotions. They also respond when we mentally rehearse an action. This instantaneous mirroring is going on all around us all the time. As little kids watching the big kids on the playground, we really were learning how to be like them. Now when we encounter people with big goals and high hope, our brains are primed to follow them.

Hope Fully

For decades the most striking object in my hometown of New Iberia, Louisiana, was a statue of the Roman emperor Hadrian. Standing seven feet tall, carved from gleaming white marble, he was magnificent, but this did not make him immune to the pranks of local teens. Many Sunday mornings, the noble emperor was adorned with vestiges of Saturday night's fun. Passing him on the way home from church, we'd conclude that Hadrian had had a great time—given the beer can in his hand and the plastic leis around his neck. After a while, I began to think of him as our town's drunk uncle. You know the type—you love him but you just don't know how he'll turn up.

Then the statue's owner, a local bank, decided to insure Hadrian in case a joke went too far. The insurance company required an appraisal. And that's when we all found out that Uncle Hadrian was a one-of-a-kind, original marble statue from ancient Greece, carved around 150 AD, and worth nearly $1 million.

I sometimes think of the Hadrian statue whenever I and other people fail to value the gifts, talents, and capacities that make us unique. It took more than 1.5 million years for us humans to develop the neurobiological hardware, consciousness of self and time, and flexible thinking needed to hope. Yet as I once did, we focus on IQ or other markers of success and take hope for granted. In the following chapter, I will offer some hard data to convince you that hope matters in your daily life.

Chapter 4

✿

Hope Matters

ONE DAY in 1975, Chuck Magerl pulled a book off a library shelf and made what to most people would have been a trivial discovery. In a thesis on midwestern industries, Chuck read that two brothers had once run a brewery just a couple of miles from where he sat in the college town of Lawrence, Kansas. The Walruff Brewery had been one of more than ninety local breweries operating statewide in the late 1800s. But Prohibition got an early start in Kansas, and the state legislature—with voter approval—shut them down in 1881. The Walruffs hung on longer than most, earning their place as the last legal beer makers in Kansas for more than one hundred years.

That day almost a century later, Chuck felt his first spark of entrepreneurism. He wanted to start his own microbrewery. But he knew he had a lot to learn. As he said, "This led me to dabble in home brewing and from there to keep track of what was slowly emerging on the west coast with small breweries like New Albion and Anchor Steam." Meanwhile, he and three friends helped open a grocery store (where Rose Naughtin, the young woman who has had two heart transplants, now works as a baker) that anticipated today's local-foods movement and became a social hub for people interested in healthy eating.

Fast-forward twelve years. Chuck's start-up brewery was off the ground, but barely. He was out of money and down to his last credit card, which he was using to charge groceries at a neighborhood gas station. In a week, he would be out of business and unable to hold off creditors. In a last-ditch effort, he set out to find investors among his friends and neighbors—people willing to bet on him and his ideas.

Money wasn't Chuck's only problem. Prohibition was long gone, but it was still illegal to sell alcoholic beverages by the glass anywhere in Kansas. That meant he also needed to convince conservative-thinking legislators to change the 1881 law that had run the Walruffs out of business. Finally, in 1989, Chuck's restaurant and beer garden, Free State Brewery, opened its doors—the first licensed brewery in Kansas in more than a century.

Today, Chuck's local supporters have only one regret. "As I've said many times, I wish I had mortgaged my house and bought all I could," one early investor lamented. "It has been such an immense success." Those who passed on the chance are reminded of their missed opportunity every time they wait for a table at Free State Brewery, surrounded by happy, chatty patrons sampling local and seasonal beers while taking in the view of the compact, fourteen-barrel brewhouse through a two-story wall of glass.

As the business grew, Chuck's friends and customers repeatedly asked him to bottle his beer so they could take it home and share it with friends. Again, there were legal hurdles—this time old laws that restricted the transport of distilled beverages within Kansas and across state lines. It took another campaign to get the laws changed, but by 2008, Free State was ready to open what Chuck's employees called a "Frankenstein" bottling plant—welded together from parts found around the world and from many different machines with mysterious past lives.

Then one night, only weeks before he would flip the switch and deliver the first six-pack, Chuck got a call from his security company, summoning him to the bottling plant. "On the drive over, from about two blocks away, I started seeing lights and smoke," he recalled. "I had that sinking feeling that it was going to be something that had a real major impact on us." The plant was on fire and all of the machinery was destroyed. Insurance covered the physical damage totaling over $1 million, but did little to address the psychological toll.

Faced with starting over almost from scratch and with the Great Recession beginning to show its effects on the economy, Chuck could easily have chosen to walk away. "You can think of one thousand different reasons not to do something," he told a local reporter. "To some extent you have to gauge those risks. On a one-year or two-year basis, this is probably a terrible time. Even before we suffered the setback with the fire, I was telling people, 'We'll know in five years whether this was a good decision.'" The one thing he was sure he had going for him: an economic downturn is great for beer sales.

Chuck took the long view and, as many small business owners do every day, chose hope again and again when it would have been easier to give up and move on. When the odds are against them, hopeful people like Chuck become even more resolute and persistent, exhibiting something like a compulsion to finish what they started. They hold fast to their vision, maintain their excitement about their goal, and, when one path or resource is shut down, find new routes to their desired future.

The Free Staters rebuilt. The bottling facility became less a Rube Goldberg operation and more a modern, energy-efficient plant, and Magerl's first batch of beer rolled off the line and into stores in May 2010. Three years later, Free State six-packs and cases are in several metro markets around the state, with distribution soon to expand to other states. At full capacity, they could brew 23 million bottles a year.

"That is well beyond anything we have planned," Magerl said. "But we have the capacity to go, and we'll take it as it comes."

Chuck says his is the "classic start-up story." But in fact it isn't. The majority of new businesses don't make it, with more than half closing down before the five-year mark. Like most successful entrepreneurs, Chuck hit hard times. But his vision for the future was crystal clear, and his commitment to making it a reality, though tested many times over more than thirty years, never wavered. Hope kept him moving toward his big, exciting goals, recruited people to his cause, and led to thriving businesses, one built (twice) and successfully launched in the heart of the Great Recession.

I love tales of successful entrepreneurs. They have a special relationship with hope. In fact, people who are in the throes of starting a company have more hope than most, and they put it on the line every day. They depend on their hope and that of others to turn a fledgling idea into a profitable business.

But for a hope researcher, stories have a downside. They can leave the impression that the only support you have for your claims is "anecdotal"—based on unique people and events. So before I share more stories and introduce strategies for increasing hope, I'd like to give you a quick overview of the quantifiable evidence of hope, including facts and figures from business, psychology, and education. If you need to persuade someone that the effects of hope can be measured, this will help you make your case.

Let me start with what I have learned through a statistical examination of more than one hundred hope studies. My colleagues (who include psychologists and educators from around the world) and I have conducted three meta-analyses, which are powerful ways to pull together the results of previous research on how hope relates to academic success, business outcomes, and well-being. All told, the science of hope shows that how we think about the future is a key determinant of success in school, work, and life. Other conditions being equal, hope leads to a 12 percent gain in academic performance, a 14 percent bump in workplace outcomes, and a 10 percent happiness boost for hopeful people. To put this in practical terms, a group of typical high-hope students scores a letter grade better on a final exam than their low-hope peers. A group of high-hope salespeople sells as much product in six days as their low-hope colleagues do in seven days. And high-hope people are just plain happier than their low-hope friends.

Specifically, hope is a key driver of five of life's most desired behaviors and outcomes. I'll start with the most basic.

Showing Up

"Eighty percent of success is showing up," said Woody Allen. Woody's statistics may be sketchy, but, no question, chronic absenteeism is a sure path to failure at school and work.

Absenteeism is one of the biggest problems facing American schools today. Researchers refer to chronic absence as a canary in the coal mine, an early indicator that students will struggle academically and possibly drop out. The data show that, by third grade, children who missed too much of kindergarten and first grade fall behind in reading. By sixth grade, missing lots of school increases the likelihood that students will drop out of high school.

Unexcused absences spike when students enter high school, have more freedom, and start to make up their own minds about the value of school in general and of certain subjects in particular. Mike Wortman, the longtime principal of Lincoln High School in Lincoln, Nebraska, confirmed that missing school in the freshman year is one of the best predictors he has that a student will drop out.

That's why my Gallup colleagues and I took a close look at the school-going behavior of a large group of Principal Wortman's freshmen. We measured the hope of students as they entered ninth grade (see Appendix for a description of the hope scales used in the studies referenced throughout this chapter), then we followed them, collecting attendance data periodically. Students with high hope missed only two days of school during their first school term. Low-hope students missed more than twice as many.

Showing up is not just a problem in schools. American businesses lose $153 billion annually because of employees struggling with chronic health conditions and billions more due to mild illnesses and family emergencies large and small. Management professor James Avey of Central Washington University believed that employees who are excited about company goals and their own future might miss less work. To test this hypothesis, he led a team that studied hope and absences among more than one hundred mechanical and electrical engineers in a Fortune 100 high-tech firm, a representative sample of the company's 179,000 workers.

This research really caught my eye because both my brother and brother-in-law are engineers. I couldn't imagine them buying that hope would have anything to do with showing up for work. I was also eager to learn if hope was associated with cost savings for a company, as Avey put a dollar value on each day of work missed.

Working with the firm's human resources office, Avey determined that the participants in his study, high hopers and low hopers combined, averaged forty-eight hours, or six full days, of sick time in a given year. (Considering the company's standard wage of $100 per hour, discounting benefits, and extrapolating to all 179,000 employees, 48 hours of absence per employee would result in a $859 million annual loss to the firm.) However, the more hopeful the engineer, the more likely he was to go to work. Over the course of twelve months, the high-hope engineers missed an average of twenty hours of work, or less than three days of work (not associated with planned leaves or vacations) with many of them missing no time at all. Low-hope engineers missed more than ten days of work each, on average. These employees cost the firm nearly four times as much as their high-hope colleagues in lost productivity due to sick days. No other workplace measure (including job satisfaction, commitment to the company, confidence to do the job) counted more than hope in determining whether an employee would show up.

Given these findings, Avey suggested that, even for professional-technical jobs that have a long list of educational requirements, including bachelor's degrees and certifications, recruiters should consider applicants' hope, along with other positive personal characteristics, in their hiring decisions.

Increasing Productivity

Imagine going to work and finding out that your colleague has left the company and you have to take her place as a project leader. Your new team is charged with solving a problem that has been hitting the bottom line hard.

Your boss is quick to emphasize the importance of the project and to point out some major obstacles: you have one team member who will undermine your authority; you need more team members but don't have the resources to hire them; your leadership style differs from that of the former project head; you now report to two supervisors; and you aren't *completely* clear on which steps to take first, since you get conflicting information from various sources.

What strategies might you use to solve these problems?

Business professor Suzanne Peterson presented this scenario to executives at a top financial services group. She gave each individual two weeks to come up with as many high-quality solutions as possible. Peterson was interested in how hope (which she had measured in each executive before the task began) was associated with the quantity and quality of problem-solving strategies. At the end of the two weeks, she then gave the list of strategies to a panel of their supervisors for evaluation, without identifying which executive submitted each solution. The bosses counted the strategies and rated the quality of each proposed solution. With all the data in hand, Peterson found that the more hopeful executives produced the better solutions. They also submitted many more solutions, possibly strategically, knowing that some of them would not be viable.

Peterson observes that hope is especially important in organizations experiencing uncertainty due to rapid changes in focus and shifts in leadership: "It may be these settings where employees' hopefulness can have a greater impact because they require the problem-solving orientation and perseverance of those with higher hope." Accordingly, in another study, Peterson found that hope was a more significant predictor of performance in start-up businesses than in more established firms. Why? Peterson put it simply: "[M]ore hopeful employees may be more likely to engage in and accept organizational change efforts."

This hope-productivity link has been demonstrated in many studies targeting various outcomes, across countries (including China, Portugal, the United States, and Switzerland) and in many professions. Hopeful salespeople reach their quotas more often; hopeful mortgage brokers process and close more loans; and hopeful managing executives meet their quarterly goals more often. To my knowledge, whenever researchers have examined hope and work performance, they have found a meaningful link. Consider, for example, a study of fast-food outlets. Each of fifty-nine managers of a nationally known fast-food chain was ranked from low to high in hope on a self-reported hope scale. With the help of the corporate office (which did not know the managers' hope scores), the researchers paired data on each franchise's overall profitability with the manager's hope level. The highest-hope managers recorded more profits than the lowest-hope managers. The same trend held for employee turnover, a crucial metric for any service industry.

It seems likely that this hope-productivity link is established when people are still in school. Indeed, research has examined the role of hope in predicting the performance of elementary, middle school, high school, and college students. In each study, hope predicted test scores and term GPA when controlling for previous grades, intelligence, and other psychological variables (like engagement, optimism, and self-efficacy).

The most compelling evidence for the added value of hope comes from four longitudinal studies. These long-term studies give us the opportunity to assess how the passage of time influences the link between hope and academic success. Three of these studies followed college students' success from their freshman year to their graduation (or their attrition or the six-year mark, whichever came first). In the fourth study, researchers examined the hope-productivity link for first-year law students.

The setup for each study was simple. Researchers recruited first-semester students to complete a standardized measure of hope along with other scales, and requested access to their personal school records for some years to come. Researchers then unobtrusively followed the students by examining student records each term or so. Statistical models determined the relationship between hope and outcomes such as GPA, on-going enrollment, and graduation. Each study controlled for the other determinants of school success, such as GPA at previous academic levels and entrance exam scores.

The findings from the studies of college students in the United States and in the United Kingdom are remarkably similar. In each study, how students think about the future predicts benchmarks of academic progress and success, including how many courses they enroll in, how many credits they earn, their GPA across those courses, their cumulative GPA, and the likelihood that they will graduate. Of note, one study showed that low-hope students are three times more likely to be dismissed from school for poor grades. Another study, which pitted hope against ACT scores, found that hope is a better predictor of ongoing enrollment and graduation than this standardized entrance exam.

The study of hope in law students provided the most surprising results. Undergraduate GPA and Law School Admission Test (LSAT) scores were collected from student records and each student completed a hope scale when they entered the program. These measures predicted academic success during what might be the most stressful semester in law school—the first. When predictors were ranked from strongest to the weakest, undergraduate GPA was the best and LSAT scores were the worst. And hope? A student's level of hope predicted his or her law school ranking better than the LSAT.

Boosting Well-being

Have you ever met a happy, hopeless person? I haven't. When Gallup asked one million people if they smiled or laughed a lot yesterday, the hopeful said yes much more often than did the hopeless. Because of this observation I decided to take a closer look at the overlap between hope and happiness with the help of psychologist Matt Gallagher of Boston University. We asked people if they were hopeful and satisfied with their lives, then measured the presence of good feelings and the absence of bad ones. According to well-being expert Ed Diener of the University of Illinois, someone who is satisfied with life, experiencing positive emotions, and not experiencing negative emotions meets the basic criteria for a happiness diagnosis. We wanted to know if being hopeful predicted (or was predicted by) these symptoms of happiness. Indeed, hope proved to be a strong, unique predictor of satisfaction and emotions. This work led us to suggest that hope is a symptom of happiness.

Anecdotal data, poll results, and correlational findings suggest that happiness and hope go together like chocolate and peanut butter. But does hope lead to happiness and well-being? And if so, how?

To date, hope research suggests that the answer is *probably*. Even a brief intervention with students designed to boost their hope led to a measurable increase in life satisfaction. Longitudinal studies of workers have also suggested that employees high in hope experience more well-being over time. And it appears that hope buffers well-being from the effects of negative life events, shielding us from adversity, protecting us from stress and sadness, and making room for happiness. For example, in a recent study of firefighters coping with the daily stress inherent in their jobs, those first responders with the highest hope were able to protect themselves psychologically from the stress that could accumulate over an entire shift. Perhaps this leaves them with less anxiety to manage when they go from firehouse to home.

Our thoughts about the future may do more than buffer us from the bad in life—they may contribute directly to meaning and purpose in life and, so, to our well-being. Studies by psychology professor David Feldman of Santa Clara University showed a correlation between hope and meaning that was the highest researchers have measured for any factor associated with hope, perhaps because hope spurs us to pursue what matters to us most, which in turn gives us a sense of control and purpose that is key to well-being.

Despite the promise of this research, the definitive studies examining a causal link between hope and happiness have not yet been done. So, for now, I will say that *hope is necessary but not sufficient for happiness.*

Enjoying Good Health

Rick Snyder, my mentor at the University of Kansas, once appeared on ABC's *Good Morning America* to conduct a live experiment showing hope in action. He started by introducing a classic research tool called the cold pressor test, which uses a tank of ice water to assess pain tolerance. Then he challenged the host, Charlie Gibson, the medical expert, Dr. Tim Johnson, and the weather guy, Tony Perkins, to dunk their right fists into the tank for as long as they could stand it. Tony pulled out his hand first, and stood shaking life back into it while Charlie and Tim continued their battle of wills. Just as the segment ended, Tim gave up, but Charlie vowed to keep his hand in the freezing water throughout the break.

When they came back from the commercial, and Charlie was declared the winner, he asked Rick what the test had to do with hope. Rick's reply: his studies had shown that hopeful people consistently tolerate more pain than their less hopeful counterparts. Then he revealed to viewers that the *Good Morning America* team had taken a standardized hope test prior to the show, and that their scores had accurately predicted the order in which each would call it quits.

Rick's work on hope and pain has since been replicated in numerous controlled experiments. In one study, hopeful people tolerated pain almost twice as long as people who were less hopeful.

These coping studies sparked research into how hope could promote healthy behaviors, including fruit and vegetable consumption, regular exercise, safe sex practices, and quitting smoking. In each case, hope for the future is clearly linked with daily habits that support health and prevent disease.

When it comes to their health, hopeful people tend to make good choices. This is true for Rose, the heart patient who closely follows her medication regimen to stay healthy. It was true for John, the farmer, when he recovered his hope and set challenging goals (for example, harvesting and baling) in order to keep his farm as well as to take better care of his day-to-day health. Finally, for the first time in his life, he accepted support from professionals, from his wife and friends, and ultimately, from his son. Each positive behavior and interaction gave John more energy, which he used to persevere.

The same is true for other people managing chronic health conditions—even for children. Professor Carla Berg of Emory University wondered if hope in young asthma patients was associated with adherence to their treatment regimen, a daily inhaled steroid. The children, diagnosed with moderate to severe asthma, completed a youth version of the hope scale and were directed to take their medication as prescribed. With all the controls in place, Berg tracked their adherence with electronic monitoring of the child's metered dose over a fourteenday period, then examined the relationship between compliance and variables, including demographic characteristics. Among all the factors studied, a child's hope was the only significant predictor of who followed doctors' orders.

How we think about the future clearly affects our health. This makes me think that my doctor should be asking me questions about my hopes and dreams. He never has. Has yours?

Living Longer

"Hopelessness Predicts Mortality." This headline about the work of medical researcher Stephen Stern grabbed my attention. As I read the story beneath it, memories of my sessions with John flooded back. I truly believe that, had John not worked so hard, hoped so hard, he would have died. If he didn't commit suicide or die of kidney disease, his hopelessness would have taken its toll some other way. I believed this when I treated John at the time, but I did not have a shred of evidence to support a link between hopelessness and mortality, or between hope and longevity. That all changed when I read Stern's research.

Scientists at the University of Texas Health Science Center in San Antonio set out to study mortality in older members of the local community. Psychiatry professor Stern and his colleagues began with a big question: "Why do some people die while others, who may be no less ill or in no less physical danger, continue to live?" Finding an answer would require following a large group of people over a long period and accounting for the many factors that could undermine each person's health.

Stern's group recruited 795 San Antonio residents, ages 64 to 79, who had taken part in a large prospective study of heart disease that began in 1979. Between 1992 and 1996, the participants added to their extensive research profiles by completing tests measuring cognitive performance as well as health markers (such as number of illnesses, blood pressure, body mass index), lifestyle factors (such as exercising, drinking, and smoking), and social well-being.

Stern set out to determine if hope is, in fact, a matter of life and death. Included in the home-based assessment was a simple question about hope: "Are you hopeful about the future?" (Or, for the many Mexican-American subjects, "Tiene esperanzas acerca del futuro?") Of the respondents, 722 people (91 percent) said "yes" while 73 people (9 percent) said "no." These two groups, the hopeful and the hopeless, proved to be equally matched in terms of their sex and ethnic makeup. No one type of person cornered the market on hope. They reported the same level of education, just under twelve years of formal schooling. Surprisingly, they even had comparable health at the time of the first home visit and no significant differences in blood pressure, body mass index, and drinking behavior.

What differences did show up? Many more of the hopeful were rated "high" in physical activity (48 percent versus 28 percent), while fewer of them were current smokers (15 percent versus 25 percent). The hopeful also scored much lower on a standard measure of depression and significantly higher on measures of social well-being and number of social contacts. The hopeful were on average one year younger (69 versus 70) and slightly better off financially.

After the study, both the hopeful and the hopeless were thanked for their participation, but they weren't told anything about their results. They received no recommendations for health care or other interventions. They were simply left to lead their lives as they chose. Meanwhile, the researchers followed the hopeful and the hopeless from a distance. Using names and Social Security numbers, they collected mortality statistics from local newspaper obituaries, San Antonio city records, and National Death Index reports. Death certificates were reviewed to determine the causes of death for each participant who passed. Finally, a certified nosologist, an expert in disease classifications, coded each cause and shared the results with the researchers.

By August 1999, the results were clear. Of the hopeless group, 29 percent had died, compared to only 11 percent of the hopeful participants. There were no cases of suicide, but 25 participants had died of cancer, and another 25 from heart disease; these diseases claimed 7.2 percent of the hopeless compared with 2.8 percent of the hopeful.

This finding—that hopelessness is a strong predictor of mortality—held up even when taking into account all the other factors measured, including ethnicity, sexual identity, drinking, perceived health, and number of medical illnesses (and the variables on which the groups differed, such as age and socioeconomic status). That is, when all other differences were statistically controlled, the people who said they felt hopeless were *more than twice as likely* to die during the follow-up period as the people who said they were hopeful about the future.

Even after more than a decade, Stern still refers to the findings as "striking." When I asked how he explained the link between hope and longevity, he said he thought it was "behaviorally mediated." In other words, hope for the future drives particular behaviors in the present that, in turn, result in a longer or shorter life. For example, he pointed out, "If you are hopeless you are less likely to keep doctor's appointments."

All of the scientific studies I've discussed in this chapter demonstrate that hope is not simply an attitude or belief that benefits us in some mysterious way. Hope can lift our spirits, buoy our energy, and make life seem worth living. It also changes our day-to-day behavior. How we think about the future has a direct impact on how well we do today. The following chapter, which wraps up the first part of this book, focuses on the link between hope and action, and why hope is so different from optimism and wishing.

Chapter 5

How Investing in the Future
Pays Off Today

AJ's MOTHER, Mary, an immigrant from Ghana, cleaned Jim Clifton's apartment building in the Georgetown section of Washington, D.C. Some Saturdays, Mary brought AJ along. He usually read while his mom worked, but one day AJ started asking Jim questions. One of the first: "Where do you work?"

Jim, the CEO of Gallup, told AJ about his job, and AJ liked what he heard. "How can I get a job there?" he asked. "Well, why don't you come over and apply?" Jim said.

A week or so later, AJ was in Jim's D.C. office for an interview, while his mother sat nervously outside. Jim opened the interview with a straightforward question: "What do you know about Gallup?" And that's when AJ's homework paid off. He'd googled Jim, he'd googled the company's name, he knew the history of Gallup and where it was headed, and he had lots of questions. As Jim later said, "This guy was going like hell to get a job here. I've asked the same question of plenty of applicants who answered, 'Not much, can you tell me about it?'"

Those applicants didn't get a job, but AJ did. "The interview went well," Jim told him. "Let's go get you some Gallup gear to wear. Then you finish middle school, high school, and college. When you graduate, your job will be waiting. Until then, when you're off school, you can work here as a junior analyst."

That's how, in the summer of 2010, at age nine, AJ became Gallup's youngest "employee," joining more than two thousand colleagues around the globe. And he became a kid on a mission. Until then, he'd been a middling student at a middling school, with vague dreams of being a radio announcer or an NBA star. Now, as he wore his Gallup gear around school, his effort skyrocketed and his grades became nearly perfect. At Jim's request, AJ reported in periodically. A typical email:

> Hello Mr. Clifton, I just wanted to give you an update on my progress in school. I aced my first math and language arts quizzes and I think I aced my first social studies quiz also. I'll keep in touch.

AJ was interning at the Gallup offices in June 2011 when I asked him to help me with some online research. We had a few email exchanges and phone conversations to set up the project. He was engaging, charming, and focused. But what really stood out was his ability to ask detailed, pointed questions. As we talked, I imagined him developing a picture, a clear image of what I needed.

I have given assignments to thousands of students, and I have time-tested expectations for what they can produce. AJ exceeded even my expectations for graduate students. He searched for and downloaded all of the available articles and summarized them succinctly. Days before his deadline, AJ delivered.

As he headed back to school in the fall, AJ told Jim, "I think I need to come in over Christmas break to work on some projects." AJ's habit of looking toward the future makes him one of my favorite examples of how hope for tomorrow changes your life today. The immediacy of return on your investment in the future is what sets hope apart from willpower, optimism, and wishing.

Connecting Today to Tomorrow

Can we inspire hope in people who don't have a Jim Clifton in their lives, no CEO of a major company ready to shape their future? Let's go back to middle school to find out. In the spring of 2009, a counselor from the University of Michigan visited a local school to give a talk about college and careers. He spoke to two groups of seventh-grade science students—295 students in all. Both groups (to which students were assigned randomly) saw a slide presentation about the university, the campus, and college majors. The second part of the talk featured real-world data about adult earnings. One group saw a graph describing the step-wise increase in salary by level of education in the state of Michigan. (Based on 2006 census numbers, the typical Michigander who graduated from high school earned $31,500 a year. Those with four years of college earned a median income of $50,900 a year.) The second group saw a graph summarizing the earnings of actors, athletes, and musicians on the 2008 Forbes Celebrity 100 list. (Musicians averaged the highest, at $63.7 million, although Oprah Winfrey, the highest-paid entertainer in the world, earned $275 million that year.)

In truth, the career information was part of a psychology experiment designed by two researchers, Mesmin Destin and Daphna Oyserman. Oyserman, professor of psychology at the University of Michigan, had previously identified a disconnect between students' thinking about the future ("I will go to college and then become a doctor") and the behavioral choices (completing and turning in assignments, preparing for exams) they were making about school and schoolwork. Why did such high expectations so often fail to turn into real achievement?

We can put numbers to this disconnect. Most American high school students (90 percent or more) believe they are college-bound, but fewer than 75 percent actually graduate from high school. Only 60 percent of *those* graduates attend college, and, in turn, only 40 percent of *those* college freshmen will ultimately graduate with a degree. By my calculations, about one of every five high schoolers who say they will seek higher education actually graduates from college. This expectation-performance gap is bad news for our young people and for our country.

Destin (now a professor of psychology at Northwestern University) wanted to devise an intervention that would help Detroit seventh graders map out their future and navigate the real barriers to success in school. The purpose of his experiment was to test future thinking associated with education (sparked by the graph of income levels by education) against future thinking that was disconnected from education (the graph of income by celebrity). Once the classroom presentation was over, the science teachers (who had not attended and hence were considered "blind" to the experiment) gave the students an extra-credit homework assignment related to information covered in their regular science class.

As Destin later told me, even he was surprised by the results. The students in the first group, who were shown an explicit link between education and income, were nearly eight times more likely than the second group to complete and turn in the optional assignment the next day. *Eight times.* It's as if they suddenly saw education as a real path to the good future they wanted. Knowing the way to a solid job that paid $50,000 a year gave these twelve- and thirteen-year olds more energy and guidance for current effort than all the fantasy fortunes of Jay-Z, LeBron James, and other icons they followed in the media.

Talking with Destin helped me realize that there is a distinction between thinking that you are college-bound (an idea that we now drum into kids) and realizing that your success in life depends on how well you do in school *today*. As he put it, these students from the Detroit middle school started "seeing schoolwork as an investment, not a chore." Like AJ, they were turned on by a vision of their future selves in a good job. When we see a direct connection between the future we want and our attitudes and behaviors today, our commitment and effort soar.

Later on, it hit me that Destin's findings ran counter to my operating instructions from childhood on. See, I graduated from "Our Lady of Perpetually Delayed Gratification." I can still see De La Salle Brother Bernard standing at the front of the gym: "Gentlemen, to be successful in the future, you must sacrifice right now." I knew that how well I would do in sports, school, work, and life depended on my suffering just a little bit every day. Throwing one hundred baseballs today would improve my pitching on game day seventy-two hours from now. Forgoing a paying job after college to go to graduate school would lead to more money down the road. Working insane hours in my first job would make me more competitive for a better job, one with more freedom and less travel.

Delayed gratification and the willpower it took to sustain it did help me succeed. (Stay tuned for more about willpower. It has an important role to play in our lives, and hopeful people know how to harness it to reach their goals.) But focusing solely on willpower ignores the psychological force that we activate when we get excited about the future. Our exhausting efforts at self-control run a distant second to knowing how to tap the generous, uplifting, and motivating energy of hope.

Resisting the Devil's Breakfast

Imagine that you have been successfully losing several pounds a month and are nearing your goal weight after a year of exercise and healthy eating. On a morning when you're feeling especially lean, you join a friend at her office for a brief meeting. As you walk in, you see them:

fresh doughnuts, one dozen shiny sugarcoated rings of glistening yum-miness, six chocolate and six glazed. A sign next to the box says "Treat yourself! You're worth it."

What will determine if you indulge? Surely this is a situation where willpower counts. And in fact, if you had a good night's sleep and a full, healthy breakfast, willpower might stand a chance. But it turns out that your ability to resist temptation depends even more on your future thinking style. Let me explain.

The teachers at my Catholic high school considered willpower a moral strength that we could build by exercising it every day. Thanks to the work of Roy Baumeister of Florida State University, we now can look into the brain and see exactly where this strength is coming from. To some extent, my teachers were right. Baumeister showed experimentally that students who were required to do things like sit up straight, exercise regularly, and speak in complete sentences later showed greater self-control in their lives. They also persisted longer in lab tests like solving difficult puzzles, squeezing a handgrip, and keep-ing their minds off sex.

However, when Baumeister tracked the physiology of self-control, he discovered that will, like a muscle, becomes fatigued with overuse. Each time we resist an impulse (whether to do something or to stop doing something), we tap the brain's energy, in the form of glucose, to tamp down that impulse. Students who had already completed one series of willpower exercises—like resisting cookies when they were hungry or ignoring a comedy video in order to track a boring computer display—subsequently gave up earlier on the puzzle and handgrip tests. In other words, willpower starts to break down whenever we're men-tally and physically depleted, whether from fatigue, overwork, hunger, or other kinds of stress.

Of course, the biggest aha that many people took from Baumeister's work was that dieting itself—through hunger and glucose depletion—undermines our ability to keep dieting. But a study led by psychologist Gabriele Oettingen of New York University complicates this picture.

Like so many people in America, a group of Philadelphia women were making another attempt to lose weight. They'd already signed up for a University of Pennsylvania study featuring a very-low-calorie diet and a year of weekly meetings designed to help them control their eating. Before the diet began, the researchers asked them how many pounds they wanted to lose. The women also answered questions about their expectations, such as "How confident are you that after the program is completed you will have lost that amount?"

But now the researchers tapped into a different kind of thinking— the stories we tell about ourselves. Each woman was asked to imagine herself as the main character in four open-ended scenarios related to food and weight loss—something like my free-doughnut challenge. Here's one of the prompts:

> You have just completed Penn's weight-loss program. Tonight you have made plans to go out with an old friend whom you haven't seen in about a year. As you wait for your friend to arrive, you imagine...

The women wrote down their thoughts and feelings, and the researchers coded these fantasy responses as positive (the women found it easy to resist food temptations, they achieved their ideal body weight) or negative (they continued to struggle with temptation).

Fast-forward one year. The women who had positive expectations for the program were much more likely to have attended the weekly sessions than the women with negative expectations. They also lost an average of twenty-six pounds *more* than the women who doubted their ability to meet their goal. In fact, the more positive a woman's expectation, the more weight she lost. The least successful of the dieters by far were the women who had low initial expectations and outrageously positive fantasies about how easy it would be to lose weight and how great they would look. Even the pessimists (women with low expectations) who acknowledged potential difficulties and struggle lost more.

The researchers concluded that the women who had foreseen challenges would actually rehearse what they would do when confronted with temptations like free doughnuts (and other pitfalls). The positive fantasies were daydreams that had no payoff in reality.

Why Wishing Can Be Bad for You

A group of newly minted professionals who were looking for their first job took part in another subtle experiment led by Oettingen. She and her team recruited students who were completing graduate school in a tough economic climate and asked them to rate their likelihood of obtaining a good job. The researchers also asked them to write down their positive and negative "thoughts, images, and fantasies" about the process of looking for and finding work and to indicate how often they had both positive and negative thoughts. Oettingen then got permission to contact the students two years later and ask them how their job searches had gone.

Stop for a minute and make your own guess about how things turned out. Is it better to "think positive," to repeatedly visualize a clear and easy path to a new job? Or should you be more realistic, accounting for the difficulties and effort involved? Which vision will charge you up and keep you going until you reach your goal?

Two years later, Oettingen found most of her recruits and asked them how many applications they'd sent out, how many job offers they'd received, and how much money they were making. A third of the participants were still without a job in their field, a testament to the toughness of the job market. The students who had the most success combined high expectations for a good job with realistic thoughts about the process of getting one. The students who had the most positive thoughts and fantasies simply hadn't tried as hard. They had sent out fewer applications, received fewer offers, and made less money when they did land a job.

In other words, hope trumped wishful thinking. When we hope, we have high expectations for the future *and* a clear-eyed view of the obstacles that we need to overcome in order to get there. We are primed for action. But wishful thinking can undermine our efforts, making us passive and less likely to reach coveted goals.

Wishing ourselves into failure and loss is bad enough. But when we push our wishful thinking onto others and call it hope it is potentially destructive.

This is what writer and activist Barbara Ehrenreich realized when she entered what she called "Cancerland" after a routine mammogram. Several years later, she fired a broadside at all the easy forms of positive thinking she encountered during her treatment, which included grueling chemotherapy. Her article, called "The Pathologies of Hope," started this way:

> I hate hope. It was hammered into me constantly a few years ago when I was being treated for breast cancer: Think positively! Don't lose hope! Wear your pink ribbon with pride! A couple of years later, I was alarmed to discover that the facility where I received my follow-up care was called the Hope Center. Hope? What about a cure? . . . Fuck hope. Keep us alive.

It pained me to read this, but who could blame her? During one of the most difficult times of her life, well-intentioned but misguided people were telling her to think about the future in a way that could actually undermine her well-being. (If you don't get better, is it your fault for not being "positive" enough?) These people were telling her to wish, not hope. And they didn't know the difference. Interestingly, the "wishiness" of her caregivers made Ehrenreich agitated and proactive, which are characteristics of a high-hope person under pressure.

Are You Hopeful . . . or Just Optimistic?

In fact, you can be both hopeful and optimistic, but, as a hope researcher, I'm a stickler about when and how I use these terms.

You're optimistic if you think the future will be better than the present. As the old song goes, you "stay on the sunny side," see the glass half full, look at life through rose-colored glasses, and generally think things will turn out well.

You're hopeful if you think that the future will be better and that you have a role in making it so. You might consider yourself a hard-nosed realist, even a pessimist—someone who sees the world in a clear, cold light—but you take action to improve any situation that's important to you.

Optimism is an attitude. It doesn't concern itself with real information about the future, and it may not have a specific goal. Some researchers call optimism an "illusion," or a "positive expectation bias."

Optimism is partly based on temperament—some babies come into the world inclined to embrace experience, while others shy away. The components of hopeful thinking are learned in early childhood; if all goes well, they're in place by age two.

Optimism can benefit us. It can foster good health and happiness, buffer stress and anxiety, and help us cope better with the present.

But when life throws us a curve, when the going gets tough, optimists can get stuck and frustrated. Hopeful people shine in negative situations. They are energized to act and they find meaning and dignity in moving ahead, whatever the challenge.

The Energy of Hope

It now looks as though wishing is impotent because it does not give us—and may actually sap—the energy we need to pursue our goals. This is the downside of passive positive thinking.

Pause a minute and think about your upcoming week. What's on your plate? What are your big responsibilities? Now imagine that everything goes amazingly well. You meet every challenge with ease. You enjoy the feeling of being in control and on top of things. You don't feel pressed for time, and yet you manage to get everything done. Wonderful, isn't it? An exercise in fantasy, right?

Heather Barry Kappes (a member of Oettingen's research team at NYU) gave this fantasy exercise to one group of research subjects—prompting them to think about a hassle-free perfect week. She asked another group to write down whatever they thought might happen in the coming week with no fantasizing. Then her team focused on the feelings of energy generated in each group, fantasy week and normal week. How excited, enthusiastic, and active did participants feel afterward? The "ideal week" group actually reported lower levels of energy. (Kappes has also researched this effect using physiological measures like systolic blood pressure, which rises whenever we're aroused to take action.)

Perhaps more surprising, when participants reported in a week later, the initial energy drain turned out to be lasting. The "ideal week" group reported that they accomplished less than the group that had written down more neutral (and realistic) thoughts. So a Sunday night filled with wishes for the upcoming week will actually *rob* you of the energy you need to get things done Monday through Friday.

Reflecting on these findings, Barry Kappes said, "When you fantasize something very positive, it's almost like you are actually living it." The mind reacts as if the goal has already been achieved. This is why fantasy "will sap job seekers of the energy to pound the pavement, and drain the lovelorn of the energy to approach the one they like." We're actually better off when we imagine ourselves surmounting obstacles, problems, and setbacks.

Beware of Mental Fast Food

Wishes are mental fast food. They are mind candy (or doughnuts) that satisfy for the moment but do nothing to nourish us for the long haul. That's why people who say "think positive" trigger my negative thinking. "Really, that's the best you can do?" Yes, I know they are trying to be supportive, but this is just lazy cheerleading. There is not a stitch of evidence that wish-fulfillment thinking ("Every day in every way I am getting better and better") improves anyone's lives in any meaningful way.

The same goes for bestselling "self-improvement" books (like *The Secret* and *The Power*) that tell us the only thing we have to change is our minds, and reality will align with our wishes. Sorry, the so-called law of attraction is not a law, and telling yourself "I will have enough money for everything I desire" will not fill your wallet, no matter how many times you repeat it.

Yet future thinking that is rich with imagery is a core ingredient of both hoping and wishing. If you are thinking about a desirable outcome, you may be hopeful. Then again, you may be just wishing. Both future visions can give you the warm fuzzies. Both are self-reinforcing—priming the pleasure pump with thoughts about a wonderful vacation will lead you to think more about that destination. Both can also help you relax and buffer you against stress, anxiety, and other negative emotions. But these benefits are fleeting *unless your thoughts spark action*. Only hope starts you thinking about ways to save money to pay for that trip to the ocean and your lodging when you get there.

In the three chapters that follow, I'm going to look more closely at how hope works in the real world. You'll see where genuine hope parts company with wishing, and how hope can stay strong even when you acknowledge your limited ability to predict or influence the future. The real world is where we face the circumstances of birth or chance or personality that could hold us back, and where we have to choose between hope and stagnation. We'll see how the three elements of hope (Goals, Agency, and Pathways, introduced in chapter 2) work together in the stories of some extraordinary individuals. I'll also alert you to the destructive messages in our culture that undermine hope, so you recognize and combat them when they come your way.

CHOOSING A BETTER TOMORROW

Chapter 6

The Future Is Ours to See

MY MIND is swirling with thoughts about the months ahead: *In the next few months, I will learn how to play harmonica. I will cook more dinners for my family and friends. I will make more trips for fun and fewer for work. I will go to church more often . . . and like it.* I have hundreds of these "in the next few months" thoughts and none of them, for the time being, has any strings attached.

Future thinking brings us wonderful freedom. It releases us from the burdens of the past and the anxieties of the present, buffers us from the stresses that come with daily life, excites the mind, and lifts the heart. That's the good news.

The bad news is that future thinking can also mislead us. Most of us overestimate how much control we have over the future and yet some of us don't exercise the bit of control we have, becoming passive about the future. When we don't act on our goals, they remain wishes—without substance or force in the real world. When we do act, we face unpredictability and chance, no matter how well we plan. That is why hope requires courage. When we hope, we are committing to a leap of faith.

Forecasting Feelings

We believe we know and understand our future selves. Because of this we usually assume we know how we'll feel if we get what we want or if we fail to get it. Right? But what *actually* happens when we get what we've hoped for, longed for, worked for? I learned the pitfalls of prediction the hard way . . . from my own family.

One of my relatives is a high priestess of wishery. She wishes hard, fixating on her big wants day in and day out. Her wish du jour might be a certain car or computer or house—not to mention pets, sofas, and trips. Then she locks in on the one thing she wants most. She had chattered on about how and why a dishwasher would simplify her life and make her happier. Then, one day while driving around town running errands, she saw "it," there, on the side of the road, with "FREE" scrawled on it, the dishwasher of her dreams. She heaved it into her car and hauled it home.

But once she got it into the kitchen, the dishwasher lost its luster and she never even hooked it up. When she moved and took the dishwasher with her, she didn't hook it up in the new house, either. Because it did have a butcher-block top, it made a handy cutting board—until it was left behind in a recent move.

Harvard psychologist Daniel Gilbert has created a science around what he calls "affective forecasting"—how we think we will feel in the future after a particular event. He warns against being cocky about our predictions, because we generally overestimate how happy we will be when, say, we move to a warm, beautiful city or get a long-sought promotion.

In one of his quirky early studies, Gilbert showed that we overestimate our emotional response to a favored candidate losing an election. (I call it the "I'm moving to Canada!" Study, in honor of a certain buddy who predicts catastrophe if his guy doesn't win a major U.S. election.)

Gilbert's team went to Texas to cover the 1994 gubernatorial election. George W. Bush, then a political newcomer, and sitting governor Ann Richards were head-to-head. The researchers stood outside a polling station and asked exiting voters how they would feel a month after their candidate won or lost. Those who had voted for Bush did not think a win would significantly influence their happiness much (a bit of a surprise to researchers). In some cases, we adjust quickly to things we expect to happen. But supporters of Richards believed that a loss would hurt them emotionally.

One month later, the researchers followed up with the participating voters by telephone. The winners were about as happy as they expected to be. On the other hand, the losers were significantly happier than they'd predicted. Some of them had even warmed up to Governor Bush since the election.

Gilbert's research resonated with my own experience. When I finished ten years of college and graduate school, I thought I would be thrilled. And I was, for a day or two, and then the reality of my new job set in. As a college instructor working toward tenure, I was sure I'd do the happy dance for months after I became bona fide—a real professor. When I got tenure, I was more relieved than ecstatic.

And what about that friend of mine who swore he'd move to Canada if "that guy is elected"? I had a beer with him recently at a local watering hole, about a thousand miles south of the Canadian border.

In chapter 9, I'll introduce some ways you can reduce your chances of affective misforecasting by bringing the future closer to you. But keep in mind that the downside of *not* choosing to take a risk on the future is the "what if" question, which can haunt us for a lifetime.

Guessing the Future

Since feelings are messy and unpredictable, maybe we should focus on the rational side of hope. We humans have managed the future well enough to become the dominant species on the planet. Even so, our day-by-day decision-making is inherently flawed. These big flaws are so hidden in plain sight that psychologist Daniel Kahneman of Princeton University won the 2002 Nobel Prize in Economics for pointing them out. In a series of brilliant experiments, he and his colleague Amos Tversky (who died before he could share the Nobel) showed just how much our thinking is guided by unconscious cues and mental processing that is lightning-fast and automatic.

In his book *Thinking, Fast and Slow*, Kahneman describes how he discovered his first cognitive illusion. "Many decades ago I spent what seemed like a great deal of time under a scorching sun, watching groups of sweaty soldiers as they solved a problem," Kahneman begins. He was doing his national service in the Israeli army, with an undergraduate degree in psychology to his credit, when he was assigned the job of evaluating candidates for officer training. In theory, the way group members responded to virtually impossible tasks would reveal leadership potential. (Think it through for yourself: Haul a log to a six-foot-high wall, then get both the log and the group to the other side. The log can't touch the ground or the wall. The group members can't touch the wall, either.)

As they watched the officer candidates struggle with the challenging group tests developed by the British army in World War II, evaluators came to the same conclusion: "The soldier who took over when the group was in trouble and led the team over the wall was a leader at that moment. The obvious best guess about how he would do in training, or in combat, was that he would be as effective as he had been at the wall. Any other prediction seemed inconsistent with the evidence before our eyes."

Doubt crept in only when the evaluators received feedback from the officer-training school, based on assessments by the commanders in charge of the cadets. As Kahneman put it, "Our forecasts were better than blind guesses, but not by much." But the real surprise was that the feedback had "no effect whatsoever on how we evaluated candidates and very little effect on the confidence we felt in our judgment. . . . We continued to act and feel as if each of our specific predictions was valid."

We are all potential victims of our overconfidence in guessing the

future. Yes, you are, too. And even if you acknowledge your own falli-
bility, you've probably bought into the notion that some other people—
"experts"—have extraordinary abilities to predict the future. Take the
50 percent of Americans who have money in the stock market. Many
believe that they are entrusting their money to skilled investors, people
who have the expertise to "beat the market." Alas, based on Kahneman's observations, these Wall Street gurus often perform no better
than dart-throwing monkeys.

The head of an investment firm whose advisers worked with very
wealthy clients hired Kahneman to give a seminar about his work.
Like any good teacher, he wanted to incorporate information about his
audience. "I asked for some data to prepare my presentation and was
granted a small treasure: a spreadsheet summarizing the investment
outcomes of some 25 anonymous wealth advisers, for eight consecutive
years," he said. "The advisers' scores for each year were the main determinant of their year-end bonuses. It was a simple matter to rank the
advisers by their performance and to answer a question: Did the same
advisers consistently achieve better returns for their clients year after
year? Did some advisers consistently display more skill than others?"

Kahneman correlated the rankings of each adviser year by year. He
had expected each adviser's results would vary, but he was still shocked
by what he discovered: "While I was prepared to find little year-to-year
consistency, I was still surprised to find that the average of the 28 cor-
relations was .01. In other words, zero. The stability that would indicate
differences in skill was not to be found."

Disturbing, eh? Yet in the tradition of overconfidence, the head of
the investment firm—and the traders themselves—simply disregarded
what the statistics showed. "Facts that challenge such basic assumptions—and thereby threaten people's livelihood and self-esteem—are
simply not absorbed," concluded Kahneman. "We are normally blind
about our own blindness. We're generally overconfident in our opinions and our impressions and judgments. We exaggerate how knowable
the world is."

Exercising a Bit of Control over the Future in the Sweet Spot of Hope

What all of this means is that genuine hope lives in a psychological sweet spot, and it requires a very special kind of mental balancing act. In the sweet spot, our thinking about the future overlaps with our thoughts about what needs to happen today. In the sweet spot, we believe in our ability to make the future better than the present, while at the same time we recognize the limits of our control.

When we live in the sweet spot, we acknowledge that we don't have access to all of our thought processes and that we can't always predict our feelings. That puts a premium on the small chunk of our thinking and behavior that directs our active attempts to shape the future in a meaningful way. We try to learn as much as we can about the situation we face, but we're aware that we can't wait until we know everything to act. We are alert to the difference between helpful critiques and challenges (which we can use as tools) and the messages that create doubt and sap our energy. We also know that the better we get at understanding our cues, habits, and thought processes, the more we can energize ourselves and others.

Messages That Undermine Hope

Start moving ahead with big plans and high energy and you are almost certain to stir up the naysayers. So brace yourself. Sometimes the negative messages come from people around you right now. Sometimes they're voices from the past. And sometimes they come from a part of you that is daunted by what lies ahead. To stay in the sweet spot of hope, you need to identify them for what they are.

You might hear from others: "You are a dreamer." "You can't fight city hall." "What makes you think you can do that?" But

I believe this kind of commentary usually reflects more on the speaker than on you or your plans. I've never known a high-hope person to try shaming someone else into a "more realistic" vision of the future. More often, high-hope people will honor your dreams or be quick to help you develop new ones.

Maybe you hear the message in your own voice: "There's nothing I can do about it anyway." "I'm too busy to think about that now." Sounds familiar? In my own head I sometimes still hear Doris Day singing, "Que Será, Será (Whatever Will Be, Will Be)." "It will work out somehow." If you recognize these thoughts, then acknowledge the fear they're coming from, and remind yourself that even the smallest effort to move forward chips away at that fear.

Bottom line: negative messages are no more "realistic" than your highest goals, and they rob you of agency.

Taking a Stake in the Future

One of the most hopeful—and riskiest—things we do in life is to have children. I know parents who start saving for their child's college tuition in the first trimester of pregnancy. Some of us commit more time to picking our children's preschools and elementary schools than we spent choosing our own colleges or shopping for our family homes. The truth is, I find myself thinking about my son's college choices almost every day—even though he only recently lost his first baby tooth.

Two of the smartest people I know are economists and colleagues of mine. They have full knowledge of the psychological and economics research that says that our behavior as parents doesn't matter as much as we like to think it does. I know—I don't like the idea of that, either—but the evidence is clear. Our small parental behaviors, based on the decisions we agonize about daily, do less to improve our children's lot in life than we want to believe. (The upside is that our little parenting screw-ups don't ruin our children's lives, either.)

And knowing this hasn't kept my colleagues from obsessing over finding just the right babysitter, enrolling their toddler in art and music classes, sending their tiny daughter to preschool prep courses, and trying to balance her academic life with her social life. Why do they do this, even though it won't have a significant effect on their daughter's intelligence, college prospects, or chances at future happiness? They do it because they want to exercise the little bit of control they do have. They do it because they are compelled to think about their child's future, and they're willing to do anything that might make her life a little bit better.

Now multiply that energy by two, then eight, then hundreds, and you have the story of a group of parents in Chicago who hit the sweet spot and made a major difference for their own children, other people's children, and their entire community.

The Roscoe Park Eight

The parents who sat around the sandbox in Roscoe Park talked endlessly about where their toddlers would go to school. Publics, privates, magnets, charters, admissions tests, lotteries for places—when did kindergarten become so complicated? Most of the moms and dads didn't even consider their neighborhood school, the Nettelhorst School, despite the fact that it was once among the most prestigious elementary schools in Chicago. As relative newcomers to up-and-coming East Lakewood, all they saw was a dark building with wire barriers over the windows, a reputation for administrative chaos, unruly bused-in kids, and terrible test scores.

But one mother, Jacqueline Edelberg, decided to visit Nettelhorst to see if it was really as bad as she'd heard. During the summer, with her two-year-old in tow, she circled the school grounds looking for an entrance. She finally found an unmarked side door where a security guard waved her in. A moment later, a woman rounded a corner and screamed at her to leave immediately.

Undeterred, Jacqueline decided to call for an appointment, which also turned out to be a challenge. Finally, after a week of phoning at various times every day, someone picked up, and she set a time to meet the principal the following morning. She took along a friend, Nicole Wagner, as backup.

To the women's surprise, Principal Susan Kurland greeted them warmly, gave them a tour of the building, and conducted a three-hour show-and-tell about school initiatives. They learned that Kurland had come to Nettelhorst two years earlier and was determined to turn it around. She'd made some headway improving student discipline, but she was struggling to get her teachers on the same page and to spark parent engagement. The latest setback was a collapsed roof that had required teachers and students to relocate. (Jacqueline then realized that the screaming woman had been shooing her away from a danger zone.)

At the end of the meeting, Kurland asked the two women a direct question: "What do I have to do to get your kids to come here?" Their stunned reply: "We'll come back tomorrow and let you know."

That afternoon, the "Big List" was born—nearly twenty stretch goals that led with two nonnegotiables: academic rigor and low teacher-student ratios. When Jacqueline and Nicole presented the list to Susan the next day, she read it through, thought for a moment, and said: "Well, girls, let's get moving; it's going to be a very busy year."

Susan was on board, but now Jacqueline and Nicole knew they needed to take stock. Did they have the energy and resources to take on this huge project? Several of the park parents insisted they'd be wasting their time on a dysfunctional school system. When they consulted a former district alderman about their plan, his first response was to laugh out loud. He said he'd tried for years to fix Nettelhorst and concluded it was a lost cause. But the principal at a successful public school nearby had a different message: "Get parents in, and you can achieve anything. Sit down with your principal and make a game plan together. Aim for the moon. If you don't reach it, you're sure to land pretty close anyway."

Despite the naysayers, Jacqueline and Nicole themselves had started to envision how bringing a renaissance to Nettelhorst could improve their lives (bye-bye competing for slots at private schools, commutes to another neighborhood, and hefty tuition bills!) and how they could also make the lives of other families better and easier. Parents united around a revitalized school could bring civic life back to their little corner of town.

Jacqueline and Nicole recruited neighborhood friends to captain teams that would each take on a specific part of the Big List. Their official title was the Nettelhorst Parents' Co-op, but they called themselves the Roscoe Park Eight. Chanting the mantra "We do more during naptime than most people do all day," they went to work.

The Roscoe Park Eight figured they had just seven months to get the school in good enough shape to woo parents and convince them to enroll their children in Nettelhorst's kindergarten the following year. They decided to begin by tackling the school's dreary façade. Soon all the exterior doors were painted bright blue; the front door was flanked by plants, and wrought-iron lamps (donated by a local store) replaced the prison-style fluorescents. Superficial changes? Sure, but at least no one would have to guess where the entrance was anymore, and it was clear that something was afoot at Nettelhorst.

No playground parents could escape the Roscoe Park Eight's pleas for volunteers, and with these extra hands, they took on a new infrastructure project green-lighted by Susan Kurland: renovate the huge, empty library, which had been neglected for years, before school opened. The Eight started cold-calling local merchants, begging for furniture, books, paint—any leftover items that a volunteer could come and carry away. Old finds were transformed into creative ways to spark the children's imaginations. The walls and ceiling were painted in sky blue with puffy white clouds. A claw-foot bathtub became the most sought after reading spot in the restocked library. There was even a sailboat with an orange sail afloat in the middle of the room. And because the volunteers worked Labor Day weekend, the library was ready for the first day of school.

Months of unremitting work later, there was a new vibe throughout the school, the halls were lined with colorful murals (both materials and talent having been donated), and a new community kitchen (also donated) was being used by teachers, students, and parents. But there were failures, too, and plenty of challenges ahead. Most of the teachers still regarded the neighborhood parents as unwelcome interlopers who were staging a hostile takeover. The parents, in turn, discovered just how hard it was to dismiss underperforming teachers, even when the principal agreed with their assessment. (Later on, many disgruntled teachers left voluntarily, and Susan invited parents to join the hiring process, resulting in a stellar faculty.) The parents' first big funding win, a three-hundred-thousand-dollar grant to establish a community center within the school, triggered chaotic scheduling and territorial problems that came close to sinking the project. And when kindergarten commitments were due for the following year, some volunteers who had given hundreds of hours to the school decided to send their own children elsewhere.

By this time, however, most of the reformers were deeply committed. They were rapidly gaining the marketing, media relations, and political skills that would spread the word about Nettelhorst and sustain the pace of change. The school grounds became the venue for public events for the entire community, including a farmer's market. Since Illinois ranked near the bottom in school funding, they recruited new volunteers to research and undertake sophisticated fund-raising from businesses and nonprofit groups.

Five years after they painted the school doors blue, the Parents Co-op had achieved every goal on their wildly hopeful Big List. They had raised more than $200,000 to renovate the science lab and auditorium. Another $210,000 came from the Chicago Blackhawks, a professional hockey team, to support the school's sports, fitness, and health programs. They had created long-term partnerships with art centers, dance schools, and businesses to make the arts and sciences curriculum among the best in the city. Test scores had more than tripled, and

Nettelhorst was named one of the top twenty schools in Chicago for academic gains.

I've focused here primarily on the Nettelhorst start-up, on how a small group of parents took a leap of faith on a project with huge obstacles and no guarantee of anything but hard work ahead. Jacqueline Edelberg and Susan Kurland later told the full story of the school's transformation in their book, *How to Walk to School: Blueprint for a Neighborhood School Renaissance*. It's an inspiring toolkit for all parents who want to stop wishing or complaining and start to build better choices for the future of their kids and themselves.

The Nettelhorst Moms and the Elements of Hope

The Roscoe Park Eight's hopeful vision was powered and sustained by the three essential elements of hope I introduced in chapter 2. Each played a crucial role in creating the vision of a better neighborhood school and the forward movement that characterizes hope in action.

Goals: More than a few Roscoe Park parents considered Jacqueline and Nicole's Big List a pipe dream, especially on a short schedule and in a bureaucratic system. But the appeal of their vision combined with the specificity of their plans drew in hundreds of volunteers over many years. A park parent who was interested in nutrition could identify immediately with the heading "Healthy, organic lunches." A book lover would want to work for the "Well-stocked, cozy library." A musician could imagine how her skills could contribute in the "Music, art, drama" category. And by making highly visible (and low-budget) changes right away, the Eight sent a powerful signal that change was possible at Nettelhorst. Each interim goal achieved and checked off inspired new, more complex and far-reaching efforts.

Agency: Many of the new families moving to East Lakeview were young professionals who prided themselves on making things happen. Jacqueline, Nicole, and the entire volunteer team were confident enough to cold-call potential donors and city bureaucrats—and keep calling. In Susan Kurland, they met an open-minded principal with a strong entrepreneurial streak who knew how to use their support. And the school's engineer, who could have been a major obstacle, got behind them from the start and helped organize many infrastructure changes. This fund of agency helped them recover from the inevitable discouragements and failures along the way. Some initiatives encountered so many obstacles that they had to be abandoned, but the group was willing to "bulldoze" (their word) when it came to their nonnegotiables.

Pathways: The eight captains each brought her own expertise to the project—from infrastructure and curriculum to special events, public relations, and marketing—based on their education and work experience. This ensured a rich mixture of priorities and plans, which were then debated and refined by the entire group every two weeks over coffee at a local diner. They also identified their knowledge gaps and recruited volunteers who could fill them. This became crucial four years into the project, when the school faced a huge budget shortfall—well beyond anything that could be made up by donated goods or neighborhood fund-raisers. A new kindergarten parent stepped up to research professional fund-raising techniques, providing a path to the new science lab and the major grant from the Blackhawks.

Ask Yourself: Five Years Ago . . . Five Years from Now

What do you see in your future? When I ask people this question, some of them respond right away with their own "Big List"—a lineup of specific goals. But there are also a lot of thoughtful folks who hesitate, all too aware of the uncertainties of life that I've touched on.

If you are looking for your Big List, here's a technique I use to reinforce hope in clients, students, and colleagues. I wait until we are celebrating a recent success or the anniversary of a meaningful accomplishment. Then I ask, "Five years ago, did you see yourself here?" This often triggers a hope retrospective, a smile and a talk about the hard times and obstacles they overcame to arrive at the present. Looking back, they are reminded of how much can happen in five years. And they almost always talk about the combination of hope, desire, determination, and luck that pulled them through. Sometimes this is the first time they see how much agency they actually had—how they were able to bend circumstances toward a desired destination.

Then I am ready with my next question: "Five years from now, what do you want your life to look like?" Try it now, and come up with as clear a picture as you can. Don't worry about probabilities or obstacles at this point; you know you will deal with them later. Put your future vision to work, and you will be surprised by how powerfully it can pull you forward.

Chapter 7

The Present Is Not What Limits Us

I WAS BORN poor and smart. When I was a child, I felt like I'd been given half of what I needed to have a good life. As I saw it, most of the other kids were born on third base and I got to first only because I was hit by a wild pitch.

How would I ever catch up with the other kids—the ones who lived in big houses on the bayou and took vacations every summer? My kid mind thought that my family and I were going nowhere fast and I would always be far behind. These thoughts made me a very anxious third grader. Most nights it was hard for me to fall asleep. I began to have stomach cramps that lasted for days at a time and caused me to miss school, which made me even more anxious and brought on more pains.

Our family doctor couldn't diagnose the problem and sent me to the hospital to see a gastroenterologist who ordered X-rays and other tests but didn't find anything wrong with me, either. My mom tried some dietary fixes, but the pain would not let up. I started to believe that the stomach cramps would be with me forever.

Out of a nine-year-old's desperation, I dreamed up my first psychological intervention: I decided to "act as if" I weren't anxious and in pain. I didn't have a clue how to do this, though, so I just started to imitate the kids who seemed happy and healthy. Sometimes I would act like my buddy Cory, who was full of confidence. Following his lead, I would walk right up to other kids and say hello rather than slinking around on the edges of groups of boys and girls at recess. My friend Bubby was always cool and laughing a lot, so I started spending more time with him. He and I got good at pulling pranks on each other. Day by day, my friends slowly rubbed off on me. I still felt lots of stress and my stomach still hurt at times, but the pain was much more manageable.

This was my first lesson in self-determination—the belief that I could act in a way that would influence my future. By changing my behavior, I could have a future with less anxiety and pain. In hindsight, third grade was when I started to believe that the arc of my life wasn't entirely determined by my current circumstances.

Kids and grown-ups alike tend to believe that their personal circumstances and characteristics are the major determinants of where they end up in life. And—let's acknowledge it right up front—to some extent, the rich do get richer and the happy do get happier. But a good bit of our future is not left to chance (see chapter 6). It is not predetermined by who we are at birth or even by who we are today. So, what does that mean for a kid who was born poor and smart? What does it mean for you? That's what this chapter is about.

Not All Smart People Are Hopeful

The one thing that I did better than most other kids was school. Because I made good grades and received academic honors, people praised me for being smart. By the time I was in junior high I believed that my intelligence—this thing that I supposedly possessed in greater quantities than others—would bring me success and even happiness.

These early beliefs followed me through grad school and the start of my career as a psychologist, as an intelligence researcher at a U.S. Department of Veterans Affairs medical center. There, although I worked with the best, the more I learned the more disillusioned I became. Smart people with bad lives came into the lab every day. One man with a genius-level IQ used his smarts in antisocial ways, cooking up schemes that took advantage of other people. Another very bright guy didn't know the basics about how to start a relationship. "How do I tell if she still likes me? What can we do on a date?" he would ask. Some smart people were unable to keep a job for more than a month or two. And many of the smartest folks seemed stuck, unable to get past problems they had been grappling with for decades.

After seeing this time and again, I started to drill deeper into the role intelligence played in success, asking, Does IQ account for most of a person's success at work? Neuropsychologists who considered intelligence alongside memory and executive functioning couldn't fully explain how people did on the job. In fact, innate cognitive ability accounted for only a fourth of the variance in success at work.

Toward the end of my time at the VA, I concluded that high intelligence wasn't always accompanied by good intentions, common sense, or motivation, and that a bulging IQ didn't guarantee success. But only after I encountered John the farmer and saw that *only when he was invested in the future* could he deal with his problems, did I begin to inquire into the relationship between intelligence and hope. John was whip-smart, but that didn't buffer him from his fears.

In the years since, I've confirmed that intelligence determines little about how we think about the future. The research on this topic is straightforward. Give a large group of people tests for intelligence and hope, then correlate the two scores. Whether you test children or adults, you'll find that *there is no relationship between intelligence and hope.* In the real world, that means not all smart people are hopeful and not all hopeful people are smart.

While these two psychological resources don't necessarily show up in high levels in the same person, they do complement each other, working together to help people achieve their goals. Economics professor Armenio Rego of the University of Aveiro in Portugal, who is a leading expert on hope in the workplace, has shown that hope and intelligence reinforce each other to increase creativity and productivity. On one hand, hopeful people benefit from intelligence because it can help them get to the root of problems and find more and better solutions and opportunities. On the other hand, intelligent people can use their cognitive strengths more creatively when they're high in hope.

Without hope, Rego points out, intelligence can be a "dormant" resource. The ability to learn from and understand the environment means little if it's not jump-started by the motivational energy of high hope. His conclusion: "Many intelligent people do not succeed precisely because they are not energized with high hope."

Hope Costs Nothing

Money buys lots of things that make our lives better. It gives us access to good food, quality education, and modern health care. It can even buy us a little happiness. But can money buy hope? Or is hope an equal-opportunity resource?

The cost of hope can be quantified by considering whether the rich have more ideas and energy for the future than do the poor. And the income threshold of hope can be determined by pinpointing the level of income at which more money stops providing more returns on hope. When I analyzed the hope in rich and poor families, there was *no relationship between hope and income*. When I compared the hope of elementary and secondary students enrolled in a free- and reduced-lunch program to the hope of students whose families didn't qualify for assistance, there were no systematic differences.

Hope costs nothing. There is no relationship between hope and money. The hopeful don't necessarily have money and the rich aren't necessarily hopeful. But I have noticed that people with lots of hope are masters at attracting resources. Remember Chuck, the entrepreneur beer brewer? People invested in him because he had a great idea and boundless determination. And in a few pages you will read about a woman whose big hopes were backed up with a seven-figure donation. So, while money does not give you hope, hope may attract money to turn big ideas into reality. In fact, if you are looking for a solid return on your money, invest big in hope.

Recent research has found no consistent findings pointing to one racial or ethnic group being more hopeful than any other. No single group of people can claim it as theirs and theirs alone. So a wealthy African-American business owner and a middle-class Hispanic college student and a poor laborer of any race or ethnicity have equal chances of being hopeful. *Yet hope is not left to chance.* What makes the difference in whether someone's hope is turned on or left inert? It depends on your mindset.

Finding the Necessary Energy in the Sweet Spot of Hope

When we're in the sweet spot of hope, we know that our present does not determine our future. In the sweet spot we are able to evaluate our present circumstances, abilities, and resources realistically, without getting discouraged if they still need to be built up. We listen to our desires and dreams because they tell us who we are, and we notice innate talents that others might miss. (Remember, some class clowns do grow up to star on *Saturday Night Live*.) We also devote time and effort to the skills we need to develop our talents. In the sweet spot, we act as if the life script we are handed at birth can be edited and improved.

Hope is not a psychological silver spoon or an automatic by-product of IQ. Entitlement and passivity are hope killers. Our energy comes from excitement about what's next and from the supporters we recruit.

Setting Your Mind to It

Imagine you're back in sixth grade, and your teacher has seated all the children in the classroom in order of their IQ. She makes it clear that for her, intelligence is the final word on character and potential. What's more, the children who have the highest IQs are the only ones who get to wash the blackboard or carry the flag during assembly. How would this affect your performance in her class? In the long term would it make you more or less hopeful?

Stanford psychologist Carol Dweck had that sixth-grade teacher. The experience sparked her career-long study of motivation, intelligence, and how we cope with failure. Although Dweck herself sat right at the front, she now believes that the effect on the kids at the top of the class was just as negative as it was for the kids at the bottom. As she recalls, "It was an uncomfortable thing because you were only as good as your last test score. . . . So the students who had the best seats were always scared of taking another test and not being at the top anymore."

Through her research, Dweck has defined two possible ways to think about intelligence and personality and how they relate to the future. "Mindset" is her word for these beliefs about ourselves. If you have a *fixed* mindset, you believe that your talents and abilities are set in stone—you have them or you don't. If you have a fixed mindset, you are less hopeful about the future. You have an upper limit, and there's nothing you can do to change it, so why try? (This was the belief of her sixth-grade teacher.) If you're one of the "gifted," you fear risk and failure because you might find out you're less talented than you thought. You internal dialogue might be "These are the only resources I have or need to get to my goal." You would start to miss cues about where you needed to make more effort or develop skills or resources to move ahead. On the other hand, if you have a *growth* mindset, you know that you can develop your talents and build your abilities. You have nothing to lose—and much to gain—if you try new ways to reach your goals.

Your inner voice tells you, "No matter what I start with, I can develop or find the resources I need as challenges pop up."

In one New York City junior high school, Dweck and her colleagues taught practical study skills to a group of students, along with how they could learn to be smart. The brain is like a muscle, they told the kids, and it gets stronger with use. A second group of students learned only the study skills. In just two months, the students in the first group leaped ahead of the second in grades and study habits. "What was important was the motivation," says Dweck. "The students were energized by the idea that they could have an impact on their mind." She recalls one boy—a notorious troublemaker—who looked at her with tears in his eyes. "You mean, I don't have to be dumb?" he said.

David Yeager, one of Dweck's former graduate students, now an assistant professor at the University of Texas, helped me make sense of that junior high boy's question. "When those with more of a fixed mindset about their traits encounter an obstacle, they are more likely to predict that it will never get better, that their life will always be this way, that they'll continue to be left out or excluded, and that their own deficient traits will cause their life to be less positive." With more of a growth mindset, that young man will have a greater desire to learn and a tendency to seek challenges, rather than avoid them.

As Yeager's comment suggests, mindset research has grown well beyond "smarts" to address all the labels we and others attach to ourselves. For example, he and his colleagues have shown that a growth mindset is key to reducing stress, depression, and aggression in adolescents who have suffered social rejection or bullying. Young teens easily think in fixed categories: They agree with statements like "Everyone is either a winner or a loser in life," and they see people in black-and-white terms as "good" or "bad." A teen who sees himself as a loser, or as someone who is just not likable, is stuck in his pain. Helpless and hopeless, he's also more likely to seek revenge on the "bad" person who has humiliated him. Simple interventions that help teens see themselves and others as "works in progress" can jump-start the coping skills they need in order to navigate high school—and give them hope for the people they will become.

In short, mindset influences every aspect of your life, from work to sports, from relationships to parenting. If you believe you can change and develop, you know you can move beyond your present limitations. This makes a growth mindset the natural companion of hope.

Messages That Neutralize Hope

Pursuing a meaningful goal is much harder when we face naysayers and devil's advocates who cast doubt on our abilities. These hope neutralizers may actually believe they are well-intentioned and only want to save us from disappointment, but their messages typically do more harm than good. Sometimes they're still echoing in our heads years after we first heard them. To stay in the sweet spot of hope, you have to put these messages to the test, use what is valid as meaningful feedback, and ignore the rest.

Beware of hope neutralizers like these: "Our kind of people just can't do that." "You're not college material." "You should be grateful for what you have." "You were never really good at that." "You have to be rich to make it." They all reflect a fixed mindset, and reinforce the destructive notion that the world is permanently divided into "haves" and "have-nots."

Maybe you're hearing the message in your own voice: "I'm not smart enough for college." "The economy is against me." "I'm too old/too young." "I don't have the connections to get the job." "People like me don't get ahead." If you recognize these thoughts, you have to carefully examine how much your view of your present circumstances keeps you right where you are.

Hopeful people are independent thinkers who crave autonomy. Paradoxically, this sometimes leads to workplace problems, especially when bosses and coworkers have fixed mindsets. Bosses who feel challenged by hopeful people may try to reinforce authority by discounting employee efforts and holding them back. Colleagues may see initiative and energy as an attempt to show them up and send hope-neutralizing messages: "What makes you so special?" "Don't be an overachiever." "You're making the rest of us look bad." When this happens, unless there's a major change in the organization, it's probably time to look for another job.

Bottom line: Negative messages deplete you, sap your agency, and keep you stuck. Disputing these messages will help you reclaim your motivation for the goals that matter to you most.

A Desire to Learn and Grow

Young Tererai was blessed with determination, curiosity, and intelligence, but in her birthplace, a small village in Zimbabwe, she was destined for poverty, illiteracy, and unending labor. Her father refused to send her to school. Girls get married, he said; boys are breadwinners. But after she did her chores, she taught herself to read and write from her brother's schoolbooks, and soon she was doing his homework for him every night. It didn't take the teacher long to notice that the homework was much better than the boy's work in class, and he pleaded with Tererai's father to let her attend school. Her father's response was to beat her for shaming the family.

The teacher didn't give up, however, and finally Tererai entered the classroom she'd longed to attend, shoeless and wearing her father's shirt as a dress. Her time there was short. After only a couple of terms, she was married off at age eleven to a man who beat her if he caught her reading—and for almost any other reason. By the time she was eighteen, she had three children.

Then in 1991, when Tererai was in her twenties, Jo Luck, the head of an aid group called Heifer International, came to her village. Heifer's mission is reducing poverty by promoting self-reliance, and Jo Luck asked the village women a question that astonished them: "What are your hopes and dreams?" Tererai still recalls that moment. "My name is Tererai," she answered, "and I want to go to America to have an education, and I want to have a B.S. degree, I want to have a master's, and I want to have a Ph.D." (She'd heard of these degrees in stories of famous African men.) Jo Luck just looked at her and said, "If you desire those things, it is achievable."

Tererai's mother encouraged her to write her goals on a piece of paper, wrap the paper in plastic, and put it in an old tin: "If you truly believe in those dreams, you'll see them grow," she told her daughter. "Cover those dreams with a rock, and they will call you back." Tererai buried her list near where she had herded cattle as a child.

In 1998, Tererai was admitted to Oklahoma State University and moved to America with her children and husband. (Coming along was his price for allowing the children to leave.) She thrived academically despite working several jobs, but the family was living in a broken-down trailer, she and the children were barely eating, and her husband was still beating her. It was only when the university tried to expel her for late tuition that an administrator, Ron Beer, discovered what was going on. He organized support from the community and arranged housing through Habitat for Humanity. In 2001, Tererai received her B.A. in agricultural education. In 2003—the year her husband was deported—she received her master's. She was working on her Ph.D. at Western Michigan University, happily remarried and writing a dissertation on AIDS prevention in Africa, when she got a surprise call from Oprah Winfrey to appear on her television show.

On October 1, 2009, millions watched as Tererai described her passion for education and her effort to end generations of poverty in her family. Then the scene shifted to Zimbabwe, and the camera showed Tererai being greeted in her home village. There she went searching for the rock that had protected her dreams for so long. Digging deep into the dirt with her hands, she unearthed the tin and unfolded the paper on which she'd written her goals. It was nearly time to check off the last one. She received her doctorate in December 2009.

Statistically speaking, Tererai is an outlier, an anomaly, an exception to every rule. Yet many people have her potential, but are not recognized and supported at crucial times in their lives. Many cut off their own future because no one has ever asked, "What are your hopes and dreams?"

In October 2011, Tererai Trent returned again to her village—this time to visit the site of the new Matau Primary School. Thanks to a grant of more than a million dollars from the Oprah Winfrey Foundation, administered by Save the Children, the school Tererai attended for less than a year will have new classrooms for 850 students, as well as new latrines and homes for teachers. It will also anchor early childhood education and literacy programs for neighboring villages. Tererai's current dream is to promote education for poor children, and particularly girls and women in sub-Saharan Africa. Her message to the children who gathered to meet her at her old school: "You have to be strong and value education and do not rush into marriage."

Tererai Trent and the Elements of Hope

Tererai seemed destined to follow the traditional paths of her culture, but developed a hopeful vision of a very different future. There is something unique and mysterious about her drive to grow, but we can also see how the elements of hope guided every step of her journey.

Goals: When Tererai discovered that she easily learned her brother's lessons, she gave a name to her longings: education. At this point, the intervention of her brother's teacher was crucial. Even though her father tried to beat her dreams out of her, another powerful adult had become her advocate and validated that her goal was good and deserved support. Later on, Tererai gave more specific names to her dreams: education in America, a B.S., a master's degree, a Ph.D. She not only named these goals, she wrote them down and buried them in a memorable ritual suggested by her mother. At the worst of times after Tererai came to America, when it seemed as if she could not continue, she could imagine those goals calling to her from under a rock in her home village.

Agency: Tererai seems to have developed a sense of agency at an early age. When she told Oprah about her wish to go to school, she said, "I just wanted to sit at a desk and raise my hand and say something." She was ready to jump in and participate, not just observe. Tererai was also ready to "say something" when Jo Luck asked the astonishing question, "What are your hopes and dreams?" Above all, Tererai knew the power of work. As a very young child, she had herded cattle, cared for her siblings, and done domestic chores. Her actions made a difference; they had consequences. In the Oprah footage, when she returns to her village, a group of young women greets her with a joyous chant. The chorus, repeated again and again: "She worked hard."

Pathways: Tererai is a hero of hope, but her story is also about the many people and organizations that gave her encouragement, opened pathways, and provided material resources when she most needed them. The quiet support of her mother was a constant in her life. Jo Luck and Heifer International gave Tererai a job as a community organizer, which funded her education in Zimbabwe. They also helped her get to America, but it took Tererai's mother going to the village elders—who urged villagers to sell some chickens and goats—to secure the last $480 of money necessary to pay for her grandchildren's airfare. At Oklahoma State University, administrator Ron Beer organized help from his church, the community, and Habitat for Humanity to keep Tererai on track for a degree. Tererai also inspired Oprah Winfrey to give a hefty grant toward rebuilding her primary school in Zimbabwe, which will create pathways for new generations of children.

Ask Yourself: Tapping the Sources of Hope

No one type of person has cornered the market on hope. It is an equal-opportunity resource available to everyone. Whatever your present circumstances, you can create some momentum toward a desired future.

I've met plenty of people who have a hard time recruiting hope, usually because they feel overwhelmed by what's going on right now. When this is the case, I ask two questions that can help them reconnect with their agency.

"Who makes you feel like you matter?" This may be someone in your life right now: a friend, a teacher, a child, a relative. It may also be a person in your past who made you feel understood, valued, and encouraged. It may even be someone who has passed away. If the person is living, make an effort to contact and spend time with him or her. If the person has died, use photos and memories to help you gain access to the warmth and energy of their support. These important people can give you the energy and determination you need to move forward. In a sense, you can borrow agency from them until you feel your own strength returning.

"What really matters to you?" This question reminds you of what is important to you and what you have to offer the world. For many people, the answer taps into their deepest values and passions. "It matters that I care about helping people." "It matters that I love my family." "It matters that I want an education." "It matters that I love to sing." Other people mention a vocation or skill. "It matters that I am a good cook (or office manager, or father, or . . .)." Sometimes people name an object or place that has deep significance to them: a family home, their church, a sports trophy, a book they loved as a child, an heirloom.

Whenever you recall what matters most to you, you reconnect with your sense of identity and purpose, which can spark you to take hopeful action.

Chapter 8

The Past Is Not a Preview

IMAGINE THAT your job is to invest millions of dollars every year in the best start-ups that come your way. The job is yours as long as you pick the successful companies and pass on the losers. What do you use for your selection criteria? How do you decide which entrepreneurs get funded and which ones don't? How much risk do you take on?

Joe Kraus, an investing partner at Google Ventures, is responsible for finding technology start-ups that dream up new gadgets and mobile and gaming services. Most entrepreneurs have their fair share of failure stories, but Kraus picks his winners by listening to plans for their new business, not stories about why their old business failed. As he puts it, "I'm first and foremost far more interested in their current idea than what happened in the past, so in the meeting with the entrepreneurs I actually don't spend a ton of time on what have they learned from their past experience. I'm much more interested in how are they thinking about their current business."

Kraus also looks for people who leverage both hope and fear about what's next. "In my mind, the ones who have no fear of failure are merely the dreamers, and the dreamers don't build great companies. The people who thread the line between vision and being able to execute and having this healthy fear of failing that drives them—not paralyzes them, but drives them—to be more persistent, to work harder than the next person—that's a magic formula." He says, in conclusion, "I think failure in the culture [of Silicon Valley] means you just haven't gotten your success yet."

The Best Predictor of Future Behavior?

When a big venture capitalist challenges a commonly held belief about behavior, I sit up and pay attention. This is because, when I was a graduate student in psychology, we were taught the following as a general truth: *Past behavior is the best predictor of future behavior.* Known as Meehl's maxim, after the University of Minnesota psychologist Paul Meehl, it has been tested and retested for more than fifty years. Study after study suggests that skilled experts using their best professional judgment couldn't predict future performance any better than (or, in many cases, even as well as) a few simple measures like past grades or recent scores on a test of ability. (This was one point of Daniel Kahneman's story—in chapter 6—about his attempts to evaluate the leadership potential of Israeli army soldiers.)

This principle has become deeply embedded in our lives, and I mean *all* of our lives, not just the lives of psychologists. It guides decision makers from college admissions committees to parole boards to loan officers. Financial experts use it to pick stocks and mutual funds. Human resources pros review applicants' job records looking for past brilliance. Law enforcement agents build current cases around a suspect's past offenses. And I'll bet you can hear some version of the same maxim on *SportsCenter, The Suze Orman Show*, and *Dr. Phil* all in the same afternoon.

Meehl's maxim is attractive because it offers a simple solution to the complex problem of selecting the right person, whether for a job or a wanted poster: *the past is the best predictor of future behavior.* For psychologists, the idea carried even more weight because of the legacy of Sigmund

Freud, whose model led psychoanalysts to spend years digging around in patients' pasts for the causes of current problems. Yet this mostly left people "unduly embittered about their past and unduly passive about their future," as University of Pennsylvania psychologist Martin Seligman, a leader of the positive psychology initiative, has pointed out.

Studying the science of hope with Rick Snyder pointed me in a new direction, as did Stern's San Antonio study, which showed that the key factor in how long people lived was how they thought about the future. Hope made the difference that standard measures just didn't capture.

In the search for sure investments, great employees, and bad apples, we have to start somewhere. The past is accessible and rich in detail. But even when the past is a predictor, it's actually not a very good one. That's because all behavior, whether it is how fast you will run a race, how well you do on a test, or how successful you will be on the job, is multiply determined. In other words, how any of us perform on a given day has more than one cause, and there are still big gaps in our understanding of what drives life's major outcomes.

Retired four-star United States Army general Colin Powell has earned numerous military, civilian, and foreign honors. He served in four presidential administrations in a variety of roles, including chairman of the Joint Chiefs of Staff and secretary of state. In his leadership book, *It Worked for Me,* he recalls that foreign military leaders often asked him, "When did you graduate from West Point?"—the obvious pedigree for someone of his accomplishments. But he didn't go to West Point, or any other famous American military institution, because, when Powell was entering college, a black person couldn't attend those schools. Powell attended the City College of New York, the free public college in Harlem, not far from where he was born. As Powell puts it in his book, "My city believed that kids like me deserved a shot at the top."

Powell says he was a mediocre student at CCNY, with one exception: his outstanding performance in ROTC. It was his A in ROTC that got his average up to just above 2.0, which allowed him to qualify for graduation.

ROTC had given Powell his vocation and he had risen to the top through the rigorous and frequent evaluation reports that determine every Army promotion. Nevertheless, "Potential, Not Just Performance" is the title of his chapter on evaluation. "Past performance alone does not adequately predict future performance," he writes. "Sure, if past performance is mediocre or worse, satisfactory or outstanding performance in the future is extremely unlikely, and if past performance ranges from better than satisfactory to outstanding, chances are good that the performance in the future will continue at that level. But it's not a sure thing."

Powell explains the qualities leaders and bosses should use to select the best candidates for a position, criteria that smack of the future focus, can-do spirit, and positive relationships demonstrated by hopeful people in every profession. They include: "Learning and growing intellectually . . . preparing for the next level" and "Reaching outside his comfort zone to acquire skills and knowledge that are not now essential, but are useful at a higher level." He writes that a person who is "[c]onfident about the next step . . . mentally prepared . . . balanced" and "[e]njoys the respect and confidence of his contemporaries" should be given special consideration.

Powell ends with a strong caution for anyone who is responsible for evaluating others: "Always be prepared to change your mind, however firmly made up, when dealing with those infinitely faceted beings we call people."

History and Hope

Because of these findings of positive psychology—and our own observations—my research colleagues and I focus on two things that add up to predict success at school and work: history and hope. We have considered how past grades and test scores plus hope predict college grades, work productivity, and staying power (graduating from school or keeping a job). In our research (introduced in chapter 4), the links between history, hope, and educational outcomes are becoming clear (see chapter 14). Indeed, in samples of grade school, high school, and college students, hope is directly related to academic achievement. Specifically, hope relates to higher achievement test scores for grade school children and higher GPAs for college and law students. The predictive power of hope adds to that accounted for by intelligence in children and by previous grades and scores on entrance exams (the ACT, SAT, and LSAT) for college and law students. In a six-year longitudinal study, the hope scores of entering college freshmen predicted better overall GPAs, adding to what is known about entrance exam scores. Maybe it is time for college recruiters to look beyond how students stack up on standardized tests and also consider how they think about big goals and go about pursuing them.

History and hope add up. The stories we tell about our future lives are, in part, a product of our past accomplishments and the identity we have created to summarize our history. Developing our best possible future selves requires an unvarnished assessment of who we have been and of how that relates to who we want to be. It also may require us to acknowledge our fears.

Hope Versus Fear

I used to believe that people could be divided into the hopeful and the fearful. I also thought that hope for the future was the primary motivator for success, whereas fear led to a seat on the sidelines of life. Then one day early in my career as a psychology professor, a colleague and I were debating what leads to a good outcome in the classroom. "Before I teach a large class," I said, "I think about the one hard-to-reach student and come up with multiple ways to make the material come alive." My colleague laughed. "When I am in front of a big room full of students," he said, "I am dreading that I look stupid. I spend a lot of time thinking about ways to not look like an idiot." It was my turn to laugh. I had to admit how much classroom energy I invested in managing students' impressions of me. Fear was part of my teaching formula, too.

A nasty case of West Nile virus was another lesson in hope and fear. During my year-long recovery, I tried to set daily rehab goals, but quickly discovered they could make my lingering pain worse and even cause new problems. Was walking down to the end of the block a doable goal? Well, I got there, but I had to sit down in a neighbor's yard for twenty minutes before I could make the sloth-like trek back to my front door.

Once I started socializing and teaching again, my hopes for connecting with others were balanced with anxiety over answering questions about an exotic illness and doing my job well. Fortunately, concern and support from my wife, friends, colleagues, and students helped me reenter my life.

It seemed that, when I was able to balance hope and fear, my health improved at a steady pace. When my high hopes weren't held in check, I exercised too much and suffered for it. When fear trumped hope, I became a recluse, withdrawing from friends, family, and profession.

Choosing hope and managing fear is hard work that never lets up. It is the work of a lifetime. We humans will always be hope-fear hybrids.

Fear signals come from one of the oldest parts of the brain, the amygdala, which automatically triggers a whole-body response that gives us the resources we need to fight back, make tracks, or play dead (otherwise known as "fight, flight, or freeze"). Fear makes us behave as if we have blinders on, seeing only the most obvious options—which may be the ones we need most.

When fear does its job, we escape what scares us. But this response is exhausting, and it comes with a host of negative emotional and physical consequences.

Hope, in contrast, depends on the youngest part of our brain, the prefrontal cortex (see chapter 3). When we attach ourselves to the future through a goal that matters to us, our brain tells us to reach out, find more resources, and get some support. In effect, hope takes the blinders off and helps us see opportunity.

No creativity comes out of fear; we just don't see possibility when we are afraid, and fear can keep us running in small circles. We have more pathways to the future when hope edges out fear. Innovation comes out of hope; we create something out of nothing, then tweak, tweak, tweak until it works just right. Hope works because it broadens our thinking *and* because it fuels persistence. Big thinking without stick-to-itiveness is not hoping, it's wishing.

Messages That Deny Hope

Everyone has been rejected. "No" stings for a long time, especially when you believe you truly were the right person for the team, club, school, job, or significant other.

"What makes you think you can do this job?" Some people open an interview with this question because they are genuinely curious about your self-assessment. When Jane Brody, then twenty-four years old, and with only two years of newspaper experience, applied for a job as a science writer for the *New York Times*, an interviewer told her she was "foolhardy." She replied, "If I didn't think I could do the job, I wouldn't be here." It was just what he wanted to hear, and she has flourished in the role for many years.

When others don't see our upside, it may be because they are stuck on our past or because their own fears keep them from taking a chance on us. Less open interviewers focus on a fixed set of criteria: "Maybe you've set the bar too high," or "Most of our associates are Ivy League graduates." Such statements suggest a fearful search for the sure thing. What interviewers forget is that sure things *just don't exist.*

The most damaging messages are those that creep into our own thinking, sabotaging us from the start: "I am scared to ask her out. She's out of my league" or "If he didn't get into that program, why would I?" or "No one will invest money in my business."

Bottom line: Critiques and self-talk like these block your entry into schools, jobs, and relationships. They alter your life course. These path-changing messages steal our self-determination.

Keeping an Open Mind

When we think about the future (in therapy or in any other change process), our emotional experiences are crucial to what we believe is possible. They can help us broaden or narrow our views; they can help us build new and durable resources or chip away at the resources we already have. This is the message of research by Barbara Frederickson, a psychologist at the University of North Carolina who calls her work "the broaden-and-build" theory of positive emotions.

Frederickson has shown that feelings like hope, happiness, and freedom are not just a welcome break from the serious stuff of life; they also have long-term survival value. Positive emotions broaden attention and cognition—when we feel safe and happy, we learn more easily and think about problems more creatively. We also become more goal-oriented and resilient.

In one experiment, Frederickson asked groups of participants to watch a film clip that induced one of four emotions—joy, contentment, anger, fear—or a control film inducing a neutral state. Afterward, the viewers were asked to list everything they would like to do at that moment. Those who had experienced joy or contentment came up with more possibilities than participants who'd watched the negative or neutral clips. When thinking about the future, they had kept open minds. They were ready to act. Those who experienced fear and anger tended to shut down their thinking.

The open-mindedness brought about by positive emotions helps us create resources, including new social bonds. It helps us maintain a sense of vital energy and then generates even more resources and pathways. Fredrickson calls this sequence the upward spiral of positive emotions. This upward spiral fuels our pursuit of the future.

Moving Past Fear

One of my most challenging psychotherapy clients, Christina had a troubled past. On the surface, she seemed to be doing fine. She was accomplished, beautiful, and intelligent. As she summed it up, "On paper I look great, but when you get to know me you realize that I'm a total mess."

When I started to work with Christina, she was doing well in a demanding MBA program, but she had no social life. Zero. The hour she spent with me was her most prolonged human contact each week. She didn't know how to introduce herself, or make small talk, or pick up on jokes, much less navigate friendships. She was oddly "off" in almost every exchange.

She had grown up as the only child of an elder in a very strict church. Religion, family, and rules dominated her childhood, along with her father's explosive rage at the slightest infraction. (I suspected more than emotional abuse, but Christina kept that door firmly closed during the entire five years I saw her.)

"What about your past can you let go, and what do you want to keep?" I asked her. Answering that question took months. Each week Christina would try to shed some of her damaged self, but it often frightened her even to think about new ways of doing things.

When she got her degree, her stellar record landed her a job with a tech firm that she'd really wanted. Her new goal for therapy was to become the person who could keep that job. She had made it through a formal interview, but ordinary give-and-take with colleagues was a daily obstacle course. If she sensed rejection, she would go into a weeks-long retreat. But over the next two years, she made slow but steady progress, and I saw her grow more confident about who she was becoming. She described feeling less burdened: "I feel more free, more open." On that note, we started the next phase of therapy.

Many psychologists, consultants, and coaches help people detach themselves from a heavy past and then stop. That fix-it approach doesn't capitalize on the growth and change generated by helping the client reach for the future. (In Martin Seligman's words, "The best therapists do not merely heal damage; they help people identify and build their strengths and their virtues.") Once Christina learned how to handle the social dynamics at her office, she set another goal. She told me she wanted to be "at the front of the room" as a trainer for her tech team. This would mean visiting the firm's branch offices to work with new groups of MBAs and engineers—a huge social challenge for her. She also wanted to start dating, because, at age twenty-eight, she had never been on a date.

Christina signed up for a course in management training, but I thought she could also recruit her skills and strengths on her own behalf. "Imagine that you're your own client," I suggested. "You're a fine strategic thinker who can sort through all the moving parts of a business. Maybe you can do the same thing with people and emotions."

Open to my suggestions for participating in a carefully selected therapy group and for experimenting with unfamiliar situations, like having dinner alone in a restaurant, Christina also started to identify her own pathways. She joined several community groups, including a more progressive church with lively younger members, and signed up for an online match service. Soon she went on her first date, and then another.

I saw her less frequently, meeting only when she needed a psychotherapeutic booster shot. When she was transferred to a training job out of state, I gave her a couple of referrals, but it was clear she was ready to try life on her own.

Making sense of our past and facing our fears frees up the psychological resources we need to invest in the future. We start to tell the story of our lives in a new way—one that includes hope.

Taking the Right Risks in the Sweet Spot of Hope

In the sweet spot of hope we have a healthy respect for the past and a passion for the future. We use the lessons (many derived from failures) and successes of the past to refine our goals, preview obstacles, and ward off hope killers.

In this sweet spot, the mind is open to what is next. Excitement and energy abound and fear becomes manageable. Pathways are plentiful when we right-size the risks in our lives.

We are naturally risk-averse creatures living in a world where risk is inescapable. Much of our risk management happens outside our awareness. For example, behavioral economists have repeatedly shown that loss aversion subconsciously motivates people even more strongly than an opportunity for gain. In other words, we are reluctant to give up a sure thing even if doing so gives us a good chance at something better.

We gain more conscious control when we become aware of our threshold for hope and our tolerance for stress associated with fear and risk. The emotional calculus done to buffer stress with hope in a risky situation is second nature to some people. For the rest of us, risk tolerance grows as we increase our pathways and resources in the face of challenges.

Risk that seems overwhelming triggers stress that can decrease mental flexibility. With fewer pathways we are more likely to become stuck or fail. To be successful in business and life, we must right-size our risk, realizing that one person's exciting hope-filled enterprise might be another person's dangerously high-risk gamble. When we take on right-risk opportunities—those that we have the requisite psychological resources to manage—we keep moving *futureward*.

Joe's Drive-In, Food Trucks, Other Right-Risk Start-ups

One Friday night in 1978 my mom stopped by our favorite restaurant, Joe's Drive-In, to pick up fried chicken and sides. As usual, the chicken was delicious. So we were all surprised when my brother, sister, and I got a gut-wrenching case of food poisoning. My dad called Sonny, the owner of the drive-in, to tell him about the bad food (which both Sonny and the health department said was a first). He invited my dad over for an apology and a few beers and told my dad that he was ready to sell Joe's and open up a new business. Dad saw this as a chance to be his own boss and leave oil field construction, which is how we came to own a low-slung cinder-block building and a few recipes.

Most businesses in America are similar to Joe's, what economists call lifestyle businesses. These restaurants, retailers, and service companies are built to provide a sustainable living for a family or two and wage work for maybe a dozen employees. Hope is vital to the day-to-day operations. Every month you have fixed expenses to cover. Anything left over is for your family. Every month you come up with new ways to make ends meet.

First-time entrepreneurs like my family have no track record. There is no past business-owning experience that would make the bank and other funders more confident about loaning money. So the investors keep the purse strings tight. As a result, first-timers have to look for a low barrier to entry into business. And that low barrier plus Americans' desire for better fast food explains the current food truck phenomenon.

With the proper license, recipes, talents, and $10,000 to $150,000, you can own your own modern-day chuckwagon. Taco trucks, which have been staples in some cities for decades, predated the food on wheels explosion. Roy Choi's opening of one of the first modern food trucks in Los Angeles, Kogi BBQ, featuring Korean short-rib tacos, started an American trend that now has caught on in Paris, one of the culinary capitals of the world. Kristin Frederick, a California native and culinary school grad, rolled out the first food truck in Paris, the hugely popular Le Camion Qui Fume (The Smoking Truck). Before she launched her burger truck, people said she would face insurmountable challenges, including the risk of trying to sell food that no one would buy. "I got every kind of push-back," said Frederick, who refers to herself as the Chief Executive Problem Solver. "People said 'The French will never eat on the street. The French will never eat with their hands. They will never pay good money for food from a truck.'" And "You will never get permission from the authorities." The naysayers were right about the Paris bureaucracies but Frederick rose to the occasion. "When someone tells me something is impossible I find it challenging." She had to navigate four agencies before she was assigned her spot and days (no roaming around allowed for French food trucks). Like most entrepreneurs, Frederick proved she could tolerate the risks of the unknown and find ways around any problems. And, from opening day, she has sold every burger on every shift.

Pop-up stores also have become a popular alternative for new entrepreneurs looking for a right-risk opportunity. Trading a full-year lease for a rental of unused space for a month or two, they offer cheap ways to generate buzz for new companies. Nate Demars became a business owner by launching a pop-up store specializing in high-quality men's suits. Demars's Pursuit targets men who need a suit for graduation, job interviews, and other special occasions with a streamlined inventory of fashionable and affordable suits. The store is near Ohio State University, where Demars hatched the idea in a business school entrepreneurship class. "It's a fresh idea in a boring old business."

To date, Pursuit has been a success. It recently moved to its second pop-up location in Columbus and Demars is open to the idea of taking the shop on the road. What other business could you conceivably move from campus to campus on a week's notice? Pop-ups are portable because risks and sunk costs are kept so low.

Food trucks and pop-up stores are start-ups that require little capital to sustain themselves. Larger start-ups, especially those that are producing or manufacturing goods, have a higher barrier to entry. Along with hope, they need a great idea, some cash on hand, sound R&D, and a little luck. Sonos had all of these when formed in 2002.

Sonos founders had one big idea: to send music from the Internet to every room in a home, wirelessly. With a small amount of capital and no track record in tech hardware design and production, they were believed to be destined for the fate of almost every other gadget tech start-up: failure. Three years after its launch, its first product, the Zone-Player 100, was delivered and well received. Sonos had a chance.

As they began to capitalize on their initial success, the recession hit and risk of failure skyrocketed. When I asked how a then-smallish company survived the downturn, Sonos CEO and cofounder John MacFarlane said that it was having a "singular vision to fill every home with music." It was that "focus that pulled us forward." With that vision and the "great energy" it inspires in its leadership and employees, Sonos continues to come up with new routes to discovery and more ways to overcome obstacles. That singular vision also kept Sonos from trying to make quick money by putting out a line of products that would sell but not necessarily fulfill the mission.

Inspired by the design and development process at Apple, Sonos has gone to great lengths to create a product that is radically simple. "There are always obstacles to overcome," MacFarlane said. "Software, mechanical, and acoustic engineers have to work together" to produce a best-in-class system.

While I have not been able to sample Frederick's burger or buy one of Demars's suits, my Sonos system has increased my enjoyment of music at least tenfold, because it made listening to music easy. Setup of the hardware took minutes and the wireless connectivity just happened. Every song I can think of is accessible through one of Sonos's partners, such as Rhapsody, Spotify, and Sirius. And its controller is on my phone (thanks to a free downloadable app), which means . . . well, it's just cool.

Sonos, a private company, continues to grow. It also has become a magnet for resources (raising $135 million in private equity funding in

June 2012) and talent (hiring a former executive of BlackBerry to be Sonos's chief commercial officer and drawing a former top Microsoft executive out of retirement and on to Sonos's board of directors). Sonos is an example of one of the many high-risk businesses that offset fear of failure with capital, talent, and hope.

Entrepreneurs and the Elements of Hope

Whether they are honchoing food trucks, pop-ups, or bigger companies, the heads of successful start-ups are the most hopeful of the enterprising bunch. Their bold goals are realized because their agency and pathways seem limitless even in the face of fear, adversity, and risk.

Goals: Many people are visited with a brilliant idea now and again, but high-hope people have a type of creativity that churns out big ideas. Their hopeful thinking spikes when they are asked to make the future better, when they grapple with today's problems, and when they realize that a big obstacle is challenging someone's progress. They also are gifted at sharing their big idea with other people, including partners, employees, investors, and consumers. They craft a right-risk vision that excites them, inspires others, and manages risk.

Agency: When the going gets tough, hopeful entrepreneurs get more energized. Their enthusiasm and confidence inspire others. Their fund of agency may seem bottomless because they are great recruiters of energy needed to get things done.

Pathways: People high in hope are adept at dealing with change. This is because they more readily experience the positive emotions that open their minds to ways they can move forward, solving problems along the way. They don't let risk run wild and create the fear that will stymie creativity. High-hope business leaders interpret obstacles as opportunities. So when they face tough problems, they come up with more and better solutions.

From Here to There

"How do I get from here to there?" In the age of GPS, MapQuest, and Google Maps, we hardly have to think about this when traveling to a new place. In daily life, however, answering this is still crucial. I've seen students, entrepreneurs, and couples fail because they had not thought beyond the first step of their plan. Without a good plan and a Plan B, you just won't find your way. And without a Plan B, you won't bounce back from setbacks or failure.

Plan B'ing is made stronger with practice. Think about a goal you are working on now. What is your plan for attaining it? That's Plan A. What's Plan B? And C? Are those the best plans you can think of? Revise each of them to make them better. Doing this each time you are in pursuit of a goal makes it easier to create pathways to your future.

In the next part of this book, we'll be looking at very specific tools, strategies, and skills for making hope happen. Many of these are backed by new research on goal-setting, on building agency, and on pathways thinking.

PRACTICING
THE THREE HOPE
STRATEGIES

Chapter 9

Futurecasting

Making Your Goals Come Alive

IF TIME machines existed, I would buy a fast one with a preview screen that shows what is happening where I'm planning to visit; I want to land on the right side of history and out of harm's way. But until Old Doc Brown works out the bugs in his DeLorean's flux capacitor, our bodies are grounded in the present. So we have to rely on the next-best thing—our capacity to travel back in time and into the future in our minds. Futurecasting—how well we can preview the future—is *the* fundamental skill for making hope happen.

Most people begin taking short mental trips into the future the moment they wake up. You might start thinking about the first sip of coffee, your 10 A.M. meeting, an important afternoon errand, a family dinner. Of the twenty thousand chunks of experience your brain registers each day, more than a third of them are spent time traveling into the future.

Our longer trips into the future, focused on big life goals, shape our choices. Should we stay on the charted path or take entertaining (but possibly unproductive) side trips? If you went to college believing that you would get a good job when you graduated, you probably visited the future, considered your many options, and then chose a major that would get you where you wanted to go. When you open a retirement account, you probably fantasize about how you will spend your savings and your much-deserved free time in the future. If you exercise and eat well today because you think it will make you live longer and better, you are a health-conscious time traveler.

So let's put your ability to move through time to the test. Imagine a ladder with steps numbered from zero at the bottom to ten at the top. The top of the ladder represents the best possible life for you, and the bottom of the ladder represents the worst possible life for you. On which step of the ladder would you say you stand at this time? On which step do you think you will stand about five years from now?

This ladder exercise, or "best possible life" question, is not something I just dreamed up. It's a tool called Cantril's ladder (after a psychologist who pioneered opinion polling). Researchers and pollsters have been using it to measure people's expectations worldwide for more than forty-five years. No matter where you start, and no matter how far off your best possible life seems, if you expect to be on a higher rung five years from now, you share the first core belief of the hopeful: "The future will be better than the present."

When I asked my best friend these questions, she found her best possible life in her own past. "I would like to be surrounded by lots of people, like I was back at college. And, I would like to be using my brain more like back then. That is what I want my future to look like." She gave her current self a 7 and then backed up to a 6.5. When I asked her about her life five years from now, she smiled, looked up at the ceiling and said, "A nine. I would like to be at a nine." She covered many years in a brief exchange. And a preview of her future self gave her a twinkle in her eye.

A Future That Draws You Forward

An athletic six feet, six inches, Andrew DeVries had spent most of his fifty-five years chasing a ball of one kind or another. So friends and family were not surprised when Andy tried out for the Michigan Senior Olympics volleyball team and made a good showing. Unfortunately, just weeks after the Olympic trials, in September 2002, Andy was riding his motorcycle on a Grand Rapids street when a car struck him. He would not step back on the court for nearly a year.

The accident crushed part of Andy's left leg. After several surgeries to try to repair the damage, doctors told him that they would have to amputate the leg at mid-thigh. They drew a black line with a Sharpie to show him where the cut would go. That's when a physician's assistant named Sarah Scholl reminded Andy how to futurecast.

Andy recalls, "As everybody was making plans for my life without a leg, a young hospitalist came up to me and said, 'Andy, what kind of golf ball do you play?'" Scholl's question brought Andy up short. Under the circumstances, he said, "talking about golf balls seemed almost idiotic." But he told her he liked the Titleist Pro V1, and the next morning, there, in the midst of all the cards and flowers in his room, was a twelve-pack of Titleist Pro V1 balls.

"She helped me stop thinking about how sorry I should feel for myself," Andy says. "And she brought a glimmer of hope." Scholl reminded him that he still had a future to think about.

When Andy woke up in recovery, he still had ten toes. The surgeons had discovered a little bit of blood flow and decided not to take the leg after all.

Sarah and Andy became very close during the rest of his hospital stay and, on the day he was released to a rehab facility, Sarah arranged to be the one wheeling him out to the ambulance. She also had a favor to ask him. She'd lost her father while she was still in high school and, when the time came for her to get married, she wanted Andy to be the one to walk her down the aisle and give her away.

Sarah had a gift for shaking up Andy's world. Here he was, going into another hospital knowing he might never get out of a wheelchair and Sarah didn't even have a boyfriend. When he pointed that out, she replied, "Someday I will." They promised to stay in touch.

Sarah wasn't the only one making plans for Andy's future. While he was still at the rehabilitation hospital, he got a phone call from John Wilder, the Senior Olympics volleyball coach. John had some good news. "Congratulations, Andy, you made the team!" Andy tried to explain the realities: the accident, the surgeries, the rehab. Coach Wilder persisted. He told Andy that he had earned the spot, and it was his, on one condition. "You get better. I'll play you if you can just stand up." The coach's promise touched Andy. "His words ignited a spark. I went at rehabilitation with a vengeance. Seven months later I was able to show up for the Senior Olympics. Although I could barely stand, John kept his word: he put me in the game. I collected myself enough to serve. We won that game and the next. As the competition intensified, the coach had to take me out, but our team went on to win the gold medal."

Like Sarah, Coach Wilder helped Andy travel through time to his future, imagining himself on the court during the Olympics. All he had to do was stand up.

Andy's story doesn't end with that team gold medal. Over the next few years, he faced several life-threatening setbacks and surgeries that would have sidelined many people permanently—including an injury caused by pushing too hard in rehab. Andy got smarter about getting stronger; he learned that slow and steady paid off. He began to look into the future again. "For the first time in five years, I subscribed to a magazine in my own name." He also began to craft a new second act for himself, becoming a fund-raiser for his beloved alma mater, Calvin College.

Then, in the summer of 2009, seven years after his accident, Andy got an email from Sarah Scholl, who had moved to Oregon. "I have a boyfriend—will you come?" Andy did not think twice. Sarah picked

Andy up at the Portland airport before the wedding. When she saw him strolling toward her, she burst into tears. It was the first time she'd ever seen him standing upright. And for Andy, "What a joy it was walking—not wheelchairing, but walking—Sarah down the aisle."

Most of us are like Andy. If we have a vision and plan for the future, we can't help but be pulled forward by life, even when our present betrays us. We start to create a narrative about a future self that competes with the old stories about ourselves. As we fill in more details and take small steps in our future direction, our energy is freed up. When we're excited about "what's next," we invest more in our daily life, and we can see beyond current challenges. That's the big point behind all the goal-setting strategies I'll discuss in this chapter.

Expecting a Better Future Is Universal

To find out if the tendency to expect a positive future is universal, two psychology colleagues and I analyzed answers to the "best possible life" question gathered from the 2008 Gallup World Poll, a representative sample of people in 142 countries. Across all countries, people said they expected to be on about the seventh rung of the life ladder in five years. The vast majority (84 percent) expected their future life to be at the midpoint of the scale (5) or above. Eighty-nine percent of people polled worldwide expected their life in five years to be as good as or better than their current life.

The people who had the most positive expectations lived in Ireland, Brazil, Denmark, New Zealand, and the United States. The most pessimistic people worldwide lived in Zimbabwe, Egypt, Bulgaria, Haiti, and Lebanon. But only one country (Zimbabwe, homeland of Tererai Trent, who had envisioned going to America for her education and Ph.D.) had negative expectations overall (a mean response of lower than 5).

We don't have an optimism problem in the world. As the

"optimism bias" predicts (see chapter 3), we are automatically inclined to look toward the positive, which makes us somewhat immune to many of the events and circumstances that could dim our views. Unfortunately, we do have a hope problem. Only half the people in the world can vigorously pursue goals that matter, keeping up their energy and finding pathway after pathway in the face of obstacles.

Creating Goals

Over the last twenty years I have gone to my share of goal-setting workshops. In the 1990s, I learned how SMART goals could make me a better student and employee. Theoretically, goals that are Specific, Measurable, Attainable, Relevant, and Time-bound get more of our attention and, therefore, are likely to be achieved. In the last decade, I also learned the hard way that juggling too many big goals undermines progress. One big goal at a time is a good rule of thumb, but it has to be one you care about deeply.

Most of the clients I work with, whether in psychotherapy or business consulting, are familiar with the kind of goal-setting rules I was taught. So I try to give them a new way to think about their aims. "Which goal are you most excited about?" I ask. "Excited?" they often ask. "Yes, excited. If you could spend your time all day on a single goal, what would it be?" One client responded, "You don't hear those kinds of questions in a goal-setting workshop."

She was right. Most people consider goal-setting to be work for diligent ants, not freewheeling grasshoppers. But the truth is, our rational, strategic thinking about goals is guided and spurred on by our emotions. As a result, we invest the most resources and make the most gains on goals we are excited about. And what if the goal that creates energy in you is not the goal your teacher, boss, or family needs you to work on right now? You do what you can to focus on two goals: one for them and one for you. You also do your best to find something that excites you about the goal that has been assigned to you.

This is where a clear and specific goal can help, because it automatically calls up more energy than a fuzzy one. Take a vague goal like "I want to feel better." How would you know where to start or what tools you need to make it happen? You can get closer to it by futurecasting. Ask yourself: "If you were feeling better, what would you be doing?" "How would your typical day change?" "How would your behavior change?" Finding workable goals is like bringing a distant object into focus with a pair of binoculars.

You boost your energy when you state goals positively. In other words, a goal should *add* to your life rather than *subtract* from it. "I want to fight less with my coworker" is clear enough, but its negative focus makes it difficult to find a workable pathway. You're looking for positive behaviors that can help change your situation. "I want to get along better with my coworker" is an additive goal. What do people who get along do? They spend time discovering common interests. They say hello and compliment good work. They laugh at the latest office absurdity. These are some ideas you can act on.

Strengths Help You Pick Your Goals

"Find out what you do well and do more of it" was Don Clifton's advice to me and many others. Gallup chairman and the father of strengths psychology, Don thought many people invest too much time and energy in overcoming our weaknesses and not enough time doing what we do best. I find that to be true of some of my clients when I talk to them about their goals. They spend much of their effort on goals that require them to work outside their strengths. I try to help these clients—individuals, schools, and businesses—figure out what they do best and find ways to do more of it.

Recently, thanks to meetings with my own strengths coach, Cheryl Beamer, and through my study of super-hopeful people, I figured out that a very hopeful person almost always outpaces a less hopeful peer because, in Cheryl's words, they "only accept A-plus opportunities." That means they dedicate themselves to goals they are excited about, that align with their strengths, and that make a big impact on themselves and others. These criteria work when choosing which sports to play as a kid, which roles to take on at a job, and which activities to engage in during retirement.

Salience: The Goals That Matter Most

There is a lot of competition for our attention and resources. We are more likely to put time and energy into the goals that stand out and grab our attention. Psychologists call these *salient goals*. I typically explain salience to audiences by asking them a question I'd like you to answer now: Have you ever washed a rental car?

Recently, out of nearly one thousand conference goers, not a single hand was raised to say yes. Why? Because 1) you don't own that rental car and 2) other things rank higher on your mental checklist. Washing the rental car is not a salient goal.

For many students at the schools I visit, graduating from high school or college is just like washing a rental car. They might give lip service to the goal, but they don't deeply identify with it or own it. Maybe nobody in their family has gone to college. Maybe their role models never mention education when they talk about their success. Maybe getting a job and making money rank a lot higher in their minds than getting a degree. Many of them are under day-to-day pressure from family problems, social relationships, dangerous neighborhoods, and turbulent schools.

Many workers also have a saliency problem. Sometimes the toughest part of their job day to day is identifying what is most important. Where should they put their time and energy? There are often competing priorities and mixed messages coming from coworkers and management. Identifying the goals that can make the most impact is essential to managing finite resources.

Leaders are expected to be salience seekers. As a leader, each goal you endorse pulls resources from other projects.

Visiting the Future: Tips for the Time Traveler

Too many of us make life-altering decisions based on images that live only in our minds (and may not be shared with anyone else on the planet—including friends and family affected by the decision). We are much better off when we upgrade our time travel to bring the future as close as we can. Here are more ways to use futurecasting to explore and refine your goals.

Picture Yourself in the Future

"People have trouble seeing their future," says Eva Quinn, vice president of corporate relations for the Principal Financial Group. "When a financial advisor says 'what are your financial goals?' people can't figure it out." That's why Principal built a simple, free mobile app called Dreamcatcher.

When you open the app, you are prompted to "[c]ollect your dreams for the future." This means taking new photos or uploading pictures that symbolize your dreams from your phone or tablet, or pulling them from other websites, and sorting, prioritizing, and labeling them. You can also add text, making your picture of Paris or an isolated trout stream even more specific. Once your Dreamcatcher reflects what you want from your future life, you are ready to start on your financial plan.

When I asked Eva Quinn about her own Dreamcatcher, she said, "There is a pottery wheel, I have a log cabin in the mountains, I want to spend my winters on the beach. There is a college graduation photo.

I need to get my little kids through college." Sharing these images with her own Principal advisor could help Eva get closer to reaching her goals.

Share Your Future Day Fantasy

Alli Rose Lopez, my wife, has a knack for getting students excited about reading, writing, and the future. As the founder and former director of the Omaha Young Writers Program, her capstone project grew out of visits with seniors at Omaha South High School. The resulting book of student essays, *In My Shoes: Teen Reflections on Hope and the Future,* captures the seniors' thoughts about what they wanted from their futures, and the many challenges that made the good life seem very distant.

As Alli was getting to know the seniors, she asked them to join her in a guided imagery exercise called the Future Day Fantasy. This exercise subtly reminds students that they are the heroes in their own life stories and primes their imaginations to create a vivid picture of a future life worth living.

Alli started by helping the students relax, prompting them to close their eyes and breathe deeply. Then she began reading the imagery aloud:

> Imagine that as you fall asleep one night, a golden, glittering grid of light suddenly surrounds you. You realize that you are in a time machine that is taking you to your own future. It is the year 2012. Two thousand and thirteen. Two thousand and fourteen. Two thousand and fifteen. . . . It is ten years in the future; you are now about to live a wonderful day, the best day in your life so far.

Most of Alli's forty-five seniors had hopeful visions of going to college, landing jobs, and starting families. A few described dreams of opening their own businesses, becoming performers, or moving to exotic places. These goals became more real when each student shared them with an adult mentor—twenty-nine volunteers Alli had recruited from local businesses, arts agencies, and colleges—and then, with a little help, drafted an essay illuminating their paths to the future. The exuberance and concerns of the students were matched with the excitement and support of the mentors, and a shoulder-to-shoulder editing process helped develop their writing skills. Even more important, the mentors listened and asked questions about the seniors' day-to-day lives, and pushed them to identify pathways to their desired futures. Over six weeks, many of the students thought harder about these issues than they ever had before.

This exercise is not for students only. Try listening attentively to your own thoughts, and then put your future fantasy on paper. You may find yourself opening up and charting a new life course. The complete Future Day Fantasy script is at www.makinghopehappennow.com.

Take Your Future for a Test Drive

On a visit to see my uncles in California, Alli and I decided to rent a small SUV so we could all travel together on day trips and still have room for our luggage. When the agent asked if we had a preference among the available cars, I said, "Not really. What would you recommend?" That's how we ended up in a Ford Escape.

This scenario is repeated thousands of times a day, and every business or vacation rental is a chance to take your future car for a test drive. Is there room for everyone and the kids' car seats? Is it easy for the kids and the grandparents to get in and out? How do you like the handling? Would it improve your commute?

Alli and I were surprised by how much we liked the Escape, which hadn't previously been on our short list. After a long drive to Lake Tahoe, Alli said, "Maybe this is our next car." And just over a year later, there was an Escape in our driveway.

I first realized the value of test-driving the future when I had to pick a college. As a first-generation student, only the second person in my family to go to college, I knew that there was a lot I did not know about this process. I had comparable scholarship offers from two state schools, University of Louisiana–Lafayette (ULL) and Louisiana State University (LSU). Many factors were tugging me first in one direction, then the other. I wanted more than a standard campus visit (too structured and too salesy) or a night on the town (too unstructured and too boozy). The plan was to travel to each school during the early spring of my senior year in high school, go to an afternoon's worth of classes, eat campus food, spend the night in a freshman dorm, and then see how I felt about the college the next morning. And I would do this without a parent, sibling, or good friend in tow. Though I wanted their opinions (and had already consulted many of them), I needed this preview to approximate a real day and night on campus. I wanted to get as close as possible to how I would feel six months later, when the fall semester started.

The college previews did exactly what I needed them to do. While I felt lonely on my visits to both schools (I didn't know anyone in the dorms where I stayed), the students at ULL seemed friendlier. Though all the classes I attended were large, I also noticed more professor-student interactions at ULL than at LSU. Finally, the advisers and counselors at ULL did a better job of helping me think about how to max out my scholarship by finishing in four years.

Taking your future for a test drive is the best way to see if it is right for you. You really want to know if a vacation spot is peaceful? Take a real or virtual tour during peak periods. Considering retiring to a different community from where you have been living? Search homeaway.com for rentals that will help you sample the new locale. Interested in pursuing a new line of work when you retire from your job? Talk to people in that town who created a second act for themselves and find out how the city supported their pursuits. Test-driving the future certainly helps you make decisions in the near term. It also can help you invest more in your long-range plans.

Consult Experienced Guides

Sometimes you have to make a decision without a test drive. If so, find people who are living the future you imagine and get their take on it. Say you are considering moving to a new neighborhood. Talk to a number of people who live there and some who recently moved away. This will give you a more unvarnished assessment than you'll get from a Realtor or from one chat with a community advocate.

If you're hunting for a new line of work, talk to as many people active in the field as you can. Who sees the work as a calling, and what does it mean to them? Who is doing it just to make ends meet? If possible, talk to people doing the same job at different companies. What satisfactions come from the work itself? Which come from the particular work environment? This kind of information is usually just a phone call, text message, or cup of coffee away.

Contrast the Then with the Now

You build on positive expectations by visiting the future. Then you go beyond visiting by actively contrasting the now—your present reality—with the then—your hoped-for future. This forces you to come to grips with the obstacles in your present. What might keep you from making that desired future possible?

For Andy DeVries, the possible future unfolded in vivid images: playing golf again, standing up with his team at the Senior Olympics, walking Sarah down the aisle. The stark contrast with his wheelchair-bound present motivated him to stick with the grueling physical rehabilitation program that put him back on his feet.

When Jacqueline of the Roscoe Park Eight took her initial tour of the Nettelhorst School (chapter 6), she immediately started comparing the sights before her eyes with her mental pictures of the school where she'd want to drop off her child in a year or two. Contrasting the then with the now helped her and the other mothers produce their wish list.

When I visited ULL and LSU, I tried to think about what I would want and need from a school not just as a freshman, but also as a sophomore, junior, senior, and graduate. Some of my thoughts about each school were reinforced, whereas some of my beliefs were challenged. But both visits gave me new information I could use to create a more accurate vision of me going to school, graduating, and then going to graduate school. Contrasting that vision with my reality of being a high school kid with only one relative that went to college helped me realize that the path to graduation would be bumpy but there would be people along the way who would help me get where I wanted to go.

Getting specific about the needs of her future self helped Lisa, a talented graphic designer, weather her first career setback. She was downsized during the recession when her firm lost a major account. It took her weeks to face the reality of being out of work and the bad feelings that come with being let go. When she first started looking again, she adopted what I call the "message in a bottle" approach to finding work. She would start her day by scanning online job boards for openings, spend hours completing generic applications, and then attach a résumé. Hitting "send" put her into the purgatory that is waiting for a response from a message set adrift by a desperate castaway. In Lisa's case, the sea was the economic downturn, and it was filled with bottles that looked very much like hers.

Lisa's turnaround came when she started to time travel. She imagined herself sharing her portfolio with the department manager at a hot new design firm she'd read about in a local business magazine. She thought she'd be a good fit for the company, and she was excited by the thought of working there. Next she made an honest assessment of the now: she realized that her portfolio needed refreshing, that she actually had little background knowledge about that design firm (or others in her area), and that she was anxious about going on interviews and meeting new people. Mentally contrasting the then with the now led to more thoughts: She needed to upgrade her wardrobe if she wanted to look right for a hipster agency. She needed to practice her interview skills with a designer friend. Lisa still didn't have a job, but instead of feeling worn-out and discouraged, she had a vision of her possible future self plus a list of positive steps she could take to get there. She was on her way from Point A to Point B.

Say Hello to Your Future Self

How well do we really know our future selves? Comedian Jerry Seinfeld, in one of his immortal monologues, captured the problem most of us face as we plan for that stranger in our future:

> I never get enough sleep. I stay up late at night, 'cause I'm Night Guy. Night Guy wants to stay up late. "What about getting up after five hours sleep?" oh that's Morning Guy's problem. That's not my problem, I'm Night Guy. I stay up as late as I want. So you get up in the morning, you're exhausted, groggy . . . oooh I hate that Night Guy! See, Night Guy always screws Morning Guy. There's nothing Morning Guy can do. The only thing Morning Guy can do is try and oversleep often enough so that Day Guy loses his job and Night Guy has no money to go out anymore.

So, how do we get Night Guy to sit down and have a conversation with Morning Guy? Better yet, how do we get them to realize they are the *same* guy?

Hal Hershfield, assistant professor of marketing at NYU's Stern School of Business, might have the answers. He researches how thinking about time can affect our decision-making and emotional experience. His work has shown that people who are primed to be aware of their future self (sometimes by as low-tech a method as visiting with an older relative) focus more on their best interest and/or the best interest of society, compared with participants who haven't made the connection between now and the future. Among other things, they choose to save more money and act more ethically.

In one study, Hershfield and his colleagues used digitally altered photos to bring undergraduates face-to-face with an image of themselves several decades into the future. As if in a mirror, they saw how the contours of their cheeks and jaws changed, how their hair whitened and their skin wrinkled. Then they were asked what they would do with one thousand dollars if they received it unexpectedly. Hershfield reported, "They allocated twice as much to a long-term savings account if they saw an older version of themselves versus just seeing themselves now."

The age-progression software Hershfield used is not available to the general public. But there are other ways to meet the future you.

Enter the Aging Booth: A trip to the mobile app Aging Booth can give you a sense of how you'll look decades from now. Download the app and age away. What financial or health decisions can you make now with the help of the older you?

Write a letter to your future self: The website futureme.org allows you to send a note to yourself months or years in the future. A note from a futureme user, "Joan in New Mexico," captures the benefits of this tool: "I love the fact that I have a ten-year plan for my future and I will receive emails periodically along the way inquiring how I am doing on some of my goals . . . it will make me reflect on this time and question my reasoning as to why I felt a certain way and if I have matured or grown from the experience."

Ask your future self's opinion: Thirty years from now (or even five), will your future self be glad you bought the expensive car, the premium vacation, or the house that's a stretch for you? (Don't assume that future self will always be a killjoy. Hershfield says that if he'd thought long term, he'd have paid extra for a sunroof; the pleasure would have outweighed the slightly higher loan payments.) When you are in the midst of making your next big life decision, seek the opinion of the future you.

Spend time with an older person: Do you have an older friend or relative who's similar to you in interests and values and positive in thought and mood? Imagine yourself looking back at your life from their perspective. How does taking the long view change your feelings about the situation you're in and the choices you face?

Trips and Goals

By taking these short and long trips, you have been practicing future-casting. Now let's put your skills to the test. Remember the question about your best possible life, five years from now? Take some time now to describe what that best possible life looks like. Be as vivid as you can. Preview the future you hope to create. Identify the goals that will help you get there. Write all this down to flesh out the details. Then say hello to your future self.

Chapter 10

Triggering Action

Putting Agency on Autopilot

Jos Van Bedoff served in the Netherlands' military before he became a maintenance man at Schiphol, Amsterdam's international airport. He'd done his share of latrine cleaning in the service, and he'd learned a trick that made the job a lot easier. How he adapted it for his new position made him a rock star among people like me who study human behavior.

Straightforward idea, really. Play offense rather than defense. Instead of figuring out faster ways to clean latrines, make it so there is less to clean. Put a red dot with a marker on the sweet spot of each urinal—to one side, not too high, not too low—and the soldier will aim. Soldiers, male soldiers that is, really don't like to miss a target.

Of course, we're not just talking about soldiers here. If you're a guy—or you've ever raised a boy—you know what I mean. If there's no red dot, a Cheerio floating in the toilet bowl will do just fine.

When Van Bedoff arrived at Schiphol, it turned out they had a serious spillage problem. The bane of maintenance workers, spillage is the technical term for the amount of urine that hits the walls and floors in a bathroom.

Van Bedoff asked his supervisors for permission to conduct an experiment. He knew a red dot made with a marker would work, but he was thinking about something more permanent. He proposed to have a realistic, life-sized fly etched into the back wall of each urinal. (Whether he knew it or not, the fly was a nod to the bees the ancient Greeks painted in the bottom of their chamber pots.) He got the okay and was given a small budget to modify a number of urinals.

And that is how a fake fly, black against white porcelain, changed the behavior of thousands of men from around the world who passed through Schiphol. Spillage was reduced by 80 percent, and the job of the Dutch maintenance workers became much easier.

Van Bedoff shaped behavior by changing one critical aspect of the environment. He did not put up signs scolding or entreating travelers. He did not invent a new, high-tech urinal. What he did was exploit a natural tendency that focused attention on a desired goal.

How does Van Bedoff's experiment relate to hope? It shows that we can create situations where it is easier to make the right choice. We can set up systems that kick in when we are too tired, too busy, or too distracted to keep our eyes on our goal. When hopeful people use these strategies, they don't have to muster up as much willpower, self-control, or agency to keep moving forward, to shield themselves from people who might undermine their efforts, or to act in line with their best interests. This chapter shows you how to hold firm to the belief that you have the power to make the future better than the present by putting hope on autopilot.

The Power of Cues and Defaults

Van Bedoff's fly was a cue—the signal X that reliably triggered response Y. Cues are the key to simple if-then plans that free up a lot of mental space and energy. They're also the basis for our good habits—you're going to bed, so of course you brush your teeth, even with your eyes half shut. And they're one of the things that make bad habits so hard to change. Hopeful people become masters at using cues in their favor.

My friend Heather wears an electronic wristband set to vibrate every twenty minutes or so throughout the day. It's a cue for her to get up from her desk, stretch, and walk down the hall or around the room for a few minutes. This cue helps Heather ward off aches and pains associated with a chronic illness.

When I was teaching college, it was a real challenge to get undergraduates to take out their earbuds, turn off their phones, and make the transition into student mode. So I put the behavior on cue. Outside the auditorium where I taught, there was a bronze statue of three kids playing. I asked my students to stop by the statue each time they came to class, give one of the kids' heads a rub, and then put away the electronics. We avoided a battle of wills over tunes and texts, the heads of the bronze kids brightened from thousands of rubs, and I had the pleasure of a class ready to pay attention.

Defaults are different from cues, but they operate just as automatically once they are set up. Hopeful people reach for this tool when they want to make an end run around indecision, procrastination, or stress. Defaults allow you to preselect a step toward your goal that goes into effect unless you take action to change it. For example, employers who sponsor 401(k) plans for retirement savings realized that employee participation lagged when each worker had to decide how much to contribute each month, and what funds to invest in. Many plans now enroll employees automatically at a preset level. Individuals can still change their terms or opt out entirely, but participation has risen—along with savings for the future.

Or say you intend to save for a specific goal, but there's never any money left at the end of the month. You set up a default by putting your paycheck on direct deposit, and then instructing the bank to transfer a defined sum to a long-term savings account as soon as the money comes in.

The people you'll meet in this chapter use many kinds of cues and defaults by setting action triggers such as goal contagions, precommitments, and when/where plans.

Create a Goal Contagion

How hard is it to pass our goals on to another person? No harder than spreading the common cold. Simply by proximity, we can infect others with the mission and excitement of our pursuits. And being exposed to others' goals primes us to adopt them. Associate with people who share your goals, or the goals you want to be more salient, and you get an automatic boost in focus and motivation.

Social psychologist Henk Aarts of Utrecht University studies the way people form goals. His research reveals how much our conscious sense of wanting and doing things depends on an unconscious foundation of habits, social cues, and environmental triggers. For example, he's shown that people who simply read stories about adopting and acting on goals soon follow suit.

Once you start looking for goal contagions, you see them everywhere. Psychologist and blogger Art Markman noticed that political yard signs sprout up in clumps during election years—many on one block, maybe none four blocks over. "One explanation for this clumping," he comments, "is that we tend to look at other people's behavior and see not only what they are doing but what they are trying to accomplish. That is, we automatically interpret the goals that people have from their behaviors." The first guy on the block who puts out a campaign sign triggers others to announce their own preference. As Markman notes, "This desire is likely to be particularly strong for neighbors of the individual with the yard sign, because those neighbors will see the sign every day." His conclusion: "To my mind, this effect is a positive one. It is crucial for people to care about the political process. One way to get people to care about this process is for others to perform actions that show they care."

Here's another example of goal contagion that relies on signs. The last time you stayed in a chain hotel, you probably noticed the sign in the bathroom telling you about the hotel's efforts to conserve energy and water. You can do your part by reusing towels and understanding that sheets won't be changed every day. These pleas for environmental virtue vary in their effectiveness.

Psychology professor Robert Cialdini of Arizona State University and colleagues collected data on more than 2,500 instances of potential towel reuse in a mid-priced hotel and discovered that small wording changes in the bathroom sign had big effects on guest behavior. When the appeal was "Help save the environment," just over 37 percent of guests complied. The message "Join your fellow guests in helping to save the environment," followed by a statement that most people reused their towels at least once during their stay, increased participation to 44 percent. The winner was a message stating that a majority of guests who had stayed in *that very room* had reused their towels. This bumped participation up over 49 percent. Even the researchers were surprised by the power of the same-room effect. The stronger the identification with "people like me," the stronger the goal contagion in favor of the environment.

The two-thousand-plus employees at my own workplace, Gallup, encounter subtle cues that promote wise choices. Signs near the elevators and stairs tell you how many calories you can burn with the proper choice. Signs at the credit union encourage you to think about the future and to make good investments today. In the cafeteria, healthful foods are featured prominently and less healthful foods tucked away.

In 2010, Gallup started playing a more strategic offense based on worldwide studies of the key elements of well-being. Each associate who chose to participate in the well-being program completed a comprehensive assessment of his current well-being in five areas: career, social, financial, physical, and community. Associates then shared their big change goals with a supervisor and one another. Some focused on financial well-being, working closely with advisers to come up with long-term plans that fit their priorities. Others set community well-being goals for contributing time, money, and talent to good causes and people. The most visible pursuit of well-being goals takes place at the company gym, where trainer Ryan Wolf acts as health-and-fitness guru to more than five hundred of his fellow professionals.

Ryan has a gift for working on your mind as he gets you to work on your body. A hopeful person in his own right, he recruits people to the gym while attending meetings or walking through the cafeteria, and he follows up with emails to those who've expressed intentions to get in shape. Once he gets them working out on a regular basis, he encourages them to set bigger goals, like participating in fun runs and races.

Ryan also encourages associates to make their commitments public. In and out of meetings, work teams talk about their training goals, diets, and weight loss plans. You can see goal contagions in action in these groups, and many informal competitions have sprung up, increasing excitement, motivation, and persistence.

These public proclamations have made a measurable difference in several of the well-being outcomes. For example, Ryan helped more associates become runners (with a 600 percent increase in the number of people participating in a local race over the last five years) and lose weight (263 people lost 1,492 pounds and 676 percentage points of body fat from January 2009 to December 2011).

Ryan is skilled at starting a wave of well-being, but his success is dependent on others getting on board and, in turn, inspiring still more people to commit to the same goals. Our decision-making and behaviors are informed many times a day by subtle environment cues and triggers, including those of our friends and coworkers. We use the power of goal contagion to our best advantage when we choose the sea we swim in.

Precommit to Hopeful Actions

One crisp winter afternoon I met Stanley Lombardo, a classics professor and Zen master, in the cozy café in our community co-op. As a translator of Homer, he's done more to make the *Iliad* and the *Odyssey* accessible than any other scholar. His versions turn the ancient Greek into lively, modern English—plain talk that I (and tens of thousands of students) can understand without getting bogged down in arcane terms and phrases.

I told Stan that the *Odyssey* is now a hot topic in the social sciences, medicine, and law. Stan was not surprised to hear that these professionals are interested in Homer's psychology. He called Odysseus "the hero of the mind," a lover of strategy, cunning, and competition. That makes him very appealing to anyone whose job is figuring out why people do what they do.

In particular, I wanted to talk to Stan about "Odysseus contracts"— agreements that precommit us to strategies that can help us maintain progress to important goals. For example, physicians refer to Odysseus contracts that bind people to a health-care plan. Advance directives (also known as living wills) precommit patients and physicians to decisions arising when the patient is no longer able to state his or her wishes.

In response, Stan launched into the classic story about how Odysseus resisted the song of the Sirens, who would surely have lured him to shipwreck and death. "Ah, Circe knew that Odysseus would want to hear the Sirens," he said. Circe, a goddess and sorcerer, had kept Odysseus and his crew on her enchanted island for an entire year. But now, as her parting gift, she told him that the Sirens tailored their songs to each voyager, preying on his unique weaknesses and selfish tendencies. "The Greek gods knew we are own worst enemies," Stan said. "So Circe told Odysseus exactly what to do."

As the ship approaches the Siren's island, she told him, instruct your crew to bind you tight to the mast, and tell them not to release you, however hard you plead. Then block the ears of every man with wax, so they cannot hear the Sirens singing. Here, in Stan's translation, is how Odysseus describes his encounter with the Sirens:

They made their beautiful voices carry,
And my heart yearned to listen, I ordered my men
To untie me, signaling with my brows,
But they just leaned on their oars and rowed on.
Perimedes and Eurylochus jumped up,
Looped more rope around me, and pulled tight.
When we had rowed past, and the Sirens' song
Had faded on the waves, only then did my crew
Take the wax from their ears and untie me.

Odysseus lived to pursue the great goal of his journey—sailing on until he reached Ithaca and reclaimed his home and wife.

Analyzing Odysseus's strategy to help us resist or defeat our modern Sirens is not as simple as tying yourself to a mast—even if you had one handy. I came up with the following precommitment rules for modern voyagers:

Know who or what your Sirens are and how they will tempt you. You may have Sirens or temptations specific to each and every goal you set. You may have weaknesses that undermine most of your efforts at change. Some common ones: (1) You don't set enough time to pursue your personal goals, and (2) You're easily distracted, so that no goal gets the focused attention it needs. Tailor your contract or strategy to avoid these temptations.

Go online to contract for change. StickK.com, developed by Yale economists, allows you to put a "contract out on yourself" by making your goals public and binding. You select your goal, set your stakes (you place a bet, risking either your money or your good name), pick a referee (who monitors your commitment and progress), and build a support team to cheer you on. The upside of stickK.com is that it functions as a commitment strategy toolkit. The downside is that it does not require you to identify your Sirens, the many challenges, probably unique to you, that you will have to overcome to honor your contract.

Assemble a support team you can count on. Who do you trust to share your hopes and goals? Who can help you refine your contract or strategy? Who knows you well enough to spot when your temptations are coming into play—and alert you to them? Who will pitch in to help you past your Sirens?

Odysseus credits Eurylochus, the leader of his crew, and Perimedes for the success of his strategy. They not only refuse to answer his self-destructive pleas; they take his frantic signals as a cue to bind him even tighter to the mast.

Don't stop at one precommitment strategy. Odysseus comes up with an ingenious new plan for every challenge he meets. That is one reason the *Odyssey* has delighted and inspired listeners and readers for more than 2,500 years.

Stan Lombardo ended our conversation on an interesting note: "Every time you use a precommitment strategy inspired by Odysseus, it becomes part of the myth of the Odyssey." You increase your own strengths and contribute to the strength of others.

Make When/Where Plans

How many times have you started a new project with a burst of energy and enthusiasm, only to wonder a few months later what happened to your great idea? Yes, a few of us make plans and just do them, but most of us need a little nudge (or series of nudges) to get things done. (Okay, some of us need a kick in the butt, and making when/where plans can help change that.)

A when/where plan uses the power of cues to prompt us to work on the long-term projects that matter most to us. A good when/where plan keeps us on track, guards us against our tendency to procrastinate, keeps us from getting overwhelmed by competing demands, and battles our personal Sirens.

Psychology professor Peter Gollwitzer of New York University has developed this strategy through a series of research studies, most notably through two I'll call the Christmas Studies. In Christmas Study #1, college students were asked prior to Christmas break to name two projects, one easy and one hard, that they intended to complete during their time off. Typical goals included writing papers, mending relationships with friends, and exercising. About two-thirds of them, with no encouragement, formed plans about when and where to get started on the project. Upon returning from Christmas vacation, participants were asked about project completion. Most of the easy projects were completed regardless of whether the student had made a when/where plan. But difficult projects were a different story. Only 25 percent of students who did not develop when/where plans in advance completed their hard projects.

In Christmas Study #2, all participants were given the same project: they were to write a report on how they spent Christmas Eve and submit it within two days of returning from the holiday. Individuals were then randomly assigned to two groups. One group was asked to create when/where plans for writing the essay; the other was not. Seventy-five percent of the group who had visited the future to specify the time and place for writing the report submitted it on time; only 33 percent of those without a plan completed the project.

Making a when/where plan is a straightforward process. Each time you get an assignment or set a goal, choose the day and time you will start working on it, and the place where you will work. For example, during last tax season, this was my plan for organizing my records from the previous year:

When: Tuesday, March 27th after morning meeting
at Pinckney school.

Where: At La Prima Tazza coffee shop. Bring W2s,
receipts, and laptop.

For those needing a little reminder of a when/where plan that kicks off thirty or more days into the future, try sending yourself a cue through futureme.org. This simple tool guarantees that you won't forget your commitment to yourself. Once at the website, plug in your email address and then write a clear and specific subject line such as "when/where plan for delivering tax paperwork to accountant" and then type in the specifics. The next step, choosing when to have the email delivered, requires you to consider whether you want the note to arrive on the day of your "when" (identified in your when/where plan) or earlier, such as day before (which is what I recommend).

A recent review of ninety-four studies that examined when/where plans found that using them made people successful at achieving an astonishing range of goals. They worked for improving time management, preparing for tests, increasing the use of public transportation, conducting monthly breast self-examinations, buying organic foods, being more altruistic, not drinking alcohol, losing weight, and recycling.

I shared one of these studies with Ryan Wolf, Gallup's athletic trainer, because it focused on people who had the goal of becoming regular exercisers. Using random assignment, half the participants were asked to plan when and where they would exercise each week. (An example: "On Tuesday and Thursday, I will do three super-sets of weights at the gym, and on Monday, Wednesday, and Friday I will do forty-five minutes of cardio at home on the treadmill or elliptical machine.") People in the second group were instructed to pursue their goal but were not prompted to create when/where plans. Remarkably, when participants were contacted months later, 91 percent of when/where planners were still exercising regularly, compared to only 39 percent of nonplanners.

One of Gollwitzer's more recent studies explores using another kind of when/where plan to protect ourselves from our Sirens. These plans are designed to shield us from unwanted thoughts and feelings that undermine our intentions. In one experiment, people were more capable of fighting off junk food cravings if they acknowledged how cravings threatened their diets and created an if/then statement that they repeated three times. (An example: "And if I think about my chosen food, then I will ignore that thought.") In another experiment, tennis players formed the intention to play each ball with concentration, and then were asked to identify four inner states that might get in their way from shot to shot (such as "feeling exhausted" or "feeling angry"). They then crafted individualized if/then statements, such as "If I feel angry, then I will calm myself and tell myself 'I will win.'" Again, tennis players who acknowledged their performance anxiety in the context of specific if/then plans played much better than in their previous matches. The new discovery here is that not only do when/where plans spur action based on external cues, but they can also be matched with internal cues that distract us and sap our emotional energy.

When/where plans work because, by and large, people have good intentions. We want to meet our obligations; we want to pursue the goals that are in our best interest. Nevertheless, our good intentions often fall victim to difficulties in initiating action and maintaining focus. We are prone to sluggish starts, fatigue, and distraction. To overcome these difficulties, we have to make our goal pursuits more automatic. First, we connect an opportunity for goal attainment with a goal-directed behavior. Having a concrete plan to execute in a well-defined situation brings hope to life. Identifying that critical situation, that opportunity to pursue a goal, helps you to marshal all of your resources at a particular point and time. Your attention and willpower become automatically focused on the goal-directed behavior, with a huge gain in effectiveness.

When We Need to Play Defense

If you were old enough to watch TV in 1984, time travel back to when MTV aired music videos twenty-four hours a day and Van Halen was played in heavy rotation. I still remember their hit "Panama," when frontman David Lee Roth and guitarist and keyboardist Eddie Van Halen let loose their wild side. The video captured both men swinging across the stage on a wire connected to waist harnesses. At one point, Van Halen dangles upside down five feet in the air while his band mates push him across the stage.

Back then, the band was at the height of its popularity and power and had developed a reputation as, well, a rock-and-roll band. They drank too much, trashed hotel rooms, and then moved on to the next town and did it all over again. Watching over the whole production was the job of tour manager Harvey Schaps, who was responsible for making sure the band showed up at their next concert safe, sound, and sober enough to perform. He was also responsible for making sure the venue organizers held up their end of the deal.

Schaps's key tool was a fifty-three-page contract, which included a backstage concert rider that was recently rediscovered by thesmokinggun .com. The rider spelled out Van Halen's offstage needs and wants in microscopic detail. The following item appeared in a list of required snacks, headed "munchies":

M&M's (WARNING: ABSOLUTELY NO BROWN ONES)

That's right. The band had to have their M&M's, and the brown ones "absolutely" had to be picked out.

When the backstage rider became public, the Internet erupted in debate. Prima donnas, the critics cried. A classic example of music industry excess. A sympathetic fan speculated that a band member was allergic to something in the brown dye. Many fans believed that a single brown M&M would trigger a backstage riot and that Van Halen would leave the venue without putting on a show.

In reality, the "no brown M&M's" clause was not a sign of the band's excess (though other contractual demands upheld that image) and it did not trigger any bad-boy rock-and-roll behavior. What it did do is keep the band safe. It was their canary in the coal mine.

Tour manager Schaps needed a way to spot-check whether the staff at each venue took the contract seriously. Many clauses focused on specifications for structural aspects of the stage, gauge of electrical wiring and amperage of outlets, and the trapeze-like rigging that enabled band members to fly at climatic moments. Schaps used a checklist when conducting a pre-concert walk-through on stage, but he also wanted an early tell that signaled how safe the setup would be. Hours before the concert, he would go to the band's suite, reach into the bowl of M&M's, and look for the brown ones. Seeing none, he would start his regular walk-through. Seeing even one, he would ask the venue manager to redo and/or double-check the stage setup.

The brown M&M's clause is an example of a defensive action trigger. We may not be swinging from wires, but we still need an alarm that tells us when the environment is not ready or our support system is failing. The trigger puts the goal pursuit process on pause until we can address serious obstacles and/or create new pathways. Which of the following triggers might apply to your situation?

The Critical Collaborator: Someone you thought was a supporter or collaborator relentlessly criticizes your goals and/or plans, predicts failure, substitutes his/her own goals for yours, and fails to offer constructive suggestions. Spending time with them makes you feel depleted and discouraged. This is a put-down artist, not a supporter, and you need to distance yourself any way you can.

The Excuse Maker: A backer or collaborator doesn't meet deadlines or deliver agreed-on money or materials. When you confront them, they are passive-aggressive and make excuses and promise to do better. Give them one more chance if you must, but start making plans to move on without them.

The Slow Responder: You haven't heard anything from the loan officer, the contractor, the HR department, the real estate agent. Waiting endlessly to hear back is not "hope," it's avoidance. Follow up politely but relentlessly. If there's a legitimate delay, most people will give you a specific date on which they'll reply.

Sirens, Canaries, and Agency

Do you have a Siren pulling your life off course or a canary in a coal mine warning you that something is amiss? Identify the Sirens and canaries that visit you most often. Defend yourself from the Sirens and listen to the canaries. This will help you maintain the energy you need to pursue your goals.

Chapter 11

Planning for Ifs

Discovering New Pathways

A LISHA MCCLUNG was a returning senior at Spelman College, a historically black women's college, when life threw her a serious curve. Like most students today, Alisha counted on student loans to pay her tuition. But in the run-up to the Great Recession, banks and loan companies were getting out of the student loan business. In January 2008 Alisha discovered that her lender, the College Loan Corporation, would not renew her loan for the fall semester. Blindsided, she called the Spelman registrar's office to find out exactly what she needed to pay to enroll. The response stunned her: "They told me my balance was zero. I thought it was a mistake."

No mistake. By late 2007, Beverly Tatum, president of Spelman College, had anticipated how the nation's growing financial crisis would affect her young women. She and her staff estimated that there would be a gap in the millions of dollars between what students would owe in tuition and room and board and what parents and loans would cover. The worse possible outcome was for an academically solid upperclasswoman with tens of thousands of dollars of school debt to leave college for a middling job that might not even pay enough to keep up with student loan payments and/or to cover her tuition for a return to school—an investment gone bad.

Tatum's answer was to establish the Spelman President's Safety Net Fund, also known as the Starfish Initiative (named after a fable in which a little girl throws beached starfish back into the ocean one by one). She and her staff approached hundreds of donors, offering each the opportunity to help one student in a unique, personal way. Putting a face and a future to a donation was powerful enticement. In one year, alumnae, parents, and friends contributed more than half a million dollars to help Alisha McClung and more than one hundred other students complete their studies at Spelman.

The Starfish Initiative enabled Alisha, a child development major who was about to begin student teaching, to increase her credit hours while cutting her work schedule from thirty-five hours per week to a more manageable fifteen. "I'm taking 22 hours this semester, so me trying to work like in previous years . . . wouldn't have worked this year at all," McClung said. "Honestly, if I hadn't got this scholarship, I don't know how the money would have been paid."

Where There's a Way, There's a Will

World-famous boxer and armchair philosopher Mike Tyson once observed, "Everyone has a plan until they get punched in the mouth." No matter how good we are at futurecasting, life throws punches. A key skill of high-hope people (like Spelman's Beverly Tatum) is the ability to plan for ifs, the ability to anticipate obstacles and create multiple pathways to each and every goal. This skill is rooted in two core beliefs of hopeful people: there are many paths to goals and none of them is free of obstacles.

Futurecasting creates momentum, the energy of hope. This energy builds on the positive emotions around our goals, our sense of personal confidence (or agency), and our willpower, or ability to persevere. But when things don't go according to plan, our energy can be quickly depleted. Maybe we try harder, earning credit for our grit. But if we stick with the same strategy, using it over and over, we'll eventually crash. Instead, we need to develop the street smarts of hope. Creating a new way gives you the will you need to press on, a boost of will that keeps you going.

In this chapter, I'm going to show you how to build hope by identifying multiple pathways from Point A to Point B and using them to navigate real and perceived obstacles. These tactics (including generating alternatives, facing down fears, filling resource gaps, building on strengths, and borrowing hope) enlist the rational mind—the planner in all of us.

Generate Alternative Pathways

In his early research on hope, Rick Snyder found that thinking about multiple pathways to a goal is a core skill of hopeful people. It is also one that can be taught.

Consider a group of Kansas City high school students taking part in what I call the Hope Camera Project (more on this project in chapter 13). Most of the one hundred high school students used donated disposable cameras to achieve the objective of telling their personal hope stories. In small groups, each armed with a camera, the students worked together and devised good plans for sharing the camera, assembling the photos, and arranging them to tell a story about hope in their lives. Only one group struggled—they lost the camera on the first day.

Many kids would have bailed at that point. But this group was excited about the project and wanted a chance to complete it. "Hey, Doc Shane, what do we do?" they asked. I told them, "Figure it out. That is what hopeful people do." That's when they started generating alternative pathways. They considered buying a new camera, but they didn't have the money. They talked about making a collage of photos cut from magazines and school newsletters but realized they didn't have enough depicting hope. Finally, they decided to check out a video camera from the school library and shoot a video telling their hope stories. The clip they produced was shared across the school and the district, creating some great discussions among the adults about how students can solve real-world problems when we give them the chance and a little nudge.

My work with the high schoolers taught me that sometimes the best hope intervention for people who are stuck is letting them figure out ways to get unstuck. As parents or teachers, what happens when a child or student hits a snag and comes to you for help? Your experience gives you the edge in problem-solving, so it's tempting to step right in with a solution, but it is not always necessary. Whenever you can, stand back and ask: "What do you think you should do? Can you think of more than one possibility? Which one would work best?" Even quite young children may surprise you with their creative ideas.

Manager and executives also need to let their new employees figure out how to solve some of the problems inherent to business. Entry-level workers need freedom to fail and enough rope to pull themselves out of trouble. Good lessons in problem-solving could make the difference between an employee developing into a contributor or a liability.

When you face your own challenges, try to devise as many coping strategies as possible. Having a surplus of pathways can help you escape a bad situation quicker or tolerate an inescapable situation better. Psychology professor Carla Berg of Emory University demonstrated the power of alternatives in an experiment where she helped people with low hope learn how to tolerate pain. All participants in her lab study were introduced to the cold pressor task and told that their goal was to hold their hand in the bucket of ice water until they could no longer stand the pain. (This is the same test Rick Snyder demonstrated on *Good Morning America* in chapter 4.) Then they were randomly assigned to one of two groups. Prior to the task, control group members were given a bland magazine article to read. The treatment group listened to guided imagery that focused on increasing the quantity and quality of strategies for coping with pain. Here are some general hope prompts that followed the pain management imagery:

> Use these steps to increase your ability to think of multiple strategies and alternative ways to reach your goals. First, think about the steps involved in reaching your goal. Second, think about the different strategies that you have for reaching the goal. And third, in your mind, rehearse what you will need to do during the pursuit of your goal to be successful in reaching it. Also, anticipate the problems you might have in reaching your goal and the alternatives you can use to overcome the problems.

Then, one by one and in private, people were asked to dunk their hands in the bucket of ice water. Participants in the guided-imagery group tolerated pain almost twice as long on average as people in the control group. Notably, they generated more strategies for dealing with pain than the control group. Some engaged in distraction techniques, like focusing intensely on objects in the room or meditating on warm thoughts or beach scenes. Others tried to flex their hand, forearm, and bicep in ways that stimulated blood flow and conceivably moved the pain around. Although both groups were low-hope at the beginning of the experiment, pathways thinking made the difference.

Face Down an Old Anxiety

When I received a postcard with a beautiful beach scene from my psychotherapy client, Ellie, I couldn't help but smile. She had made it to Hawaii. This was a real victory of hope over fear, because Ellie was terrified of flying.

Ellie came to me because her husband had been promoted to a great new position at a military base in Honolulu. He had already moved out there and the government had paid for the family's possessions to be loaded onto a container ship. Ellie's job was to fly herself and the kids, ages five and seven, from the Midwest to their new home—in less than three weeks. "I've got to do this, but I don't know if I can," she told me. "I haven't flown in ten years and I promised myself I would never do it again." Her last flight had been the kind that could turn normal fears into a full-blown phobia—multiple boarding delays, turbulence from takeoff to touchdown, a long wait on the tarmac before being released from the cabin. But Ellie was determined. She saw the move as a big adventure for the family, and she didn't want her children to suffer from her fears, or worse, to learn them for themselves. "I picked up this anxiety from my mom," she said. "I don't want the kids to get it from me."

Ellie and I drew up a plan based on a preferred treatment for phobias called systematic desensitization. We would start with a good dose of relaxation training and then expose her to imagined fears of flying, first introducing the least threatening and escalating gradually. At each stage, her fearful images would be countered by relaxation techniques until her anxiety went away or at least became more tolerable.

A good plan—until we hit a snag. The relaxation training gave Ellie a new set of skills, but she couldn't make the simulated threats feel real enough for the desensitization to work. I thought hypnotherapy might help, but since I wasn't trained in the technique, I referred her to a colleague. Ellie agreed to attend the session if I would join her. At the end of a marathon meeting with the other therapist, we still did not know if the treatment had worked. Ellie's postcard was proof that she had succeeded in getting from Point A to Point B.

Fill a Resource Gap

On the evening of April 29, 1992, much of America was watching television, taking in the violent images from the Los Angeles riots. That night, John, living in Southern California, was closer to the action than most but still safe in his home. A young black man himself, John related somewhat to Rodney King and the rioters. He understood why people were angry: King's beating by a band of cops had been captured on video, swift justice was promised, and then the court let King's assailants skate. But John knew violence wasn't the answer.

That Wednesday night in California, the rioters chose fear and then they chose rage. Millions of TV viewers across the nation chose fear and retreated into their homes, only to watch nonstop news coverage of looting and beat-downs. John chose hope over fear. And he has done so again and again, every day for the last two decades.

Just a few days after the riot, on May 5, 1992, John, a twenty-six-year-old from Compton who had experienced the highs of acting alongside child stars and the lows of living in his Mitsubishi Montero for six months, became an activist and a social entrepreneur. His desire to help kids was grounded in an important post-riot discovery that shaped his philosophy about growing people and changing communities: "Three thousand buildings were burned or vandalized during the riots. None of them were homes. You don't burn what you own." What if kids learned how to *own* their futures?

John wanted to give young people a voice and create pathways to a secure financial future through a start-up community organization. John Hope Bryant's small community center, Operation HOPE, struggled in the beginning. But in twenty years, it has grown into three-hundred-plus city centers serving youth, helping them learn the skills and language of money and believe in the promise of the future. To date, thanks to John's hands-on hope, more than one million young people have learned the ways of personal finance. Nearly $1.5 billion has been raised to address urban poverty, and nineteen thousand Hope Corps volunteers have been mobilized into service. Now John takes his message on the road. He says he teaches people how to build "hope capital" through the "magic of compounded hustle." He advocates for the financial futures of American kids and young people around the world. At the heart of every service and speech that John and his colleagues provide is that if you are financially literate you have more pathways in life. If you do not use a bank and instead frequent check-cashing centers, the financial system works against you, limiting your options with high interest rates and no opportunities to accrue wealth. If you have some knowledge about how to manage your own finances and work with a local bank, you can usually find ways to save for the future and make ends meet today.

Build Pathways from Strengths

School report cards, annual reviews at work, and investment portfolios typically are mixed, providing some good news and some bad. We gravitate to the bad news and tend to skim over the good. What happens when we study what we do best before we focus on our deficits? That approach opens up more pathways to success.

At the beginning of my teaching career, reading student evaluations was torturous. Students must have figured the new guy needed plenty of feedback. I can still quote the comments that really rocked me. In 1993, it was "You have poor diction." That's exactly what a south Louisiana transplant didn't want to hear. In 1998, another student wrote, "Sometimes I can't follow you." That came after I spent months trying to make course material accessible and easy to follow. In 2005, "You seemed to play favorites in class" made me question how inclusive an educator I was.

Working on diction, giving lectures in a more lockstep fashion, and including more students in class discussions made me a less flawed average teacher. But the fix-it mentality took only me so far. When I began to pay attention to what students saw as my strengths, my growth accelerated, and I became an award-winning teacher at my university. For example, students noted that I was able to bring material to life with case studies and stories. That feedback led me to write down more accounts of my clinical and consulting work so that I had more ready-to-share stories that illustrated points. I also chose supplemental readings from nonfiction books and magazines to show students how concepts played out in the real world. Finally, when I couldn't find a textbook that brought positive psychology to life for students, I wrote my own and filled it with vignettes and exercises.

Thinking about how to do more of what you do best can lead you to many pathways to growth. Focusing on your strengths first also keeps your mind open to fixes for your weaknesses. Say your child comes home with a report card with four A's, a B, a C, and an F. Leading with a discussion of the A's and B will help you and your child come up with lots of ideas for making sure the F doesn't show up again. Jumping on the F first will shut your child down emotionally, and that will undermine her pathways thinking.

Turn Work into Play

Writer Dave Eggers is best known for his book *A Heartbreaking Work of Staggering Genius* and his screenplay for *Where the Wild Things Are*. He's also known for his untiring and creative support of other writers. But if you enter the Pirate Supply Store at 826 Valencia Street in San Francisco, you won't see any writers at work—at least not right away. You have to walk to the back of the store, to the big room behind the shelves filled with items like beard extensions, dolphin tears, eye patches, skull-and-crossbones dice, remedies for scurvy, and wooden planks by the foot. Then you will understand why pirates also need the many colorful books on display.

What you find at 826 Valencia is a tutoring center that mentors young writers—or perhaps a mentoring center that provides help with writing. It makes a caring adult available to every child who walks in. Its mission is "supporting students ages 6–18 with their writing skills, and to helping teachers get their students excited about the literary arts." The 826 mentors accept students at all levels of skill and work with them shoulder to shoulder on school assignments, college essays, and creative projects. The students' final creative work is then published in the books, magazines, and newspapers on sale in the store and online. All programs are free of charge.

Eggers was a struggling writer living in Brooklyn when he first spotted the resource gap that led to the founding of 826. As he recalls, "So many of my friends who were teaching in city schools were having trouble working with their students, keeping them at grade level, in reading and writing in particular." Eggers asked his friends what they needed to help the kids. Their answer: "More people, more bodies, more attention, more hours, more expertise from people who have skills in English and can work with these students one-on-one."

Eggers knew many writers with flexible daytime hours who could share their love of words and storytelling. What was needed was a way to connect writers, students, and teachers. He took the idea with him when he moved to San Francisco, and there, with a dozen or so friends, he found a storefront at 826 Valencia Street, where they planned to set up a tutoring center. One big problem: the space was zoned for retail; the landlord said they had to sell something. Eggers and his buddies were stumped until someone pointed to the old wooden beams overhead: "It really kind of looks like the hull of a ship." Which became the spark that ignited inspiration: San Francisco's "only independent pirate supply store" opened its doors in April 2002.

Despite the weeks of setting up the center and the sign out front offering "help with all your English needs," no students showed up. Not one. Eggers filled this new resource gap by persuading seasoned educator Ninive Calegari to join the team. Calegari knew how to spread the word to local schools, teachers, and parents, and soon, with the pirate supply shop paying the rent, Eggers and his band of merry tutors were sitting shoulder to shoulder with kids, listening to their ideas and helping them put those ideas on paper.

The next big leap came when the writer-volunteers realized that the students were just like them: they got more excited about writing if their work ended up in a published book rather than in a bin of forgotten essays. The 826 team learned in a couple of months what it took me years to discover: not a single kid in America wakes up excited about the opportunity to raise his school's reading, writing, and math scores.

Children want to learn skills that matter. They will learn what we have to teach them if those skills are attached to a meaningful product or outcome. The staff started designing projects that would teach groups of students, whether at the 826 storefront or at their neighborhood school, how to write essays and stories worthy of being bound in a book and sold. "Now we're sort of addicted to the book thing," Eggers said in 2008. "The kids will work harder than they've ever worked in their life if they know it's going to be permanent, know it's going to be on a shelf, know that nobody can diminish what they've thought and said, that we've honored their words, honored their thoughts with hundreds of hours of five drafts, six drafts—this attention that we give to their thoughts."

Eggers and Calegari cofounded 826 National, which now includes eight affiliated centers in cities across the country. On a recent work trip to Washington, D.C., I visited the Museum of Unnatural History. Dana Carlson, the museum curator, greeted me. She is responsible for artifacts that include saber-tooth dental floss, mega-sand, and primordial soup, all of which are for sale to visitors. Dana then introduced me to Joe Callahan, the executive director of 826 DC, who told me that 1,039 local volunteers had provided more than 11,500 hours during the 2010–2011 school year, serving some 1,547 students in the D.C. metro area. On the day of my visit, twenty mentors were sitting alongside students—helping with homework, discussing drafts of new short stories, or just chatting. I was struck by the buzz in the tutoring room, a sound of happy engagement that we don't often associate with school classrooms.

My next stop is the 826 Los Angeles location. The Echo Park Time Travel Mart is a convenience store for time travelers. Their motto: "Whenever you are, we're already then." Seems like a hope researcher ought to visit that one.

Borrow Hope

You've explored one alternative after another. You've filled every gap you can identify. But you still don't have the resources you need to get from Point A to Point B. There's one more secret weapon used by hopeful people: borrowing the hope of others.

When I was twenty years old I was determined to go to a good graduate school (out of Louisiana) and get a Ph.D. in psychology, followed by a great job. I had good grades, adequate test scores, and strong letters of recommendation. Trouble was, I did not know how to type (which made filling out fifteen applications challenging), I was a poor writer (my essays were atrocious), I had rarely been out of Louisiana, and I had never been on a plane. To make my dream come true, I had to risk letting lots of people know about my goal—and then ask them to invest in it by sharing their resources with me. My girlfriend and her mom stepped up by typing my applications (while I was learning to type). My older brother helped me answer questions about myself and my future and then proofed and reproofed my essays. Friends at work who had taken to calling me "college boy" gave me the confidence to apply far and wide. A family friend who had accumulated hundreds of thousands of miles on sales trips donated the airline ticket so I could visit my top-choice school. And my mom put "Shane getting into graduate school" on her prayer list at church.

This kind of old-fashioned, time-tested family and community support can still help you get where you want to go. Many caring adults in our neighborhoods, schools, and sports and mentoring programs see it as their job to lend hope to young people, knocking down an obstacle here or filling a gap there. Folks do tend to rally around you when your needs are made clear.

But I also know I was lucky to be surrounded by people who believed in me and in my goal. Today, when many of us live far from our hometowns, social entrepreneurs are pioneering new models for borrowing hope. Within just a few years, crowdsourcing has given us access to a vast neighborhood of millions of people around the world. I'll describe just a few of these new ways to negotiate for the skills, resources, and encouragement you need to keep your hope in high gear.

TimeBanks.org, with three hundred active TimeBanks in twenty-six countries, makes it easy to exchange your time, spent doing what you do best, for the time of others in your community, doing what they do best. Everyone's time is valued alike. If I spend an hour providing math tutoring, I might exchange that "time credit" for sixty minutes of dog walking. In the words of their website, "We are all assets. We all have something to give."

For example, TimeBanksNYC connects individuals across the five boroughs of New York City in an attempt to identify untapped skills of people in each neighborhood, develop a sense of connection and community, and promote the sharing of resources. Staten Island resident Mary Barbieri was injured while running an errand near the World Trade Center on September 11, 2001. A few months later, she was preparing for a move to a new apartment when she became emotionally overwhelmed at the prospect of packing. She called the local office of TimeBanksNYC, and the organization sent six people to help her pack, move, and unpack. Mary was more than willing to pay it forward. "Anything they need me to do. If somebody needs a lunch and they can't get out of the house, I'll bring them lunch," she said.

Crowdrise.com, founded by Robert Wolfe and a cast of characters including actor Ed Norton, has a different focus. It helps individuals and groups raise funds to bankroll a community project or charity. Once you sign up on the website, you can enlist friends, family, community members, and all other members of Crowdrise to get excited about your cause. The website also offers many suggestions for making your appeal fun and engaging, putting the age-old power of a compelling story to work in a new way.

On my latest visit to Crowdrise.com, I checked out projects in the "human services" category. There I saw the faces of some celebrities (Sophia Bush, Will Ferrell, Jonah Hill), and many other people like you and me who were creating something out of nothing with the help of the crowd. Hill, an actor known for his roles in quirky comedies, was fund-raising for Nothing But Nets, a project with a goal of sending 150,000 bed nets to villagers in the Horn of Africa—a simple, practical way of protecting people from the mosquitoes that carry malaria. This cause has multiple sponsors, but over eight months, Hill's entry alone has brought in more than sixty-five thousand dollars and counting, mostly in very small amounts. Watch the list of donations scroll down your computer screen, and you see the power of the crowd in action.

ChallengePost.com should be on your list if you work for a government agency, nonprofit organization, or software company that needs to generate top-flight ideas from around the world on a limited budget. This site allows you to tap into the innovation of millions of people who are more than willing to compete for the opportunity to fill your gap. Here's how it works. First, you describe the details of your challenge. (For example, the city of New York challenged the world to develop software applications that would make the city "more transparent, accessible, and accountable," based on masses of available data.) Next, you post a reward for the best entry. The product or idea that is judged to meet your challenge or solve your problem is then given the reward. (New York posted a reward of twenty thousand dollars and received eighty-five apps, valued at more than $4.5 million.) Communities form around some challenges, sparking discussion and more ideas for development. Innovative participants have also attracted venture capitalists.

In another example, the U.S. Department of Agriculture initiated "Apps for Healthy Kids," which made available nutrition data for a thousand commonly consumed foods and challenged students, software developers, and entrepreneurs to create Web-based and mobile games to teach young people how to use the information to make good choices. The aim was to fill the gap that exists between what kids know (this food is good for me and this is not so good) and what they do (I will eat a lot of this and a little of that). With prize money totaling only sixty thousand dollars, some of it donated by General Electric, ninety-five games worth about $5 million were created in response to the challenge.

Whatever your hopeful goal, you can probably find a site to support it. Kickstarter.com has become the go-to source for financing creative projects. DonorsChoose.org allows classroom teachers to fund projects (some very modest) that their own school or district can't afford. Crowdsourcing literally brings the world's resources to your computer.

From Borrowing to Sharing Hope

Through the pursuit of individual success at school and work, we learn the how of hope. Then we lead hopeful lives, accruing more personal success, amassing more hope. But hope can do more than make you successful and lead to personal well-being. Hopeful individuals can share their wealth of hope, making the lives of others better. Imagine what could happen if we shared some of that hope surplus, making our personal hope a public resource. Could we create a culture and spirit dedicated to solving our biggest problems and making our communities better?

CREATING A
NETWORK OF HOPE

Chapter 12

Leading with Hope

*F*ollowers—*students, employees, congregants, citizens—all need hope.*
There it is. I just summed up the last century's worth of schol-
arly works on leadership. It is worth repeating. *Followers need hope.*
Whether you are following a teacher who is showing you how to solve
a problem, a boss who is trying to win a company-saving contract, or a
preacher who is working to strengthen your community, *you need hope.*

Of course, there are some caveats to that statement. I will address
one of them right here: followers have other needs that they look to
leaders to meet. Gallup discovered followers' need for hope and other
intangibles when it asked people to identify the most influential leaders
in their lives. Here, play along with the nation by answering the following question:

> What leader has the most positive influence in your daily life? Take
> a few moments to think about this question if you need to. Once
> you have someone in mind, please list his or her initials. _____

Now, please list three words that best describe what this person contributes to your life.

_____

_____

_____

A random sample of more than ten thousand people shared their thoughts during telephone interviews. Through the hard work and insight of a Gallup research team, each word describing a leader was compared and contrasted with other responses. Ultimately, the coding process rendered clear results about the needs of followers. Then the twenty-five most frequently mentioned words were studied carefully. Surprisingly, words we often associate with leadership, such as *wisdom* or *humility,* were nowhere near the top of the list.

Followers, whether referencing spiritual leaders, great leaders from the past, good bosses, or today's community leaders, say they want the people they serve to meet four psychological needs: compassion, stability, trust, and hope. In return, followers give their commitment, creativity, mutual trust, and engagement.

A leader's hope is especially valuable to followers during tough times. Gallup research, however, suggests that the vast majority of leaders do not spend enough time on making hope happen. Even leaders of large groups of people spend more time reacting to problems than initiating a better future.

Types of responses did not differ by type of leader. So, a manager is no less on the hook for providing trust than a spiritual leader. A CEO is no less responsible for giving love to followers than a parent. And political leaders are as responsible as other leaders for meeting the hope needs of their followers.

By studying hopeful leaders and talking to their followers, I found that people who want to spread hope and motivate followers need to practice these three tactics:

* Create and sustain excitement about the future.
* Knock down existing obstacles to goals and don't put up new ones.
* Reestablish goals—regoal—when the circumstances demand it.

Leaders don't necessarily have the budget or staffing that they need or want, but they do have infinite resources—hopeful thinking—in every one of their followers. Followers look to leaders to capitalize on the spirit and ideas of the times, to dream big, and to motivate them toward a meaningful future.

Creating Excitement About the Future

When people have a boss who makes them feel hopeful about the future, they are more committed to their jobs. Specifically, when Gallup asked followers whether their leader at work (typically a manager) made them enthusiastic about the future, of those who said yes, 69 percent were engaged in their jobs, scoring high on a measure of involvement in and excitement about work. These engaged employees are the products of hopeful leadership. They are more innovative and productive than others, and they are more likely to be with the company for the long haul.

Of those followers who said their leader did not make them enthusiastic about the future, a mere 1 percent were committed and energized at work. These disengaged workers are a threat to business, coworkers, and themselves. They not only fail to make meaningful contributions; they undermine the hard work of others, and they are likely to be more physically and mentally unhealthy than their coworkers. And, for good and bad, it is somewhat likely that they won't be with the company one year later.

Inspired by Gallup's leadership findings, I tried to learn more about hopeful leaders by talking to their followers. Here is what JerLene, a workplace consultant for the same company for twenty-five years, had to say about the leader of her consulting group.

> **JerLene:** I just love her. She knows what I am good at, and she lets me do it. Why can't everyone have a boss like her?
>
> **SJL:** Besides letting you do what you do best, what does she do to keep you so fired up?
>
> **JerLene:** She wants to make people's lives better. That's what I want, too. That's what we all want here. And she doesn't let foolish trends and fads distract us from what we are doing.
>
> **SJL:** How does she make your life better?
>
> **JerLene:** Well, let's see. She calls me before a big trip to ask me what I want to share with the client. She emails me after my meetings for highlights. I look forward to those calls and emails. She encourages me to work with other consultants and researchers who can make me better. And she understands that I am trying to be a great consultant and a great mom, and sometimes that will require flexibility on her part.

JerLene and other followers of strong leaders talk about their shared vision for the future (focusing more on "we" goals than "me" goals), the chance to use their talents to make change happen, and an energy that sustains them and gets them through down times. They feel a day-to-day excitement and hope. There's no fear in their interactions.

Shortly after an F5 tornado with 200-mile-per-hour winds decimated 95 percent of the city of Greensburg, Kansas, at 9:45 P.M. on May 4, 2007, a group of community leaders realized that they had to create a bold new vision of the future for their city, one that would get the nation's attention. Within twelve hours of the storm, then-mayor Lonnie McCollum told the media that the people of the city had decided to rebuild. Upon her visit to Greensburg, then-governor Kathleen Sebelius met with city leaders. When she left the closed-door meeting she announced to the world that "[w]e talked about having Greensburg be the greenest rural community in America."

Just days after the south-central Kansas city was turned into rubble, city council members and state officials signed a resolution announcing that Greensburg would rebuild as America's greenest city, making it environmentally and economically sustainable. Steve Hewitt was city administrator, and so it became his job to rally the community and turn big ideas into LEED-certified public buildings, businesses, and homes—a sort of living science museum that would bring more people to town than its other big attraction, the world's deepest hand-dug well. I asked Steve how the city's plan, collaborations, and hard work had restored morale to a group of people who had lost everything. He told me, "Everybody needed a story of recovery," and explained that the Greensburg recovery story came together as the community contributed to it, as real planning began, and as the long-term picture started to look better than the past.

Mayor Bob Dixson, who took office in the wake of the storm, helped Hewitt follow through on the plan, declaring, "We live in exciting times here in Greensburg, and we need to be moving boldly into the future." Dixson continues to lead Greensburg toward its status as America's greenest city, with the goal of providing some inspiration to the rest of America. (For more information see Greensburggreentown.org.) And when the city of Joplin, Missouri, got hit with an F5 in May 2011, Greensburg city officials passed on all they had learned to those city leaders and townspeople in Joplin.

If we aspire to lead with hope, like the city leaders in Greensburg, we need to support our story in every message we share with our followers, from strategic plans to the details of everyday communications.

All exchanges—including texts, emails, tweets, reports, speeches, interviews—must, individually and in total, communicate trust and stability to create and/or maintain excitement about the future. Followers see fear as the enemy, and when fear infects the words of their leaders, it can make them doubt their commitment to a project or even to a company. Auditing or vetting messages for hope and fear can help keep employees engaged.

This doesn't mean memos filled with exclamation marks, smiley faces, and goofy emoticons. The goal is a straightforward and engaging message that the future will be better than the present, that every recipient has a role in making it so, and that the paths to the future will require the group's commitment and effort. That is what I saw in a recent communication from Steve Rasmussen, CEO of Nationwide Insurance, who rose through the ranks in the insurance business and led his company through the Great Recession, to his thirty-six thousand associates. In his letter, he explained that they had many opportunities to expand their business and he wanted their help in promoting that growth. He closed by writing:

> Thanks for all you're doing to help build our momentum. Associates are why Nationwide has been so successful in serving members and building the communities where we work, and why I'm sure we'll continue to be so in the future.
>
> My request is to help us take full advantage of the opportunities before us. Also, please learn how your role or team provides value to the entire organization. Understand how all the pieces fit together to activate our New Mutual strategy. And know that you're working for a winning organization that is on the move—one whose noble purpose is fulfilled through our actions and commitment to our members, communities and associates every day. I'm proud of how far we've already come, and for what I know you'll do to help us leverage our competitive advantage in the future.

Rasmussen's closing statement creates a sense of energy and forward motion. He includes all of Nationwide's associates in the mission and then makes a request of each of them. He reminds them of their purpose and their responsibilities—all in 150 words.

Leaders like Rasmussen know that their personal hope is a public resource. *If you can't make followers excited, you are no longer a leader.*

The hope or fear created by our daily communications doesn't change just the overall climate of our homes, schools, or workplaces. It affects the emotional and cognitive psychology of each person, making them either more open or more closed. Excitement about the future, whether it's experienced as calm encouragement or something bordering on exuberance, expands what a person feels like doing right now and can do in the future. According to psychologist Barbara Fredrickson, these positive emotions can create an upward spiral where pathways and energy fuel one another.

Leaders who are burned-out, fearful, or demoralized tend to shut down their own thinking. They struggle to solve old problems or deal with the crisis of the moment, leaving little energy for coming up with fresh ideas and flexible plans. With blinders on, they are more concerned with surviving the now than with preparing for the then. Through their anxiety-laced communication (or worse, no communication at all), they infect their followers with negative emotion, narrow vision, and their own disengagement.

At their core, great leaders are great storytellers. Some are quiet, some are flamboyant. But they all create a picture of a meaningful goal, and they describe a path—filled with both struggles and exciting challenges—to get there. It's the story of a journey we want to share, one that demands our best skills and efforts and expands our own sense of what we can accomplish.

Knocking Down Obstacles

Leaders lose influence when they make our lives harder. Whether it is a small-town high school principal adding extra obstacles to graduation, or a politician creating more red tape in the way of getting what you need, we don't respond well to hope killers.

Hopeful leaders make our lives better and easier. With instrumental support (a helpful hand in a time of need), influential leaders knock down obstacles to goals, giving followers their best shot at doing what they do best. Fairness and balance also come in here, because getting rid of some obstacles can create new bumps in the road for someone else.

For leaders who are willing and able to put themselves in the shoes of their followers, knocking down obstacles is one of the quickest ways to build hope. Unfortunately, too many leaders distance themselves— their followers tell you they "don't have a clue." How many high school counselors, bankers, and college financial aid counselors have recently completed the Free Application for Federal Student Aid that paves the way for many students to attend college? How many college presidents have logged into a mock student account and tried to enroll in a class? How many CEOs have struggled to duct-tape together child care for their kids during holidays and summers? How many senators have waited all day in a free clinic to get a referral to another clinic to get basic health care?

John Fetterman has a clue. At six feet, eight inches and more than three hundred pounds, a bald and heavily tattooed Fetterman could easily use his street cred and a little fear to get his way. But as mayor of Braddock, Pennsylvania, Fetterman hardly uses his brawn in his attempts to turn his adopted hometown around. He uses hope as a hammer.

Like many industrial towns, Braddock, an old steel town outside Pittsburgh, had its glory days. The first A&P grocery store in America opened there. It was home to the Carnegie Foundation's first public library in the United States. But when Fetterman moved there in 2001, it was nearly dead, having lost 90 percent of its population and 90 percent of its buildings.

Mayor Fetterman has a knack for eliminating obstacles. With no community center or playground, Fetterman struck a publicity deal with Levi's jeans. The company set a national ad campaign in Braddock, used local talent, and, most important, donated a $1 million community center that was named in honor of a slain child.

With no grocery stores or restaurants, Braddock was a food desert. Fetterman helped locals develop a two-acre urban garden that provides produce for families and extra vegetables for sale in nearby towns.

Fetterman works daily to make the townspeople and outside investors enthusiastic about the future of small-town America. He believes that a leader should give people more options. "Creating as many different opportunities and allowing people to define their success is crucial." Supporters refer to the Fetterman Effect, which led to Braddock getting more attention and resources than other struggling towns in the Rust Belt. Despite his appeal, his progress is slow and he is not without critics. But lifelong resident Jeremy Cannon sums up Fetterman's efforts: "He's one of the few people that gave us hope for the future. He gave us opportunities with jobs. He just gave us a reason to wake up every day and a place to go."

Regoaling

A leader's greatest challenge is regoaling, which reclaims willpower from the pursuit of unattainable goals. Regoaling requires you to change course after days, months, or years of convincing others that you were on the right path and then realizing that you weren't.

Regoaling is where hope meets courage. Leading with hope is easy when the odds are in our favor or when we can recruit a team and develop a plan that can help us beat the odds. It is a different matter when the odds are truly insurmountable. In the face of such odds, some leaders engage in conspiracy and silence, deluding themselves and others about what might happen, while they cling to goals that are no longer viable or realistic. Other leaders—the ones we want in our lives—guide us toward choices that balance our rational and emotional interests. They are at their best in the worst of times.

I learned how great leaders face the toughest of circumstances from an unlikely source: a pediatrician. Chris Feudtner, who works at the Children's Hospital of Philadelphia, is not your typical kid doc. He is one of a few dozen palliative pediatric care physicians in the world. That means he spends every day helping families who are losing their fight for the lives of children.

Years ago, Dr. Feudtner realized that hope is what sustains families who are working toward one vital goal: keeping their child alive. Then, when all forms of treatment have been tried and all tests point to failing health and imminent death, Feudtner teaches families to reinvest their hopes in a new goal: helping their child die peacefully. In one of our discussions, he convinced me that there is one right we should all have when we are out of treatment options. "You have to pick your modus exodus, the way that you die," Dr. Feudtner said.

When Feudtner's families regoal, they take the support and energy they have devoted to keeping their child alive and redirect it to letting the child go peacefully. Every day, Feudtner helps parents face the hardest decision they will ever make, framing the options in real terms, preparing families for what is probable and what is possible. "I ask them, 'What is the best way to love your child now?'" This opens up one of the hardest conversations imaginable. Dr. Feudtner has been shoulder to shoulder with hundreds of families who have grappled with that question. How they answer it can make the difference between a grief that rips the remaining family apart, or allows them to heal slowly together.

My conversations with Chris Feudtner about his patients taught me a hope lesson that I will not soon forget. That is: regoaling requires us to let go of some of our dreams to make our best possible future. If parents facing an unimaginable loss learn to regoal, I can learn to do it as well.

In daily life, regoaling requires us to let go of hopes that no longer serve our future. And sometimes we have to revisit old goals that we thought were in our rearview mirror. That was the case for Sandy Lewis, who shelved her own plans to get a beloved community senior center back on track.

With multigenerational programming, fund-raising, and new facilities and partnerships, Sandy had helped turn the Champlain Senior Center in Burlington, Vermont, into a community resource and a national model for promoting the independence and well-being of older citizens. Just a few years after Sandy resigned as the president of the board, the phone started ringing. Sandy's friends and colleagues had bad news. The center was falling into disrepair and not meeting the needs of the seniors. Sandy felt compelled to visit and see for herself what was happening.

She was appalled at what she found. There was graffiti on the walls, trash in the hallways, dog hair lining the cafeteria floors, and the financial forecast was bleak. What was once a community hub was now a ghost town: it seemed as if only those who had nowhere to go remained. Saddest of all, it looked like the seniors had given up. Still passionate about the mission and purpose of this organization, Sandy put the launch of a start-up on hold and prepared to go to work. But first she knew she had to "reengage the seniors in the ownership of their beloved center."

Here is her account of a regoaling session with some very angry clients:

I had about 70 infuriated people in the room, with much shouting and cane waving—all directed at me. It had been a long time since I was publicly afraid for my safety, but I soldiered on and they got the picture. Once they settled down, I shared the financial data and my hope for the future. Then I asked them what they wanted for the center, what their goals might be and asked them to work with me to achieve them. What do you hope to see for the center? What will the center look like in 5 years? What is your vision for the center? What programs would you like to see here? How would you like to help?

I was very clear that it was *their* center and that I was their agent. I promised to keep them abreast of the financial and political picture, and they agreed to work with me to return the center to its glory days. I kept the focus on the future and only addressed the vision that I knew was possible. I wanted to make sure that they were going to work hard to improve the center and after the tenor of this initial meeting, I was pleased that they were passionate.

Hopeful leaders like Sandy rise to the occasion when they are needed most. They are straight shooters whose honesty creates trust and helps us build a new version of the future.

Spreading Hope

No matter how high it is, our individual hope sometimes gets bottled up by powerful personal or social forces. That is when we most need hopeful leaders. Their hope becomes a public resource for tackling the problems we face.

When we are at our lowest point at work or school or in our personal lives, hope is a force multiplier. It can turn even a tiny amount of energy into mojo for the future. Nothing good happens when we are demoralized. The leaders who care about us most know this. That's why they work so hard to give us a glimmer of what's possible. And *that* is why people follow them.

Chapter 13

Teaching Hope to
the Next Generation

WHEN I first started to bring hope programs into public schools, I wasn't sure how much students would benefit. But I was certain that our hope team could engage the kids and get them thinking about the future. So when a handful of high school freshmen were tuned out and a couple seemed flat-out annoyed by us, I had to figure out what was going on.

I went quietly over to Steve, a longtime classroom teacher, who seemed to have a good connection with the students. I was curious about one boy in particular. "What's up with that kid? Why's he blowing us off?" What Steve shared rocked me: "You guys are talking a lot about the future. I think he would say he doesn't have one. Some of his cousins and friends died before they hit fifteen. He says he is living on borrowed time."

This student—I will call him Carlos—lived every day the way my former VA client John did in those terrifying days after his medical diagnosis. Carlos saw himself as a boy with no future. Why should he spend an hour a week talking about something he didn't have? I realized that our first job was to reconnect Carlos—and a few other students in his class—with a believable future, and as quickly as possible. Our team would need to make a special effort with those students, helping them trade a fast-life strategy of reacting and spending for one that relied on planning and investing.

Steve also touched on a struggle that many more students were having. "Even those who believe that they have a good future ahead of them—they don't see how school will help them get there." *Whoa!* As we know from Destin and Oyserman's study in the Detroit middle school (see chapter 5), this connection between school and who and what we want to be when we grow up is fundamental to the success of our children. This became another key focus for the hope team, and I believe that it is the central challenge for our educational system today. We have to help students see that school is relevant to the future they want for themselves.

I've now spent almost two decades researching hope in young people. Since 2009 I have measured hope in more than one million students through the Gallup Student Poll. I have worked with thousands of America's most hopeful teachers. And I have taught hope programs to children of every age. I now believe that to teach hope to our children, in and out of the home, we need to do the following:

* Link children's current thinking, efforts, and learning to their future lives.
* Teach children specific, multiple pathways to meaningful goals.
* Conduct community audits to preserve and recruit extra agency for children.

But there's a caveat: These three tactics work only if the young person is already connected to the future. And that connection, in turn, is created if, and only if, a child has at least one caring, hopeful adult in his or her life, and if the child is excited about at least one thing in the future.

Being close to a caring, hopeful adult paves the way and prepares the heart for hope. All children are not born into loving families, but even one caring adult can buffer a child from the pains of the past and the fears of the present. Only with that support and protection can our youth invest in the future. Only with the help of a caring, hopeful adult do our young people have the luxury to imagine a better future.

I've known many teachers, counselors, coaches, and mentors who became the primary caring, hopeful adult in children's lives. But even when children are well supported at home, anyone who works with them needs to convey hope to make sure that the next generation is in hot pursuit of the future.

Children also need something to hope for. They need to be excited about one thing in the future . . . then another, then another. That one thing can be big or small, novel or run-of-the-mill, close at hand or far in the future—as long as it teaches them to look forward with positive expectation. The content hardly matters (a weekly visit to the park, a family trip, a sporting event, a school dance) as long as thoughts about it are energizing to the young person. Lessons about pathways or agency don't stick unless they're aimed at something meaningful.

Another thing: In most cases, that one exciting thing, that thing that gives hope a spark, *can't be assigned by the adults*. That exciting thing can be *uncovered* by caring adults only as we are getting to know the young people in our lives.

This shouldn't come as much of a surprise, since we, the adults, don't like it when someone assigns us a task, either. No middle school student wakes up squealing with glee, "I get to raise the school district's reading scores today!" No college student in America jumps out of bed and says, "Today, I will do my part to raise the graduation rate at my school!" They don't care about our institutional goals. They are excited about personal goals that create a promising future for themselves. Our job is to do all we can to make sure that the present readies them for it.

Linking Learning to Life

In most school systems, education has a relevancy problem. Students are picking up on the fact that they are being prepared for a twenty-first-century world with a twentieth-century curriculum. According to the Gallup Student Poll, only half of Americans students, grades five through twelve, say that their teachers make them feel that their schoolwork is important. Perhaps due to school reforms hyperfocused on assessment, relevance has been swapped for efforts to increase rigor and accountability.

Whatever the cause, education no longer addresses a deep "felt need" among students. Many students just don't hunger for what today's schools provide. They don't see how education will fix any of their current or future problems. That needs to change. It *can* be changed. And it can be changed quite easily.

What if students consider today's work as an investment in their future self? The more (and earlier) we prime students to make connections between their college-bound selves and their K–12 selves, the more they invest in hard work today. Furthermore, the effectiveness of Destin and Oyserman's brief psychological intervention (chapter 5) suggests to me that we should use such small interventions more frequently (as the benefits are real but short-lived) rather than building big school reform or youth development programs that use massive amounts of time, energy, and money we can't get back.

Here are some ways my colleagues and students have connected students of all ages to their future:

Fantastic Future Me. Developed by the Omaha Children's Museum with the help of Gallup and Phenomblue Labs, Fantastic Future Me is an interactive computer tool that helps children ages three to eight imagine themselves in a future career. When a child walks up to the buzzing, whirling display, it snaps a head shot and then prompts her to try on one of twenty careers ranging from archeologist to video game designer. The child selects from dozens of clothing items and tools (some children try on every single accessory before choosing) to complete their future image. They then email, text, or print out the image, which is accompanied by a basic description of the educational path that would take them from their present to their future job. The Future Me message, sent to Mom, Dad, a favorite teacher, or some other caring adult, can kick off more conversation and exploration of a particular career path.

Mentoring for the future. The TeamMates Mentoring Program is a one-to-one school-based mentoring model that pairs school-age youth in Nebraska and Iowa with adults in their community. One hour of mentoring per week gives the mentor and the mentee plenty of time to talk about the hassles of the day and the possibilities that the future holds. In a partnership with Gallup and the Clifton Strengths Institute, TeamMates developed hope cards that nudge the mentors to link school to life and prime this discussion about the future. Together, adults and students come up with new ways to solve current problems and clear the way for goals that excite them. The mentor then sends a hope postcard to the student's school or home to remind the student of the next steps to his or her goal.

New-style career days. Schools across America are revamping career days to make them more relevant and engaging. Some schools are inviting local men and women who love their jobs (according to Gallup research, only 1 in 5 workers do) to discuss how classroom topics relate to their work today. Folks who are enthusiastic about their work tend to be innovative in how they use their knowledge and skills, and capable of telling a good story about what they do to almost any audience. These are the people who should be attending career days and recruiting students into internships. Students become more active participants when they have their own questions to prime the discussion. When we hosted Kids Day at the Gallup Omaha campus, the youngsters who attended were prepared with the following questions: (1) What do you like to do each day at work and why?, (2) How does your best friend at work make each day better?, (3) How do you feel when you get to do what you do best at work and why?, and (4) How does your work make the world a better place?

Project-based learning. Project-based learning is engaging to students, and it builds knowledge and mastery. Students like Philadelphia's Azeem Hill get hooked on learning when we demonstrate how today's (and every day's) classroom experiences are associated with real work and real life. "People seem to believe that . . . that if you can't learn at a desk in a row, and if you can't take a test, that you're not smart. But some people learn better when they're able to go to the shop and see it in action." Azeem's high school teacher, Simon Hauger, agrees. An electrical engineer turned inner-city math and science teacher in West Philadelphia, Hauger helped fifteen high school students build a "badass hybrid" car. The students wanted to create a cooler car, one that was fast and fuel efficient, that would be popular with young drivers. Hauger bought into their goal and worked with them every afternoon applying science, technology, engineering, and math principles far beyond what they were learning in class.

The car, their 160-miles-per-gallon Factory Vive GTM biodiesel, made it to the semifinals of the Progressive Insurance Automotive X Prize and won the "Next Generation Award" from *Popular Mechanics*. The students received special recognition from President Obama for their work. During the launch of a 2010 STEM (science, technology, engineering, and mathematics) education initiative, the president said, "They didn't have a lot of money. They didn't have the best equipment. They certainly didn't have every advantage in life. What they had was a program that challenged them to solve problems and to work together, to learn and build and create. And that's the kind of spirit and ingenuity that we have to foster. That's the potential that we can harness all across America. That's what will help our young people to fulfill their promise to realize their dreams and to help this nation succeed in the years to come."

Hauger capitalized on the success of the after-school project-based learning program and got permission and support from the school district and funders to open the Sustainability Workshop. The workshop functions as a school that models how to "unleash the creative and intellectual potential of young people to solve the world's toughest problems."

Demystifying college costs. Students need real, understandable information about the costs of college. Many don't know the details about how often-quoted tuition, room, and board expenses can be offset by the amounts available from scholarships, grants, and loans. Destin Mesmin points out that students who know that need-based financial aid can make college more affordable are more likely to spend time on homework today. The United States government is creating a college scorecard to give students a more realistic assessment of what a degree costs at each college and the amount of debt they might accrue. This online tool will help compare college after college on expenses and graduation rates. With real information about resources and expenses, students are less likely to dismiss further education because "I (my family) can't afford it."

Bridging high school and college. Traditional college visits in junior and senior year come too late to motivate many students. Take freshmen and sophomores to the local college to meet some of the school's best professors. Arrange for them to sit in on a class, take notes, and prepare to report on how the class material could be applied in the real world. Then invite the professors to join the students for lunch. Facilitate a discussion about what you are teaching in class or at home, how it relates to the professor's field, and how that connects to tomorrow's job requirements. The professional staffs of the federally funded programs Educational Talent Search and Upward Bound are masters at bringing the future into the present with campus visits. They help students as young as ten to attend college courses. Students in their early teens can live on campus during six weeks in the summer, immersing themselves in college life and connecting their current experiences with their future at college and work.

Once a student is future bound, she starts entertaining goals beyond school. The goals that are most salient to young people are the same ones that captivate most of us caring, hopeful adults. Specifically, they want a good job. It is the image of having a good job that pulls people through the years it takes them to finish their high school and undergraduate education. And they want that good job to provide security for the second outcome they are pursuing: a happy family. Although ideas about what a happy family looks like differ vastly from person to person, young people and adults covet an image of a group of people coexisting and helping one another in daily life. It is these goals—the good job and happy family—that help young people overcome the rigors of high school and college. These expectations, the foundations of a good life, are what draw us forward.

Matching the Will with the Ways

Many young people dream the American dream, believe it can be achieved, and don't have a clue how to make it a reality. Their will often exceeds their ways, which hamstrings their hope.

Students generally are confident and think "I can do anything!" According to a 2003 study by the Organisation for Economic Co-operation and Development, American kids are number one in the world in confidence. For the most part, students have adequate will and say they are willing to put in the hard work to pursue a future they are excited about.

The big problem is that they lack the ways or necessary strategies to reach the big goals, such as graduation and employment. In 2009 the Gallup Student Poll showed that 92 percent strongly believed that they would graduate from high school, but only 62 percent of them strongly believed that they could come up with many ways to get good grades. Nearly half of American students strongly believed that they would find a good job after graduation, but only a third of them (35 percent) strongly believed that they could find ways around any problem that might arise in life.

I believe that our young people lack the ways of hope because the how of school, work, and life doesn't get the attention it warrants. Perhaps because of the intense pressure to teach and learn content in each class during each school year (driven by well-meaning commitment to excellence or fear-based compulsion to do well on state testing), the process of getting good grades and solving daily problems may remain a mystery. Parents may recognize and praise a test score or a win on the field but may not explain or emphasize the how of goal pursuit.

Student hope may be enhanced by small efforts to teach them the ways to study for tests, prepare for the examination period, track grades over time, solve interpersonal disputes, compete in athletics, pursue career interests, and interview for jobs. When students have both the will and the ways, they are more likely to reach their goals.

My all-time favorite way to teach the ways of hope is to do it on the sly, before people realize I am working hard to get them to think more strategically about the future. I use the Hope Camera Project, which was originally developed for use in a children's hospital and then adapted for use in a school-based hope program. A description of a recent application of the Hope Camera Project illustrates how a project-based assignment can teach ways of hope.

School counselor Jennifer Magnuson-Stessman gave her thirty-six fifth graders and sixth graders disposable cameras and a week's time to document hope in their lives. She enticed them into action by promising them to display their work at a community art show for their friends, family, educators, and other community members.

Jennifer kicked off the project by laying out the steps that would lead the students to a fun and rewarding night at the art opening. First, each student would capture images of hope in their daily lives in twenty-eight photos. In consultation with Jennifer, they would pick the one photo that best represented hope to them. Next, they were to write a brief essay, to be edited and reedited with her, to tell their story. Finally, the students would print the photos, crop them, mat and frame them, hang them along with their essay, then rehearse for the art show.

Jennifer walked each student through each step. She nudged them to think about multiple ways to make the progress they wanted. Then one night in April 2011, hope was on display during the art show in the school gym. My wife and I attended the unveiling with about one hundred school officials, students, and family members who sampled apple juice in wineglasses, with fresh strawberries and cubed cheese. As Alli and I viewed the photos, read the essays, and chatted with the students, we realized that some of them had considered their project to be a harbinger of hope over the course of the past winter and spring. Family strife struck most, academic struggles slowed down many, and health problems plagued several students or their siblings. No matter what students were grappling with, they had "the project." We were impressed by their ability to figure out how to get things done and experienced a palpable sense of hope that night—a feeling that I still remember fondly today.

The Hope Camera Project can be replicated in any youth development setting and can be modified in ways that make the exercise more appropriate for particular purposes. For example, a career development spin could be put on the project. Each student would take pictures of people who love jobs that they themselves might want to do one day. By meeting numerous people in jobs they love, students could become familiar with the pathways specific to a particular career or, more generally, to making a decision about a college major.

The project costs about thirty dollars per student to complete. This covers the disposable camera and prints, the matting and the hanging of the selected photos, and the finger foods and apple cider for the student and guests. For a thousand dollars, thirty-three students can learn how to create pathways and share hope with dozens of friends and family.

This is just one way we can teach people how to match their will with their ways. Once students learn how to think flexibly and create alternative strategies to reach their goals, they can use this skill for a lifetime.

Conducting Community Audits

A community audit is one of the most effective ways to buffer large groups of students from hope killers and to recruit extra willpower for kids in need. Surveying school and neighborhood assets and deficits, both physical and social, helps to determine what resources are available to children and what problems need solving.

An audit might lead to a high schooler creating a no-bullying campaign on her block. A mother asking a well-intentioned friend to stop speaking to her child in a punitive manner. A neighbor lobbying city leaders to eliminate safety problems or blight. It might spur a principal to guide ineffective and hopeless teachers to better work. Extra willpower for students might come from efforts to improve school lunches, provide more mentoring, or add extracurricular activities that help children learn to regulate their own behaviors.

Nancy Oberst, a highly skilled community auditor and one of my heroes, has dedicated her life to making kids' lives better. As a classroom teacher, she helped elementary students look over the horizon and think beyond their neighborhoods and the limits placed on them by others. To do this, she surveyed what her students and school community needed. Then she provided the necessary instrumental support by enlisting the help of people from all corners of her Omaha community.

As principal of Liberty Elementary, Nancy turned the school into a community center valued by the entire neighborhood. She got to know the locals by spending summers canvassing neighborhoods and visiting schoolchildren's homes. When she found health and safety issues were undermining her students' efforts at school, she wasted no time in addressing them.

To tip the health and safety scales in the favor of the kids, she got the school written into a grant that set up a health clinic in the school. She shielded students walking to school from the violence of the neighborhood with help of vigilant neighbors and assertive safety officers.

Nancy also struck a deal with the local prostitutes to conduct business away from Liberty Elementary and the children's favorite walking route. In response to Nancy's respect and diplomacy, some prostitutes took on a motherly role and worked hard to make sure that students crossed streets safely and steered clear of neighborhood trouble.

Nancy says, "I never turned anyone down when they offered to help." She accepted raincoats for the students, even when all of them had bad weather gear, because she knew the students' siblings could use them. She took all the food that people offered the school, because she knew that the neighborhood adults could use an extra meal. She did this in order to create goodwill—which would keep the givers connected to the school in a way that made their assistance more reliable in times of need.

When need does arise, Nancy says that "[e]veryone just kind of gets pulled in." People are quick to show up if you build the kind of hope super-network that Nancy built at Liberty.

Parents, teachers, and principals tend to know the communities around their school better than do people without children and many city officials. Given their direct responsibility for the safety, welfare, and development of children, they have a special vigilance for what makes a kid's life better or worse. By conducting community audits, they can locate and resolve problems that sap students' energy and create conditions that promote student effort. Whether they are setting up a Walking School Bus program or enlisting neighbors to sit on the front stoop when kids are going to or from school, educators and other adults can help create communities that make learning easier and bright futures more likely.

Connecting the Dots

There is a real disconnect between what kids need to do tomorrow and what we teach them in school today. There is a troubling gap between how confident our kids act and how competent they are. And there is a hole where the community support for our young people should be. Despite the vast majority of U.S. children who have hopeful, caring adults in their lives, our Gallup Student Poll suggest that a few million almost certainly don't.

To make hope happen today, conduct a small-scale community audit on your next neighborhood walk or drive to the local store. Find one thing that might be getting in the way of a child's success, health, or happiness. Then use your hope to make that obstacle go away.

Chapter 14

❀

Networking Hope

C HARITY ESCOBAR, a hardworking teacher, is dedicated to help-ing her adult students—among them an elderly man, a maid, a carpenter, and an ex-convict—learn how to read. She remains com-mitted to her work, though wooed by Arturo, a wealthy man with an amnesic wife, who loves her and wants to take her away from toil and poverty. Daily, she charms, cajoles, and tutors her students, celebrating the small steps toward literacy. At first they read only small words, then short sentences, and finally entire paragraphs. Slowly, her students, overcoming many obstacles, transform their lives by learning to read. And they battle numerous villainous people who try to thwart their growth.

Sound like a soap opera? It is. Well, it was—but with a twist. *Ven Conmigo* (*Come With Me*) was developed by Miguel Sabido, once a producer for one of Mexico's largest commercial television networks, specifically to promote enrollment in adult literacy classes offered by the national government. Airing for thirty minutes a day, five times a week, it ran for 280 episodes in the mid-1970s, drawing larger audiences than the network's regular telenovelas. Each episode ended with a thirty-second epilogue from a noted Mexican celebrity who emphasized the primary point it made and encouraged viewers to apply the lesson in their own lives. One episode-epilogue combo was supposedly so provocative that it created a traffic jam in Mexico City as thousands of people rushed to pick up a pamphlet about a national literacy program at a government office. *Ven Conmigo* was credited with increasing participation in literacy courses by 63 percent, to more than eight hundred thousand students.

The show was based on a sophisticated methodology for using dramatic media to promote social change. Sabido wove his approach together by analyzing the success of a Peruvian soap opera called *Simplemente María* (*Simply Maria*), believed to be first telenovela aimed at increasing literacy. He also drew on the work of legendary Stanford psychologist Albert Bandura, whose pioneering studies showed how social influences could increase personal motivation.

These soap operas for good, many of which continue to be aired on television and radio today, turned entertainment media into an educational tool for grown-ups, modeling positive behavior and lifestyles that directed the viewer toward self-improvement and the common good. The soap opera stars who typically have the most impact on viewers, in Sabido's design, are the transitional characters. These characters are the ones who seem most like us. They are in a battle between their old selves and their new ones and demonstrate that hope can change us. These transitional characters help viewers learn to move from a life defined by bad behaviors, daily struggles, and physical or psychological impoverishment through a process of difficult change to a life filled with what matters most.

You can make hope contagious for your friends, workplaces, schools, and communities by building a network of hope through three tactics:

* Model hope through stories and deeds.
* Provide hope through instrumental or intrusive support.
* Become a Super Empowered, Hopeful Individual.

The tagline for this chapter could be "Hope . . . pass it on!" because hope *is* contagious. As explained by network scientists Nicholas Christakis and Stephen Fowler in their book *Connected,* your friend's friend's friend can influence your hope and happiness. (They call this the "Three Degrees of Influence Rule.") Christakis and Fowler examined the social networks of thousands of people who had participated in a longitudinal study of health. After reviewing decades' worth of medical and psychological data, they discovered that "contagions" and "emotional stampedes" run through our social circles—shaping everything from how much we weigh and how much we smoke or drink, to our voting patterns, daily feelings, and goals for the future.

These three degrees of influence and these emotional stampedes need not be left entirely to chance. You can surround yourself with hopeful people. Your friend's hope has the greatest impact on you, but your hope is also affected by your friend's friend's relationship with the future. Your hope is actually dependent on your entire social network, including best friends, role models, and secondhand associates. And your hope can be shared with others. While it might be hard to believe, your hope, in a small but meaningful way, is related to the hope of someone you may never meet.

Modeling Hope

Hope models are all around us. The runner who just passed my window suggests to me, "Hey, I should go for a run." The lunch mate who chooses salad over a burger subtly reminds me to eat healthy. The boss who devotes an hour a week to quietly and sincerely rewarding and recognizing employees encourages me to praise the people in my office. As

I discussed in chapter 11, our behavior is primed, often unconsciously, by the actions of others in our social network.

Our subconscious brains are more purposeful and intentional than we once thought. They scan the people, places, and things around us to answer a question that nags us day in and day out: "What do I do next?" We are primed to set and move toward goals by everyday sights and experiences. So when positive role models pop up at the right place and time, they help us answer that "next" question in a way that nudges us toward goals that matter. The priming is not wholly left to chance when we surround ourselves with people who model desirable behavior.

Hopeful people have a habit of showing up when others need them. They seem primed to pick up the feelings of someone who could use help knocking down an obstacle or filling a gap. I have seen school custodians, parents, teachers, and local businesspeople modeling hope to children all in the same day, with each seemingly stepping in when a child could use a little guidance. I have watched CEOs, managers, and rank-and-file employees crowd around new employees and interns, vying for the chance to help them learn the business and, as a by-product, showing them how to pave the way for the next batch of new recruits.

To learn more about how people come to model hope, I started asking them how hope was taught to them. Yano Jones, the most hopeful youth mentor I have met, told me the story of his hope model.

As a young man growing up in the streets of North Omaha, I was told I was a statistic and that I wouldn't go to college. I was also told that I wasn't smart enough to handle college. At one point I began to think like that, until a person who believed in me stepped into my life and inspired me. This person saw the potential in me and worked hard to make me understand that I can do whatever it is I want to do in life. I was told that it wouldn't be easy. I was told that you will deal with adversity and you will make mistakes.

Yano met his mentor, Dick Davis, while working a summer job. As a boy in Nebraska, Yano had never known an African-American man who had founded a company and earned public respect for his business acumen.

One day I had the opportunity to sit down with Dr. Davis and talk about how he came to own the Davis Companies, where I worked summers in college. Dr. Davis warned me of the harsh realities that I might face as I begin to look for jobs upon graduation.

He explained to me that every day in life for him is the opportunity to prove people wrong. To show people that he can and has worked just as hard as the next man. He made sense to me. It's as if he had experienced a lot of the things I had seen and faced the obstacles I had faced.

So what I started to do is watch every move he made, not really saying much, but just observing how he handled himself around people, how he dressed, what his communication was like. He taught me what to do and what not to do. He helped me understand the importance of networking and treating everyone around me with respect and high regard. He left me with a lot of things that helped me to be the man I am today—understanding the importance of hard work, dedication and commitment. He helped me to realize that even if you make a mistake, figure out what you did wrong and learn from that situation.

Classic epics like Homer's *Odyssey* are the model for "the hero's journey" that has taught life lessons to numberless generations. Today, we can find many modern heroes who look a lot more like us. And just as Yano learned from Dick Davis, their stories about how to move toward a perceived destiny still captivate listeners, inviting us—subconsciously or consciously, implicitly or explicitly—to join them on their journey.

Providing Hope Through Support

Reading between the lines of stories about rugged individualism, self-reliance, up-by-the-bootstraps success, you'll usually discover a supporting cast of caring people who provided crucial help in the form of money, time, and other assistance. Social scientists call this instrumental support. Most folks, like Seth Reams, just call it helping your neighbor.

At the depths of the Great Recession, after many depressing months of unemployment and a nudge from his girlfriend, Michelle King, Seth decided it was time to put his diverse talents developed as a concierge to use. He would offer his services to people in need in their Portland, Oregon, community and organize other volunteers through his website, http://wevegottimetohelp.blogspot.com. Within sixteen months of the site's launch, more than a hundred WGTTH volunteers (most, like Seth, people who had lost their jobs) provided assistance with nearly four hundred projects ranging from moving furniture to painting houses and building fences. WGTTH provides no financial support and accepts no payment, except to ask that recipients "pay it forward." Reams says, "One of the biggest things we offer is hope."

Seth's good works and hope network buffered him from the demoralization of long-term unemployment. It may also have given him the initiative he needed to invest in one of his entrepreneurial ideas. In 2010, Seth and Michelle decided to turn their hobby, making feed for backyard birds, into a business. A month after they put up a website, their product was in eight stores. A year later, their revenue was up 300 percent. "I love what I do. . . . I couldn't ask for anything more." When we emailed about his current path, Seth's enthusiasm for the future just jumped off the computer screen. "It has been a wild ride and we look forward to the future."

Corporate America has realized the real and marketing value of hopeful support. McDonald's leveraged hope in a 2011 TV campaign that highlighted how a portion of the money from each Happy Meal purchased was donated to the Ronald McDonald House, a charity that provides a place for families to stay as they care for their hospitalized child. These commercials, with adorable children looking for a thing called "hope" in the iconic McDonald's box, suggested that hope is real and that it can be shared with other children.

My favorite example of how a business can spread hope through its advertising, products, or services comes from Tide, the laundry detergent company that is part of Procter & Gamble. Tide sponsors the Loads of Hope program, supporting communities that have been devastated by tornadoes, hurricanes, and earthquakes. Tide realized that a family's need for clean clothes becomes critical in such a crisis. They would help preserve the dignity of people who have lost so much by providing a simple but much-needed service.

Loads of Hope was launched in November 2005, in response to Hurricane Katrina's devastation along the Gulf Coast. Tide built a mobile trailer packed with thirty-two energy-efficient Frigidaire washers and dryers and coordinated a team of American Red Cross volunteers who, along with Tide employees, spent days washing, drying, and folding clean clothes for families trying to bounce back. In five visits to the Gulf Coast (in response to both Katrina and Hurricane Gustav in 2008), Loads of Hope staff washed 13,871 batches of laundry for 10,950 families over the course of fifty-nine days.

Then in 2010, when a catastrophic earthquake struck Haiti, Tide partnered with Operation Blessing to help survivors. A Port-au-Prince hospital, devastated by the quake, needed just about everything, but third on their wish list, right after clean water and radiology equipment, was laundry services. In response, Loads of Hope sent ten washers and ten dryers to the National Hospital and the Zanmi Beni orphanage. The washer-dryer sets at the orphanage freed up staffers, who had been washing clothes by hand, enabling them to provide additional care for more than forty special needs children.

Back in the United States, after Hurricane Irene hit the eastern seaboard in September 2011, Loads of Hope went to the coast, working in towns such as Cobleskill, New York. "Hurricane Irene has unfortunately left many without access to clean water, power, and the ability to clean their clothes," said Sarah Pasquinucci of Tide. "We hope that by restoring the basic need of clean clothing, we can help give hope to those who need it most."

Of course, thousands of nonprofit organizations also provide instrumental support to devastated communities, but today there is a growing debate about the long-term effectiveness of some interventions. What kind of help not only alleviates the immediate problem, but also increases the self-sufficiency (or agency) of the recipients? In other words, can aid be designed to create a hope contagion?

Heifer International, which provided Tererai Trent with support early in her educational journey, links donors to people in need through a "catalog" of gifts filled with smiling children cradling adorable (and clean!) piglets, chicks, goats, and other livestock that can add to the nutrition and income of impoverished small farmers. They make each gift feel very concrete by attaching it to a specific animal or "flock of hope," even though the fine print makes it clear that the money goes into a general fund. (You cannot expect to visit your llama in Bolivia.) Their materials stress the many steps they take to make sure your gift creates pathways to a better life: "Heifer recipients receive months of training in how to care for their animal; sell the milk, eggs or other products at market; and restore the environment." Recipients are also expected to "pass on the gift" by sharing their knowledge and animal offspring to others in their community. Donors are told, "Your generosity just sparked a cycle of giving . . . a cycle that will transform lives for generations to come. Passing on this knowledge as well as the offspring of the gift animal is at the heart of Heifer's model."

How do you give hope to those who need it most? Esther Duflo, a development economist at the Massachusetts Institute of Technology, is now evaluating randomized controlled studies that test how and why aid works—or doesn't. The participants are people stuck in a "poverty trap" who seem almost immune to the help provided by some organizations. They are so poor that other extremely poor folks see them as destitute. They don't just need aid. They need escape hatches out of extreme poverty.

Duflo recently evaluated a program in the Indian state of West Bengal that is built on the notion that effective aid should jump-start long-term change in the lives of poor families. Judged to be unable to payback a microloan, these families were given a productive asset (that is program-speak for a cow, goat, or chickens), training to tend to the animal, sell the milk or eggs, and manage their households, and a small stipend to tide them over until the animal was profitable. This combination of choice, an asset, support and training, and a stipend triggers people to open their minds to the future rather than to spend all of their mental resources on mere survival. (And while each piece of the aid package is valuable, the support and training might foster hope. Specifically, the support ups the will to continue work with the asset and the training provides the ways to be successful.)

The results of this controlled study were compelling. Eighteen months after the program began (and some time after the training and stipend were discontinued), the families randomly assigned to receive the aid plus hope were earning 20 percent more money, eating 15 percent more and skipping fewer meals, and experiencing fewer depressive symptoms than people in the control group. Participants were also working an hour more per day than the controls, saving some money and making more plans. Overall, their income gains were strikingly larger than the value of the aid they received. Duflo's explanation is that hope for the future paid off in investments in the present.

People who get aid plus hope work harder today. Duflo's findings are summed up by *New York Times* columnist Nicholas Kristof's observation: "Assistance succeeds when it gives people a feeling that a better outcome is possible, and those hopes become self-fulfilling as people work more industriously and invest more wisely."

When people are stuck, overwhelmed by obstacles, and other kinds of help have failed, and/or volunteer organization or corporate aid is not available, they may need to contract out for hope. Intrusive support, which is instrumental support on steroids, is the most active and direct assistance for someone who wants to keep moving toward a challenging goal. With their implicit agreement, a supporter establishes a contract that gives permission to "butt into" their lives to keep them on track, even when or especially when they're ready to give up. When people show signs of not meeting their obligations, those ready and able step in and try to get them back on the right track using whatever means necessary.

Yano Jones is a master of intrusive support. He works as one of nine "talent advisors" at Avenue Scholars, an Omaha program founded to offer an avenue of success for students of talent and need from high school through community college or university, and eventually on into the workplace. He relates to the mentees in his program because their current experiences were his past experiences.

Yano's job is to help them realize their talent and overcome the obstacles associated with growing up impoverished and without the right kind of role models. More practically, Yano does everything he can to make sure that the fifty Avenue Scholars in his care go to school every day, do their homework, stay out of trouble, finish high school, enroll in college, and earn their degree.

Some mornings Yano wakes up as early as 4:30 to drive his students to football practice, stays up late to attend a school theatrical performance, and then taxis a student safely home. Of course, Yano is not just there to ferry students from Point A to Point B. Lots of supportive chats take place when Yano transports his "babies." He is on the front lines whenever he senses that a young man or woman is falling behind at school, encountering a major obstacle at home, or has exhausted the resources or strategies they need to move ahead. These are signals for him to step even more forcefully into their lives.

Yano told me about a student who came to him with both hope and need. "She also came into my class with an attitude like no other. You see, she didn't care about anything. She didn't care about school; she didn't care about what her mom had to say. She was going to do what she wanted to do. I have to admit, it was very frustrating at first, but I knew just as with young people that I have worked with in the past, that if you show them you sincerely care, they will show you the same, in their own way."

Positive modeling and providing instrumental and intrusive support require us to join forces with others, and to share our future desires and pursuits. Today, new social networking tools can also play a role in mobilizing the most hopeful among us.

Become a Super-Empowered, Hopeful Individual

Yano Jones, Andy DeVries (chapter 9), and Rose Naughtin (chapter 2) are among the most hopeful people I know. I consider them charter members of the tribe of Super-Empowered, Hopeful Individuals, or SEHIs—people who believe the future will be better than the present—for everyone—and that they can make it happen. They believe that changing the world is a realistic goal despite every obstacle imaginable. They spread hope every day. Are you ready to be a SEHI?

Game designer Jane McGonigal coined the SEHI acronym in her book *Reality Is Broken*. Subtitled *Why Games Make Us Better and How They Can Change the World,* it explores the power of alternate reality games to improve real lives and solve real problems. One of McGonigal's technology-based collaborative games was World Without Oil, where more than 1,900 players and 60,000 active observers collaborated on ways to survive the first thirty-two weeks of a global oil crisis triggered when demand exceeded supply. Together they not only imagined the personal impact of such an event in rich detail, but also came up with many practical suggestions to help prevent it from happening. Other McGonigal games such as Superstruct and EVOKE (developed with the World Bank Institute) have been used as training tools for social change. They provide ways to practice hope virtually, in the belief that we can generalize the knowledge and skills learned in the game to real life.

In 2009, when a traumatic brain injury threatened to sideline her, McGonigal decided to make a game of her recovery. Today the Super-Better game and app allows players to customize a program to meet their medical and psychological challenges, recruit the support of allies, and find relevant scientific research. As they progress from one stretch goal to another, players are told, "You surprise yourself" and "You are a hero to others." The game worked for McGonigal, a super-user of her own technology: "It made me feel optimistic and like I had agency."

McGonigal's games provide a model for how SEHIs of all kinds can mobilize followers. First, highlight an urgent problem. In a typical school or work week, we may not feel a heightened, focused demand for our contributions. A big, meaningful goal that demands attention and resources now provides that urgency. Second, provide continuous feedback. People will keep working relentlessly on a cause if they are receiving real-time feedback on their progress. Feedback also provides guidance and quick course correction when we're trying something bold or new. Third, foster a community of trust. Common goals, hard work, and the heat of urgency forge powerful social bonds. SEHIs support and celebrate this process. Finally, remember that pursuing a big goal on a tight timeline alongside trusted friends and colleagues has a payoff that goes beyond winning and losing. That payoff is meaning.

We can see this kind of call to action following disasters, when people like those from groups such as the American Red Cross and Tide swoop in to help those in need. After the F5 tornado in Greensburg, Kansas, SEHIs in the city council used these principles and capitalized on these conditions to mobilize their neighbors, recruit the green industry, and attract support from people across the country. By creating the pathways for hope, SEHIs invent and spread their own humanitarian missions. They don't wait around for the world to save itself.

Hope to Spare

The people in this book are kindred spirits—not just because they are hopeful, but because they have hope to spare. When shared, that spare hope goes a long way in the world today.

Please build up your hope. Then with hope to spare, help others build a future that is better than the present. Much better.

What happens if we the hopeful make small tweaks to television shows, video games, foreign aid, and mentoring programs so that they are more effective at spreading hope? I look forward to finding out.

Epilogue

Ripples of Hope

Each time a man stands up for an ideal, or acts to improve
the lot of others, or strikes out against injustice, he sends
forth a tiny ripple of hope, and crossing each other from a
million different centers of energy and daring, those ripples
build a current which can sweep down the mightiest walls of
oppression and resistance.

—ROBERT F. KENNEDY, JUNE 6, 1966

Tiny Ripples: Which Will Be Yours?

The tiny ripple of hope you set in motion can change the path of someone's life. It can make their future better.

You don't have to take a big, bold action or raise a ton of money to spark change. You can start small. You merely need to create momentum where there was none.

Making ripples starts with you. You know that irksome feeling you get when you see a problem that no one is doing anything about? Or the pang you feel when someone is left behind by life? That's where you start.

To spread hope, you have to get off the sidelines. Sure, you can influence people and events from a distance, but starting a ripple of hope requires some action, some force. Here is what you need to do:

* Catch yourself thinking or saying "I wish someone would do something about that" or "I wish that problem would go away" or "I wish that person would catch a break." Turning that wish into hope starts a ripple.

* Recruit one or more friends to help you define and address the problem. You may need to borrow their hope when confronting the issue. You will give each other energy as you develop your plan.

* Make one visible change that addresses the problem. Ripples of hope stand out. They grab attention. They inspire others to start ripples of their own.

Create a ripple of hope in your home, school, business, or community. At the very least, tell your own story of hope. You will find people who want to hear that things can be better, that we can be more, that our lives can be lived for greater meaning.

Appendix

Hope Scales Used in Research

Since the late 1990s these two hope scales have been used by hope researchers around the world. The Adult Trait Hope Scale is given to people fifteen years old and older. The Children's Hope Scale is used with children eight to fourteen years of age.

The Adult Trait Hope Scale

Directions: Read each item carefully. Using the scale shown below, please select the number that best describes *you* and put that number in the blank provided.

1 = Definitely False	2 = Mostly False	3 = Somewhat False	4 = Slightly False
5 = Slightly True	6 = Somewhat True	7 = Mostly True	8 = Definitely True

____ 1. I can think of many ways to get out of a jam.

____ 2. I energetically pursue my goals.

____ 3. There are lots of ways around any problem.

____ 4. I can think of many ways to get the things in life that are most important to me.

___ 5. Even when others get discouraged, I know I can find a way to solve the problem.

___ 6. My past experiences have prepared me well for my future.

___ 7. I've been pretty successful in life.

___ 8. I meet the goals that I set for myself.

Scoring: Tally 1, 3, 4, 5 for a Pathways score and 2, 6, 7, 8 for an Agency score. Add the Pathways and Agency scores to determine the Hope total score.

The Children's Hope Scale

Directions: The six sentences below describe how children think about themselves and how they do things in general. Read each sentence carefully. For each sentence, please think about how you are in most situations. Place a check inside the circle that describes *you* the best. For example, place a check (✓) in the circle (○) above "None of the time," if this describes you. Or, if you are this way "All of the time," check this circle. Please answer every question by putting a check in one of the circles. There are no right or wrong answers.

1. I think I am doing pretty well.

○	○	○	○	○	○
None of the time	A little of the time	Some of the time	A lot of the time	Most of the time	All of the time

2. I can think of many ways to get the things in life that are most important to me.

○	○	○	○	○	○
None of the time	A little of the time	Some of the time	A lot of the time	Most of the time	All of the time

3. I am doing just as well as other kids my age.

○　　　○　　　○　　　○　　　○　　　○

None of　A little of　Some of　A lot of　Most of　All of
the time　the time　the time　the time　the time　the time

4. When I have a problem, I can come up with lots of ways to solve it.

○　　　○　　　○　　　○　　　○　　　○

None of　A little of　Some of　A lot of　Most of　All of
the time　the time　the time　the time　the time　the time

5. I think the things I have done in the past will help me in the future.

○　　　○　　　○　　　○　　　○　　　○

None of　A little of　Some of　A lot of　Most of　All of
the time　the time　the time　the time　the time　the time

6. Even when others want to quit, I know that I can find ways to solve the problem.

○　　　○　　　○　　　○　　　○　　　○

None of　A little of　Some of　A lot of　Most of　All of
the time　the time　the time　the time　the time　the time

Scoring: The total Children's Hope Scale score is achieved by adding the responses to the six items, with "None of the time" = 1; "A little of the time" = 2; "Some of the time" = 3; "A lot of the time" = 4; "Most of the time" = 5; and, "All of the time" = 6. The responses to the three odd numbered items are totaled for the Agency score and the responses to the even numbered items are tallied for the Pathways score.

Scales reprinted with permission.

Snyder, C. R., Harris, C., Anderson, J. R., Holleran, S. A., Irving, L. M., Sigmon, S. T., Yoshinobu, L., et al. (1991). The will and the ways: Development and validation of an individual-differences measure of hope. *Journal of Personality and Social Psychology*, 60 (4), 570–585. doi:10.1037/0022-3514.60.4.570.

Snyder, C. R., Hoza, B., Pelham, W. E., Rapoff, M., Ware, L., Danovsky, M., Highberger, L., Rubinstein, H., and Stahl, K. J. (1997). The development and validation of the Children's Hope Scale. *Journal of Pediatric Psychology*, 22, 399–421.

Recommended Reading
and Resources

Chapter 1: What the Man with No Future Taught Me About Hope

C. R. Snyder, *The Psychology of Hope: You Can Get There from Here*. New York: Free Press, 1994. The first practical and scientifically based introduction to hope and how it works in real life. From the distinguished psychologist whose research is the basis for much of today's understanding of the subject.

Chapter 2: Looking for Hope

Jerome Groopman, *The Anatomy of Hope: How People Prevail in the Face of Illness*. New York: Random House, 2003. A physician's compassionate telling of how he has seen patients facing serious illness use their hope to survive and thrive.

Chapter 3: Nexting and Prospecting

Tali Sharot, *The Optimism Bias: A Tour of the Irrationally Positive Brain*. New York: Pantheon, 2011. A neuroscientist's lively inside-the-brain view of why most people are optimistic or hopeful about life.

Chapter 4: Hope Matters

Studs Terkel, *Hope Dies Last: Keeping the Faith in Troubled Times*. New York: New Press, 2003. A collection of interviews that shows why hope matters in the lives of all people, especially those facing adversity.

Chapter 5: How Investing in the Future Pays Off Today

Roy Baumeister and John Tierney, *Willpower: Rediscovering the Greatest Human Strength*. New York: Penguin Books, 2011. A new way to look at our powers of self-control, including many illuminating real-life examples as well as practical, research-based strategies for resisting temptation and reaching our most important goals.

Chapter 6: The Future Is Ours to See

Jacqueline Edelberg and Susan Kurland, *How to Walk to School: Blueprint for a Neighborhood School Renaissance*. New York: Rowman & Littlefield, 2009. The complete inspiring story, including a detailed how-to, many cautionary tales, and a toolkit for setting up an independent, not-for-profit fund-raising company to benefit your school.

Daniel Gilbert, *Stumbling on Happiness*. New York: Knopf, 2006. A tour of what scientists have discovered about the uniquely human ability to imagine the future and about our capacity to predict how much we will like it when we get there.

Daniel Kahneman, *Thinking, Fast and Slow*. New York: Farrar, Straus & Giroux, 2011. A challenging, entertaining, and enlightening book that sums up the author's Nobel Prize–winning research and offers many techniques for avoiding the mental glitches that get us into trouble.

Chapter 7: The Present Is Not What Limits Us

Carol Dweck, *Mindset: The New Psychology of Success*. New York: Random House, 2006. Dweck explains why it's not just our abilities and talent that bring us success, but whether we approach them with a fixed or growth mindset.

www.mindsetonline.com. An overview of mindset applications for parents, teachers, and coaches. Includes valuable suggestions on how—and how not—to praise children.

www.mindsetworks.com. Specifically for schools and educators. Includes an introduction to Brainology, a program that shows students how to grow their minds.

Chapter 8: The Past Is Not a Preview

Barbara Frederickson, *Positivity: Groundbreaking Research Reveals How to Embrace the Hidden Strength of Positive Emotions, Overcome Negativity, and Thrive.* New York: Crown Archetype, 2009. Frederickson offers concrete strategies for increasing positive emotions so that we gradually shift the ratio of positivity to negativity in our lives.

www.positivityratio.com/single.php. An easy-to-take test you can complete and score online as often as you wish, enabling you to track progress toward more positivity.

Chapter 9: Futurecasting: Making Your Goals Come Alive

Omaha Young Writers Program, *In My Shoes: Teen Reflections on Hope and the Future.* Omaha, NE: WriteLife, 2011. A moving example of what can happen when adults ask teens what is going on in their lives, build trust, and then really listen. Written by two classes of inner-city high school seniors with the guidance of volunteer writing mentors from across their community.

http://dreamagain.principal.com/dreamcatcher/preregistered/home.html. A free program that allows you to create a visual collage of the images that capture your life goals.

Chapter 10: Triggering Action: Putting Agency on Autopilot

Dan Ariely, *Predictably Irrational: The Hidden Forces That Shape Our Decisions.* Revised and expanded edition. New York: HarperCollins, 2009. A highly entertaining book that opens our eyes to all the ways we overpay, underestimate, and procrastinate. It may even help you make better decisions about the future.

Robert Cialdini, *Influence: The Psychology of Persuasion.* Revised edition. New York: HarperBusiness, 2006. A now-classic book describing six universal principles of persuasion and showing how they can be used ethically to create personal and social change.

Charles Duhigg, *The Power of Habit: Why We Do What We Do in Life and Business.* New York: Random House, 2012. Why do some people and companies struggle to change while others seem to remake themselves overnight? Through many revealing stories and scientific insights, this book shows you how to create the habits necessary to reach your goals.

Homer, *Odyssey*. Translated by Stanley Lombardo. Indianapolis, IN: Hackett, 2000. This fast-paced, colloquial, accessible translation enables today's readers to appreciate the wily Odysseus as a "hero of the mind."

Tom Rath and Jim Harter, *Wellbeing: The Five Essential Elements*. New York: Gallup Press, 2010. The research underlying Gallup's well-being initiative, with suggestions to help you improve well-being in each of five key areas of your life.

Richard Thaler and Cass Sunstein, *Nudge: Improving Decisions about Health, Wealth, and Happiness*. New York: Penguin Books, 2009. An eye-opening analysis of how our biases drive our decisions, sometimes to our detriment, and how environmental cues can be used to help guide us toward choices that will support us in the future.

Chapter 11: Planning for Ifs: Discovering New Pathways

www.ted.com/talks/dave_eggers_makes_his_ted_prize_wish_once_upon_a _school.html. Dave Eggers cracks up and inspires the audience with his stories about the founding of 826 Valencia, the first in a network of eight imaginative and innovative writing and mentoring centers across the country.

Chapter 12: Leading with Hope

Tom Rath and Barry Conchie, *Strengths-Based Leadership: Great Leaders, Teams, and Why People Follow*. New York: Gallup Press, 2009. Based on thousands of interviews with leaders and followers, this book identifies three keys to being an effective leader and shows how each person's unique strengths and talents can drive their success.

Chapter 13: Teaching Hope to the Next Generation

Martin E. P. Seligman, Ph.D., *The Optimistic Child: A Proven Program to Safeguard Children Against Depression and Build Lifelong Resilience*. Boston: Mariner Books, 2007. For anyone who has children or works with children. Seligman uses anecdotes, dialogues, cartoons, and exercises to create a practical program for teaching the positive strength of optimism, which he calls "a sunny but solid future-mindedness that can be deployed throughout life."

Chapter 14: Networking Hope

Abhijit Banerjee and Esther Duflo, *Poor Economics: A Radical Rethinking of the Way to Fight Global Poverty*. New York: PublicAffairs, 2011. Meticulous research into how very poor people—the millions who exist on less than ninety-nine cents a day—make decisions about how to spend their energy and resources.

Nicholas Christakis and James Fowler, *Connected: The Surprising Power of Our Social Networks and How They Shape Our Lives*. New York: Little, Brown, 2009. Striking evidence for our profound influence on one another's taste, health, wealth, happiness, and even weight.

Jane McGonigal, *Reality Is Broken: Why Games Make Us Better and How They Can Change the World*. New York: Penguin Press, 2011. How to use the power of cooperative games to improve real lives and fix what is wrong in the real world.

Tina Rosenberg, *Join the Club: How Peer Pressure Can Transform the World*. New York: Norton, 2012. Stories from around the globe about how social entrepreneurs have created change by tapping humanity's most powerful and abundant resource: our connections with one another.

Notes

Chapter 1: What the Man with No Future Taught Me About Hope

5 *Fortunately, after a few hours*: I was trained to use cognitive therapy for depression. In cases where a client is thinking about suicide, I provide support and compassion while examining the thoughts and feelings associated with the suicidal ideation. For John, who had no history of mental illness or suicidality, his diagnosis and treatment plan threatened his autonomy. This was enough to create a downward spiral that resulted in his suicidal thinking. As I was able to help him consider how he could maintain a modicum of control over his life, he was able to think about life with a kidney ailment and dialysis. For a detailed description of cognitive therapy, see A. T. Beck et al., *Cognitive Therapy for Depression* (New York: Guilford Press, 1987). For a layperson's guide to the basics of cognitive therapy, see Martin Seligman, *Learned Optimism* (New York: Knopf, 1991).

6 *Though still entertaining suicidal thoughts*: For clients with ongoing suicidal thinking the primary goal is to reduce the risk of self-harm. At the very least, means of harm are removed from the home, and friends and family provide necessary support. In some cases, clients are admitted to a psychiatric treatment unit for their own safety. John's plan for suicide involved highly lethal means, so inpatient admission was considered. However, he became more stable over time, had a wealth of social support, and the weapons were removed from his home. John did sign a behavioral contract indicating that he would contact emergency services if he was again suicidal but he would not have been released if his wife and friends had not been available to support and monitor him.

6 *After an hour or two*: C. R. Snyder, *The Psychology of Hope: You Can Get Here from There* (New York: Free Press, 1994). This book summarizes Rick's think-

226

ing about hope. I refer to it often and recommend it to readers interested in how hope theory came to be.

6 *"Just as our ancestors did"*: Ibid, p. 6.

8 *His GFR (glomerular filtration rate)*: Glomerular filtration rate (GFR) is a test used to check kidney functioning. Specifically, GFR estimates how much blood passes through the filters in the kidneys, called glomeruli, each minute. http://www.nlm.nih.gov/medlineplus/ency/article/007305 .htm.

9 *Turns out, smart is not enough*: Y. Choi and R. Veenhoven, "IQ and happiness," working paper, happiness research group, Erasmus University Rotterdam, 2005.

11 *Since my experience at the VA clinic*: Over the course of the book, I will describe research conducted with my students at the University of Kansas, and with and by my colleagues at Gallup and around the world.

11 *Through my own research and Gallup polls*: Ibid.

11 *Recently, I began identifying*: Additional studies using Gallup data focus on the most hopeful K–12 and college students and workers, with a special emphasis on teachers. S. Marques, S. J. Lopez, A. M. Fontaine, and J. M. Mitchell, "Benefits of very high hope among adolescents" (under review).

11 *Although some people still believe*: Hope is now widely regarded as an appropriate construct to study in social sciences, but this wasn't always the case. As with other positive constructs such as happiness and optimism, journal editors in the 1980s needed convincing that hope could be operationalized and carefully examined. Thanks to pioneers including Rick Snyder, Ed Diener, Michael Scheier, Chuck Carver, and others for paving the way with their creativity and fortitude.

11 *In addition, while only half*: S. J. Lopez and V. Calderon, "The Gallup Student Poll: Measuring and promoting what is right with students," in S. I. Donaldson, M. Csikszentmihalyi, and J. Nakamura, eds., *Applied Positive Psychology: Improving Everyday Life, Schools, Work, Health, and Society* (New York: Routledge, 2011), pp. 117–34.

Chapter 2: Looking for Hope

17 *Sometimes I was fantasizing*: My thoughts about future thinking have long been influenced by the work of Gabriele Oettingen. G. Oettingen and D. Mayer, "The motivating function of thinking about the future: Expectations versus fantasies," *Journal of Personality and Social Psychology* 83, no. 5 (2002): 1198–1212.

17 *I called my grad school professor*: In 1993 Rick taught a social psychology course that I took in graduate school at the University of Kansas. He lectured with great passion about his new work on hope. In 1998, when I became a professor at KU, Rick served as my faculty mentor.

18 *The first belief*: For discussion of optimism, see M. F. Scheier and C. S. Carver, "Optimism, coping, and health: Assessment and implications of generalized outcome expectancies," *Health Psychology* 4 (1985): 219–47. For additional perspective, read M. W. Gallagher, S. J. Lopez, and S. D. Pressman, "Optimism is universal: Exploring the presence and benefits of optimism in a representative sample of the world," *Journal of Personality* (2013). For an explanation of the differences between hope and optimism, read C. R. Snyder, S. C. Sympson, S. T. Michael, and J. Cheavens, "The optimism and hope constructs: Variants on a positive expectancy theme," in E. Chang, ed., *Optimism and Pessimism* (Washington, DC: American Psychological Association, 2000), pp. 103–24.

18 *The Gallup World Poll*: The Gallup World Poll was initiated in 2005 and annually surveys approximately 1,000 individuals from over 142 countries around the world, providing a representative sample of 95 percent of the world's population. Information about the development, ethics, and survey procedures used for the World Poll can be obtained online at http://www.gallup.com/consulting/worldpoll/24046/About.aspx. Gallagher, Lopez, and Pressman, "Optimism is universal: Exploring the presence and benefits of optimism in a representative sample of the world."

18 *Regardless of age*: T. Sharot, *The Optimism Bias: A Tour of the Irrationally Positive Brain* (New York: Pantheon, 2011).

18 *The second belief*: E. L. Deci and R. M. Ryan, *Intrinsic Motivation and Self-determination in Human Behavior* (New York: Plenum, 1985). See also http://selfdeterminationtheory.org/.

18 *Two more core beliefs*: Snyder was the first to discuss the roles of pathways thinking as part of hope. He also acknowledged that hopeful people had a keen awareness for the obstacles in their path. Snyder, *The Psychology of Hope*.

19 *"Today we will talk about hope"*: I have used the head, heart, holy test of hope with hundreds of audiences. Take the "test" yourself and share with others.

21 *Fear gives us only three behavioral options*: The fight-or-flight response was first discussed by W. B. Cannon, *Bodily Changes in Pain, Hunger, Fear and Rage: An Account of Recent Research into the Function of Emotional Excitement* (New York: Appleton-Century-Crofts, 1929). A short time later this

article popularized the term: H. Selye, "A syndrome produced by diverse nocuous agents," *Nature* 138 (1936): 32. The freeze response, which may in fact come before fighting or fleeing, was described in detail by J. A. Gray, *The Psychology of Fear and Stress* (Cambridge, UK: Cambridge University Press, 1988).

21 *It's Aesop's fable*: B. Sneed, *A Modern Retelling of Classic Fables* (New York: Dial, 2003). Includes beautiful and original illustrations.

22 *Jerome Groopman, M.D.*: I enjoy reading Dr. Groopman's books and articles. He is an excellent storyteller, as you will discover as you read his book *The Anatomy of Hope: How People Prevail in the Face of Illness* (New York: Random House, 2003).

24 *To attain hope, you need to create momentum*: This three-part conceptualization of hope was first discussed in detail in Snyder, *The Psychology of Hope*.

Chapter 3: Nexting and Prospecting

33 *On our morning walks*: The term *nexting* was used in a related, yet different context in D. Gilbert, *Stumbling on Happiness* (New York: Knopf, 2008). Gilbert says that nexting occurs when "brains are continuously making predictions about the immediate, local, personal future of their owners without the owners' awareness" (p. 6). As it relates to hope, nexting occurs when vivid images of the recently visited future are shared and refined.

35 *The story begins 1.6 million years ago*: T. Suddendorf and M. C. Corballis, "Mental time travel and the evolution of the human mind," *Genetic, Social, and General Psychology Monographs* 123 (1997): 133–67; T. Suddendorf, D. R. Addis, and M. C. Corballis, "Mental time travel and the shaping of the human mind," *Philosophical Transactions of the Royal Society of London B: Biological Sciences* 364 (2009): 1317–24.

35 Standing man: Suddendorf and Corballis, "Mental time travel and the evolution of the human mind."

35 *This cognitive leap*: E. S. Savage-Rumbaugh, "Hominid evolution: Looking to modern apes for clues," in D. Quiatt and J. Itani, eds., *Hominid Culture in Primate Perspective* (Niwot: University Press of Colorado, 1994), pp. 7–49.

35 *Fast-forward 1. 5 million plus years*: S. L. Kuhn, M. C. Stiner, D. S. Reese, and E. Güleç, "Ornaments of the earliest Upper Paleolithic: New insights from the Levant," *Proceedings of the National Academy of Sciences* 98 (2001): 7641–46. For a more critical discussion of whether Neanderthals buried their dead and believed in an afterlife, see S. Ralph, "Shanidar IV, a Neanderthal flower

burial in Northern Iraq," *Science* 190, no. 4217 (1975): 880–81, and R. H. Gargett, "Grave shortcomings: The evidence for Neandertal burial," *Current Anthropology* 30 (1989): 157–90.

35 *They dedicated a special site*: Ibid.

35 *These practices are an early sign*: Ibid.

35 *With big brains*: C. A. Banyas, "Evolution and the phylogenetic history of the frontal lobes," in B. L. Miller and J. L. Cummings, eds., *The Human Frontal Lobes* (New York: Guilford Press, 1999), pp. 83–106.

36 *According to psychology's Bischof-Köhler hypothesis*: D. Bischof-Köhler, "Zur Phylogenese menschlicher Motivation," in L. H. Eckensberger and E.-D. Lantermann, eds., *Emotion und Reflexivität* (Vienna: Urban und Schwarzenberg, 1985), pp. 3–47; D. Bischof-Köhler and N. Bischof, "Is mental time travel a frame-of-reference issue? Open peer comment to: Suddendorf T. & Corballis M.C.: The evolution of foresight: What is mental time travel and is it unique to humans?," *Behavioral and Brain Sciences* 30, no. 3: 316–17.

36 *In December 1994, during a hike*: *Cave of Forgotten Dreams* is a Werner Herzog film. Werner Herzog's website, including his appearance discussing the documentary on *The Colbert Report*: http://www.wernerherzog.com/index .php?id=64.

36 *art in Chauvet Cave is now preserved*: http://www.culture.gouv.fr/culture/arc nat/chauvet/en/.

37 *Neuroscientist Tali Sharot*: T. Sharot, *The Optimism Bias: A Tour of the Irrationally Positive Brain* (New York: Pantheon, 2011). This is a neuroscientist's lively inside-the-brain view of why most people are optimistic or hopeful about life.

37 *Even more surprising is how creative*: "The Evolving Minds of Humans," interview with Antonio Damasio on *Science Friday*, National Public Radio, Nov. 12, 2010, http://www.npr.org/2010/11/12/131274187/the-evolving-minds -of-humans.

38 *Our special awareness*: A. Varki, "Human uniqueness and the denial of death," *Nature* 460 (2009): 684; L. L. Carstensen, D. M. Isaacowitz, and S. T. Charles, "Taking time seriously: A theory of socioemotional selectivity," *American Psychologist* 54 (1999): 165–81.

40 *For example, accounts*: E. Tulving, D. L. Schacter, D. R. McLachlin, and M. Moscovitch, "Priming of semantic autobiographical knowledge: A case study of retrograde amnesia," *Brain and Cognition* 8 (1988): 3–20.

42 *This work is done in a brain area*: D. R. Addis, A. T. Wong, and D. L. Schacter, "Remembering the past and imagining the future: Common and distinct

neural substrates during event construction and elaboration," *Neuropsychologia* 45 (2007): 1363–77.

42 *The most meaningful episodes*: A. Damasio, *Self Comes to Mind: Constructing the Conscious Brain* (New York: Pantheon 2010).

42 *This "prospecting" function of the hippocampus*: Addis, Wong, and Schacter, "Remembering the past and imagining the future."

42 *When we anticipate a new situation*: Ibid.

42 *Training in our brain's simulator*: Ibid.

43 *Now the prospection pipeline*: Ibid.

43 *Your rACC*: Ibid.

43 *The final key station*: Banyas, "Evolution and the phylogenetic history of the frontal lobes."

44 *The prefrontal cortex functions*: E. K. Miller and J. D. Cohen, "An integrative theory of prefrontal cortex function," *Annual Review of Neuroscience* 24 (2001): 167–202.

44 *One recent study*: S. J. Peterson, P. A. Balthazard, D. A. Waldman, and R. W. Thatcher, "Neuroscientific implications of psychological capital: Are the brains of optimistic, hopeful, confident, and resilient leaders different?," *Organizational Dynamics* 37, no. 4 (2008): 342–53.

45 *Emotions are as contagious*: E. Hatfield, J. T. Cacioppo, and R. L. Rapson, "Emotional contagion," *Current Directions in Psychological Science* 2 (1993): 96–99.

45 *They've begun to map systems of "mirror neurons"*: G. Rizzolatti and L. Craighero, "The mirror-neuron system," *Annual Review of Neuroscience* 27 (2004): 169–92. For a more accessible summary of this work, see D. Goleman, *Social Intelligence: The New Science of Human Relationships* (New York: Bantam, 2006).

45 *For decades the most striking object*: Mary Tutwiler, "Hadrian's waltz out of New Iberia," *Independent*, May 6, 2008, http://www.theind.com/index .php?option=com_content&task=view&id=2456&Itemid=96; Holly Leleux-leux-Thubron, "Hadrian sells for nearly $1 million," *Daily Iberian*, Dec. 10, 2008, http://www.iberianet.com/news/hadrian-sells-for-nearly-million /article_7bed4996-8f75-5b36-97fa-40487d54fdc6.html; Christie's listing: http://www.christies.com/LotFinder/lot_details.aspx?intObjectID=5157992.

Chapter 4: Hope Matters

47 *The Walruff Brewery*: Paul Cauthon, "Everything old is brew again: The Old Walruff Brewery was killed by prohibition, but its legacy lives on in Free State,"

Lawrence Journal-World, May 27, 2010, http://www2.ljworld.com/news/2010/may/27/everything-old-brew-again/; illustration from 1880: http://www.world west.net/photos/2010/may/27/192620/.

47 *"This led me to dabble"*: Ibid.

47 *Meanwhile, he and three friends*: http://mercarchives.wordpress.com/about/.

48 *Chuck's start-up brewery was*: Chad Lawhorn, "Free State Brewery's success built on humble beginnings of founder Chuck Magerl," *Lawrence Journal-World*, May 25, 2010, http://www2.ljworld.com/news/2010/may/25/free-state-brewerys-success-built-humble-beginning/.

48 *Today, Chuck's local supporters have only one regret*: Ibid.

48 *It took another campaign*: Mark Fagan, "Free State to start bottling beer: New production center in east Lawrence to enable regional distribution," *Lawrence Journal-World*, Nov. 30, 2007, http://www2.ljworld.com/news/2007/nov/30/free_state_start_bottling_beer/.

49 *Then one night, only weeks*: Sophia Maines, "Firefighters extinguish two-alarm blaze at new Free State Brewery facility in east Lawrence," *Lawrence Journal-World*, Oct. 6, 2008, http://www2.ljworld.com/news/2008/oct/06/electrical_engineer_help_determine_cause_free_stat/.

49 *The bottling facility became less a Rube Goldberg operation*: Phil Cauthon, "Free at last: After months of anticipation, bottles of Free State beer on sale Friday," *Lawrence Journal-World*, May 20, 2010, http://www2.ljworld.com/news/2010/may/20/free-last-after-months-anticipation-bottles-free-s/.

50 *Chuck says his is the "classic start-up story"*: Lawhorn, "Free State Brewery's success built on humble beginnings of founder Chuck Magerl."

50 *All told, the science of hope*: B. Reichard, J. Avey, S. J. Lopez, M. Dollwet, and S. Marques, "Having the will and finding the way: A review and meta-analysis of hope at work," *Journal of Positive Psychology* (2013); S. J. Lopez, B. Reichard, M. Dollwet, and S. Marques, "Relation of hope to academic outcomes: A meta-analysis" (under review); J. Cheavens, M. W. Gallagher, and S. J. Lopez, "The relation of hope to depression and anxiety: A meta-analysis" (in progress).

51 *"Eighty percent of success is showing up"*: http://www.quotationspage.com/quote/1903.html.

51 *Absenteeism is one of the biggest problems*: http://www.schoolleadership20 .com/profiles/blogs/let-s-focus-on-chronic-absenteeism-by-hedy-chang -and-robert-balfa.

51 *The data show, that by third grade*: Ibid.

51 *We measured the hope of students*: S. J. Lopez, *All-American High School* (Omaha, NE: Gallup, 2009).

52 *Showing up is not just a problem in schools*: http://www.gallup.com/poll/150026/Unhealthy-Workers-Absenteeism-Costs-153-Billion.aspx.

52 *Management professor James Avey*: J. B. Avey, J. L. Patera, and B. J. West, "The implications of positive psychological capital on employee absenteeism," *Journal of Leadership and Organizational Studies* 13 (2006): 42–60.

53 *Given these findings*: Ibid.

53 *Your new team is charged*: S. J. Peterson and K. Byron, "Exploring the role of hope in job performance: Results from four studies," *Journal of Organizational Behavior* 29 (2008): 785–803.

54 *Accordingly, in another study*: S. J. Peterson, F. O. Walumbwa, K. Byron, and J. Myrowitz, "CEO positive psychological traits, transformational leadership, and firm performance in high-technology start-up and established firms," *Journal of Management* 35, no. 2 (2008): 348–68.

54 *This hope-productivity link*: Relevant articles include the following: F. Luthans, B. Avolio, J. Avey, and S. M. Norman, "Positive psychological capital: Measurement and relationship with performance and satisfaction," *Personnel Psychology* 60 (2007): 541–72; F. Luthans, B. Avolio, F. Walumba, and W. Li, "The psychological capital of Chinese workers: Exploring the relationship with performance," *Management and Organization Review* 1 (2005): 249–71; K. Luthans and K. Jensen, "The linkage between psychological capital and commitment to organizational mission: A study of nurses," *Journal of Nursing Administration* 35 (2005): 304–10; F. Luthans, S. M. Norman, B. J. Avolio, and J. B. Avey, "The mediating role of psychological capital in supportive organizational climate–employee performance relationship," *Journal of Organizational Behavior* 29 (2008): 219–38; P. R. Magelleta and J. M. Oliver, "The hope construct, will, and ways: Their relationship with self-efficacy, optimism, and general well-being," *Journal of Clinical Psychology* 55 (1999): 539–51; S. Mansfield, "The relationship of CEO's and top leadership teams' hope with their organizational followers' job satisfaction, work engagement, and retention intent" (Ph.D. diss., Regent University, 2008), available from ProQuest Dissertations and Theses database (UMI No. 3292257); S. J. Peterson and K. Byron, "Exploring the role of hope in job performance: Results from four studies," *Journal of Organizational Behavior* 29 (2008): 785–803; S. J. Peterson and F. Luthans, "The positive impact and development of hopeful leaders," *Leadership and Organization Development Journal* 24 (2002): 26–31; S. J. Peterson, F. O. Walumbwa, K. Byron, and J. Myrowitz, "CEO positive psychological traits, transformational leadership, and firm performance in high technology start-up and established firms," *Journal of Management* 35

(2009): 348–68; A. Rego, C. Marques, S. Leal, F. Sousa, and M. P. Cunha, "Psychological capital and performance of civil servants: Exploring neutralizers in the context of an appraisal system" (manuscript submitted for publication, 2010); A. Rego, F. Sousa, C. Marques, and M. P. Cunha, "Authentic leadership promoting employees' psychological capital and creativity" (manuscript submitted for publication, 2010); A. Rego, F. Sousa, C. Marques, and M. P. E. Cunha, "Hope and positive emotions mediating the authentic leadership and creativity relationship" (unpublished, 2010); A. Rego, F. Machado, S. Leal, and M. Cunha, "Are hopeful employees more creative? An empirical study," *Creativity Research Journal* 21 (2009): 223–31.

54 *a study of fast-food outlets*: Peterson and Luthans, "The positive impact and development of hopeful leaders."

54 *Indeed, research has examined*: S. P. Buckelew, R. S. Crittendon, J. D. Butkovic, K. B. Price, and M. Hurst, "Hope as a predictor of academic performance," *Psychological Reports* 103 (2008): 411–14; J. Ciarrochi, P. C. Heaven, and F. Davies, "The impact of hope, self-esteem, and attributional style on adolescents' school grades and emotional well-being: A longitudinal study," *Journal of Research in Personality* 41 (2007): 1161–78; L. A. Curry, C. R. Snyder, D. L. Cook, B. C. Ruby, and M. Rehm, "Role of hope in academic and sport achievement," *Journal of Personality and Social Psychology* 73 (1997): 1257–67; M. W. Gallagher and S. J. Lopez, "Hope, self-efficacy, and academic success in college students," poster presented at the annual convention of the American Psychological Association, Boston, 2008; R. Gilman, J. Dooley, and D. Florell, "Relative levels of hope and their relationship with academic and psychological indicators among adolescents," *Journal of Social and Clinical Psychology* 25 (2006): 166–78; S. C. Marques, J. L. Pais-Ribeiro, and S. J. Lopez, "The role of positive psychology constructs in predicting mental health and academic achievement in children and adolescents: A two-year longitudinal study," *Journal of Happiness Studies* 12, no. 6 (2011): 1049–62. Related research also includes the longitudinal studies listed subsequently.

55 *The most compelling evidence*: C. R. Snyder, H. S. Shorey, J. Cheavens, K. M. Pulvers, V. H. Adams III, and C. Wiklund, "Hope and academic success in college," *Journal of Educational Psychology* 94 (2002): 820–26; L. Day, K. Hanson, J. Maltby, C. Proctor, and A. Wood, "Hope uniquely predicts objective academic achievement above intelligence, personality, and previous academic achievement," *Journal of Research in Personality* 44 (2010): 550–53; S. J. Lopez and M. W. Gallagher, *Academic Trajectories* (under review).

55   *Three of these studies*: Ibid.

55   *In the fourth study*: K. L. Rand, A. D. Martin, and A. Shea, "Hope, but not optimism, predicts academic performance of law students beyond previous academic achievement," *Journal of Research in Personality* 45 (2011): 683–86.

56   *When Gallup asked one million people*: Unpublished analysis of data from the Gallup-Healthways Wellbeing Index and the Gallup Student Poll.

56   *Because of this observation*: M. W. Gallagher and S. J. Lopez, "Positive expectancies and mental health: Identifying the unique contributions of hope and optimism," *Journal of Positive Psychology* 4 (2009): 548–56.

56   *According to well-being expert Ed Diener*: E. Diener, "Subjective well-being," *Psychological Bulletin* 95 (1984): 542–75.

56   *Even a brief intervention*: S. C. Marques, J. P. Ribeiro, and S. J. Lopez, "Building hope for the future: A program to foster strengths in middle-school students," *Journal of Happiness Studies* 12 (2011): 139–52.

56   *Longitudinal studies of workers*: J. B. Avey, F. Luthans, R. M. Smith, and N. F. Palmer, "Impact of positive psychological capital on employee well-being over time," *Journal of Occupational Health Psychology* 15 (2010): 17–28.

57   *For example, in a recent study of firefighters*: L. Steffen, "The relationship of dispositional hope with daily stress and affect in fire service" (under review). For a general discussion of goal shielding, see A. Achtziger, P. M. Gollwitzer, and P. Sheeran, "Implementation intentions and shielding goal striving from unwanted thoughts and feelings," *Personality and Social Psychology Bulletin* 34 (2008): 381–93.

57   *may contribute directly to meaning and purpose*: D. B. Feldman and C. R. Snyder, "Hope and the meaningful life: Empirical and theoretical associations between goal-directed thinking and life meaning," *Journal of Social and Clinical Psychology* 24 (2005): 401–21.

57   *Rick Snyder, my mentor*: For a complete account see C. R. Snyder, S. J. Lopez, and J. T. Pedrotti, *Positive Psychology: The Scientific and Practical Explorations of Human Strengths* (Thousand Oaks, CA: Sage, 2010).

58   *Rick's work on hope and pain*: C. R. Snyder et al., "Hope against the cold: Individual differences in trait hope and acute pain tolerance on the cold pressor task," *Journal of Personality* 73 (2005): 287–312.

58   *In one study, hopeful people*: Ibid.

58   *These coping studies*: N. Nollen, C. Befort, K. Pulvers, A. James, H. Kaur, M. Mayo, Q. Hou, and J. Ahluwalia, "Demographic and psychosocial factors associated with increased fruit and vegetable consumption among smokers in public hous-

ing enrolled in a randomized trial," *Health Psychology* 27 (2008): 252–59; R. Floyd and D. McDermott, "Hope and sexual risk-taking in gay men," paper presented at the American Psychological Association, San Francisco, August 1998; K. Pulvers, L. Cox, S. J. Lopez, J. Selig, and J. Ahluwalia, "Hope for coping with the urge to smoke: A real-time study," poster presented at the Society of Behavioral Management, San Diego, 2008; K. Pulvers, L. Cox, S. J. Lopez, J. Selig, and J. Ahluwalia, "Hope for coping with the urge to smoke: A real-time study" (under review); C. Feudtner, "Hope and the prospects of healing at the end of life," *Journal of Alternative and Complementary Medicine* 11 (2005): 23–30; C. Feudtner, K. W. Carroll, K. R. Hexem, J. Silberman, T. I. Kang, and A. E. Kazak, "Parental hopeful patterns of thinking, emotions, and pediatric palliative care decision-making: A prospective cohort study" (manuscript submitted for review, 2010).

58 *Professor Carla Berg*: C. J. Berg, M. Rapoff, C. R. Snyder, and J. M. Belmont, "The relationship of children's hope to pediatric asthma treatment adherence," *Journal of Positive Psychology* 2, no. 3 (2007): 176–84; A. D. Branstetter, C. J. Berg, M. S. Rapoff, and J. M. Belmont, "Predicting children's adherence to asthma medication regimens," *Journal of Behavior Analysis in Sports, Fitness, and Medicine* 1, no. 3 (2010): 172–85.

59 *"Hopelessness Predicts Mortality"*: S. Stern, R. Dhanda, and H. Hazuda, "Hopelessness predicts mortality in older Mexican and European Americans," *Psychosomatic Medicine* 63 (2001): 344–51. Similar evidence for the hope-longevity link can be found in S. A. Everson, D. E. Goldberg, G. A. Kaplan, R. D. Cohen, E. Pukkala, J. Tuomilehto, and J. T. Salonen, "Hopelessness and risk of mortality and incidence of myocardial infarction and cancer," *Psychosomatic Medicine* 58 (1996): 113–21.

Chapter 5: How Investing in the Future Pays Off Today

63 *AJ's mother, Mary*: Portion of AJ's story was shared in J. Clifton, *The Coming Jobs War* (New York: Gallup Press, 2011).

64 *"Hello Mr. Clifton"*: AJ sends frequent updates to Jim and other Gallup associates. In July 2012 I got the chance to visit with him. He is excited about the future and is surrounded by people who will help him get there.

65 *Let's go back to middle school*: M. Destin and D. Oyserman, "Incentivizing education: Seeing schoolwork as an investment, not a chore," *Journal of Experimental Social Psychology* 46 (2010): 846–49.

65 *The second group saw a graph*: http://www.forbes.com/lists/2008/53/celebrities08_The-Celebrity-100_EarningsPrevYear.html.

68 *Thanks to the work of Roy Baumeister*: R. Baumeister and J. T. Tierney, *Willpower: Rediscovering the Greatest Human Strength* (New York: Penguin Books, 2011).

68 *But a study led by psychologist Gabriele Oettingen*: G. Oettingen and T. A. Wadden, "Expectation, fantasy, and weight loss: Is the impact of positive thinking always positive?," *Cognitive Therapy and Research* 15, no. 2 (1991): 167–75.

70 *A group of newly minted professionals*: G. Oettingen and D. Mayer, "The motivating function of thinking about the future: Expectations versus fantasies," *Journal of Personality and Social Psychology* 83, no. 5 (2002): 1198–1212. For more about how to make fantasies more functional, see G. Oettingen, D. Mayer, J. S. Thorpe, H. Janetzke, and S. Lorenz, "Turning fantasies about positive and negative futures into self-improvement goals," *Motivation and Emotion* 29 (2005): 237–67.

71 *This is what writer and activist*: B. Ehrenreich, "Pathologies of hope," *Harper's*, February 2007, available at http://www.barbaraehrenreich.com/hope.htm. For a broader discussion of her views on optimism and happiness, see B. Ehrenreich, *Bright-Sided: How the Relentless Promotion of Positive Thinking Has Undermined America* (New York: Metropolitan Books, 2009).

72 *The components of hopeful thinking*: C. R. Snyder, "Genesis: Birth and growth of hope," in C. R. Snyder, ed., *Handbook of Hope: Theory, Measures, and Applications* (San Diego: Academic Press, 2000), pp. 25–57.

73 *Heather Barry Kappes*: H. B. Kappes, G. Oettingen, and D. Mayer, "Positive fantasies predict low academic achievement in disadvantaged students," *European Journal of Social Psychology* 42 (2012): 53–64; H. B. Kappes and G. Oettingen, "Positive fantasies about idealized futures sap energy," *Journal of Experimental Social Psychology* 47 (2011): 719–29.

73 *Reflecting on these findings*: http://www.scientificamerican.com/article.cfm?id=the-pitfalls-of-positive-thinking.

Chapter 6: The Future Is Ours to See

80 *Harvard psychologist Daniel Gilbert*: Daniel Gilbert, *Stumbling on Happiness* (New York: Knopf, 2006).

80 *In one of his quirky early studies*: D. Gilbert, E. C. Pinel, T. Wilson, S. J. Blumbert, and T. P. Wheatley, "Immune neglect: A source of durability bias in affective forecasting," *Journal of Personality and Social Psychology* 75 (1998): 617–38.

82 *In his book* Thinking, Fast and Slow: D. Kahneman, *Thinking, Fast and Slow* (New York: Farrar, Straus & Giroux, 2011).

82 *"The soldier who took over"*: http://www.nytimes.com/2011/10/23/magazine/
dont-blink-the-hazards-of-confidence.html?pagewanted=all. Here is the
leadership task and solution as described by Kahneman. "Think it through
for yourself: haul a log to a six-foot-high wall, then get both the log and the
group to the other side. The log can't touch the ground or the wall. The group
members can't touch the wall, either." This is how Kahneman described the
typical approach to getting to the other side: "A common solution was for
several men to reach the other side by crawling along the log as the other men
held it up at an angle, like a giant fishing rod. Then one man would climb onto
another's shoulder and tip the log to the far side. The last two men would then
have to jump up at the log, now suspended from the other side by those who
had made it over, shinny their way along its length and then leap down safely
once they crossed the wall. Failure was common at this point, which required
starting over."

82 *"Our forecasts were better"*: http://www.nytimes.com/2011/10/23/magazine/
dont-blink-the-hazards-of-confidence.html?pagewanted=all.

83 *The head of an investment firm*: Ibid.

83 *"While I was prepared to find"*: Ibid.

83 *"Facts that challenge such basic assumptions"*: Ibid.

85 *In my own head I sometimes still hear Doris Day*: J. Livingston and R. Evans,
"Que Será, Será (Whatever Will Be, Will Be)" (1956), Doris Day rendition
available at http://www.youtube.com/watch?v=xZbKHDPPrrc.

85 *Our small parental behaviors*: B. Sacerdote, "How large are the effects from
changes in family environment? A study of Korean American adoptees," *Quarterly Journal of Economics* 121 (2007): 119–58. For a delightful discussion of
the economics of parenting, listen to http://www.freakonomics.com/2011/08
/29/the-economists-guide-to-parenting-economist-kids-photo-gallery/
and http://www.marketplace.org/topics/life/freakonomics-radio/freakonom
ics-how-much-influence-does-parent-have-childs-education.

87 *"Get parents in, and you can achieve anything"*: J. Edelberg and S. Kurland,
How to Walk to School: Blueprint for a Neighborhood School Renaissance (New
York: Rowman & Littlefield, 2009), p. 29. The entire account of the Nettel-
horst transformation draws on this book.

90 *Jacqueline Edelberg and Susan Kurland*: Ibid.

91 *Some initiatives*: Ibid.

Chapter 7: The Present Is Not What Limits Us

94 *This was my first lesson in self-determination*: E. L. Deci and R. M. Ryan, *Intrinsic Motivation and Self-determination in Human Behavior* (New York: Plenum, 1985). See also http://selfdeterminationtheory.org/.

95 *Whether you test children or adults*: C. R. Snyder et al., "The will and the ways: Development and validation of an individual-differences measure of hope," *Journal of Personality and Social Psychology* 60 (1991): 570–85; C. R. Snyder et al., "The development and validation of the Children's Hope Scale," *Journal of Pediatric Psychology* 22 (1997): 399–421.

96 *Economics professor Armenio Rego*: Personal communication, May 22, 2012; A. Rego, F. Machado, S. Leal, and M. P. E. Cunha, "Are hopeful employees more creative? An empirical study," *Creativity Research Journal* 21, no. 2 (2009): 223–31.

96 *Without hope, Rego points out*: Ibid.

96 *there was* no relationship between hope and income: "Relationships between hope, income, and teacher-student ratio in March 2009 Gallup Student Poll," unpublished data, 2009.

97 *Recent research has found no consistent*: S. J. Lopez et al., "Hope for the evolution of diversity: On leveling the field of dreams," in C. R. Snyder, ed., *Handbook of Hope: Theory, Measures, and Intervention* (San Diego: Academic Press, 2000), pp. 223–42; L. M. Edwards, A. Ong, and S. J. Lopez, "Hope measurement in Mexican American youth," *Hispanic Journal of Behavioral Sciences* 29 (2007): 225–41.

98 *Stanford psychologist Carol Dweck*: C. Dweck, *Mindset: The New Psychology of Success* (New York: Random House, 2006).

98 *"It was an uncomfortable thing"*: L. Trei, "New study yields instructive results on how mindset affects learning," *Stanford Report*, February 7, 2007.

99 *"You mean, I don't have to be dumb?"*: Ibid.

101 *Young Tererai was blessed*: Tererai Trent's story was first shared by Nicholas Kristof. See both his article "Triumph of a Dreamer," *New York Times*, Nov. 14, 2009, and his book for more details. N. D. Kristof and S. WuDunn, *Half the Sky: Turning Oppression into Opportunity for Women Worldwide* (New York: Knopf, 2009).

101 *Then in 1991, when Tererai*: http://www.oprah.com/oprahshow/Tererai-Trents-Story-Video. http://www.oprah.com/world/Tererai-Trents-Inspiring-Education/3 www.oprah.com/world/Tererai-Trent-Returns-to-Zimbabwe.

103 *In October 2011, Tererai Trent returned*: T. Mukwazhi, "Tererai Trent Pursues Her Dream," www.dailnews.co.zw, Oct. 13, 2011.

Chapter 8: The Past Is Not a Preview

107 *Joe Kraus, an investing partner at Google Ventures*: http://www.npr
     .org/2012/06/19/155005546/failure-the-f-word-silicon-valley-loves-and
     -hates.

108 *Known as Meehl's maxim*: P. Meehl, *Clinical vs. Statistical Prediction* (New
     York: Appleton Century Crofts, 1954). Additional research supported
     Meehl's findings: W. M. Grove, D. H. Zald, A. M. Hallberg, B. Lebow, E. Snitz,
     and C. Nelson, "Clinical versus mechanical prediction: A meta-analysis," *Psy-
     chological Assessment* 12 (2000): 19–30. The findings have been widely cited
     and have been taught in universities for about half a century. See http://whar
     tonmagazine.com/blog/moneyball-for-managers-paul-meehls-legacy.

108 *Study after study suggests that skilled experts*: Kahneman, *Thinking, Fast and
     Slow*.

109 *"unduly embittered about their past"*: M. E. P. Seligman, *Authentic Happiness*
     (New York: Free Press, 2002), p. xii.

109 *In his leadership book,* It Worked for Me: C. Powell and T. Koltz, *It Worked for
     Me: In Life and Leadership* (New York: Harper, 2012).

109 *"When did you graduate"*: Ibid., p. 271.

109 *"My city believed"*: Ibid., p. 273.

110 *"Past performance alone"*: Ibid., p. 67.

110 *"Learning and growing intellectually"*: Ibid., p. 68.

110 *"Always be prepared to change your mind"*: Ibid., p. 70.

111 *Indeed, in samples of grade school*: S. P. Buckelew, R. S. Crittendon, J. D. But-
     kovic, K. B. Price, and M. Hurst, "Hope as a predictor of academic perfor-
     mance," *Psychological Reports* 103 (2008): 411–14; J. Ciarrochi, P. C. Heaven,
     and F. Davies, "The impact of hope, self-esteem, and attributional style on
     adolescents' school grades and emotional well-being: A longitudinal study,"
     Journal of Research in Personality 41 (2007): 1161–78; L. A. Curry, C. R. Sny-
     der, D. L. Cook, B. C. Ruby, and M. Rehm, "Role of hope in academic and
     sport achievement," *Journal of Personality and Social Psychology* 73 (1997):
     1257–67; M. W. Gallagher and S. J. Lopez, "Hope, self-efficacy, and academic
     success in college students," poster presented at the annual convention of the
     American Psychological Association, Boston, 2008; R. Gilman, J. Dooley,
     and D. Florell, "Relative levels of hope and their relationship with academic
     and psychological indicators among adolescents," *Journal of Social and Clini-
     cal Psychology* 25 (2006): 166–78; S. C. Marques, J. L. Pais-Ribeiro, and S. J.
     Lopez, "The role of positive psychology constructs in predicting mental

health and academic achievement in children and adolescents: A two-year longitudinal study," *Journal of Happiness Studies* 12, no. 6 (2011): 1049–62.

112 *Fear signals come from*: M. Davis and J. P. Aggleton, eds., *The Amygdala: Neurobiological Aspects of Emotion, Memory, and Mental Dysfunction* (New York: Wiley, 1992).

112 *Hope, in contrast*: S. J. Peterson, P. A. Balthazard, D. A. Waldman, and R. W. Thatcher, "Neuroscientific implications of psychological capital: Are the brains of optimistic, hopeful, confident, and resilient leaders different?," *Organizational Dynamics* 37 (2008): 342–53.

113 *When Jane Brody*: http://well.blogs.nytimes.com/2012/05/21/a-richer-life-by-seeing-the-glass-half-full/.

114 *This is the message of research*: B. Fredrickson, *Positivity: Groundbreaking Research Reveals How to Embrace the Hidden Strength of Positive Emotions, Overcome Negativity, and Thrive* (New York: Crown Archetype, 2009).

114 *In one experiment, Frederickson asked groups*: B. L. Fredrickson, "What good are positive emotions?," *Review of General Psychology* 2 (1998): 300–19.

116 *"The best therapists do not merely heal"*: M. E. P. Seligman, *Authentic Happiness* (New York: Free Press, 2002), p. xiv.

117 *We are naturally risk-averse creatures*: For a discussion of how this is manifested in daily life, read the discussion of loss aversion in Kahneman, *Thinking, Fast and Slow*.

118 *With the proper license*: Erin Zimmer, "So you want to start a food truck?," Openforum.com, Dec. 20, 2010, https://www.openforum.com/idea-hub/topics/innovation/article/so-you-want-to-start-a-food-truck-erin-zimmer.

118 *Roy Choi's opening*: Katy McLaughlin, "The king of the streets moves indoors," *Wall Street Journal*, Jan. 15, 2010, http://online.wsj.com/article/SB10001424052748704842604574642420732091490.html.

118 *Kristin Frederick*: Julia Moskin, "Food trucks in Paris? U.S. cuisine finds open minds, and mouths," *New York Times*, June 3, 2012, http://www.nytimes.com/2012/06/04/world/europe/food-trucks-add-american-flavor-to-paris.html?pagewanted=all.

119 *I got every kind of push-back*: Ibid.

119 *Nate Demars became a business owner*: http://www.columbusalive.com/content/stories/2011/09/15/fashion-pursuit.html.

119 *"It's a fresh idea in a boring old business"*: Ibid.; http://www.businessinsider.com/17-most-creative-pop-up-stores?op=1#ixzz1yuRQH4fb.

120 *Inspired by the design*: http://www.cultofmac.com/174696/sonos-subs-shape-was-designed-by-the-public/.

Chapter 9: Futurecasting: Making Your Goals Come Alive

125 *But until Old Doc Brown*: http://en.wikipedia.org/wiki/Back_to_the_Future.

125 *Of the twenty thousand chunks of experience*: http://www.abc.net.au/radio national/programs/allinthemind/nobel-laureate-daniel-kahneman-toward -a-science-of/3546434.

126 *This ladder exercise*: This exercise was developed by Hadley Cantril. It is formally referred as the Cantril Self-Anchoring Striving Scale. H. Cantril, *The Pattern of Human Concern* (New Brunswick, NJ: Rutgers University Press, 1965).

127 *An athletic six feet, six inches*: "A Health Approach Replaces Self-Pity with Promise," Nadia Reiman, producer, for NPR Storycorps, Oct. 21, 2009. http:// www.npr.org/templates/story/story.php?storyId=113830758;http://www .mlive.com/news/grand-rapids/index.ssf/2009/10/man_keeps_promise_ after_physic.html.

129 *two psychology colleagues and I*: M. W. Gallagher, S. J. Lopez, and S. D. Pressman, "Optimism is universal: Exploring the presence and benefits of optimism in a representative sample of the world," *Journal of Personality* (2013).

130 *In the 1990s, I learned how SMART*: Though frequently attributed to goal theorists or management experts, it is unclear who first used the acronym SMART.

131 *You boost your energy when you state goals positively*: C. J. Roney, E. T. Higgins, and J. Shah, "Goals and framing: How outcome focus influences motivation and emotion," *Personality and Social Psychology Bulletin* 21 (1995): 1151–60.

132 *Psychologists call these* salient goals: S. Ratneshwar, L. W. Barsalou, C. Pechmann, and M. Moore, "Goal-derived categories: The role of personal and situational goals in category representations," *Journal of Consumer Psychology* 10 (2001): 147–57.

132 *Have you ever washed a rental car?*: See http://www.economist.com/blogs/de mocracyinamerica/2011/06/neoliberalism for a discussion of when and how this term is used. For more discussion see Terry Anderson and Laura E. Huggins, "No one washes a rental car," *Defining Ideas: A Hoover Institution Journal*, November 5, 2008, http://www.hoover.org/publications/defining-ideas/ article/5498.

133 *That's why Principal built a simple*: http://dreamagain.principal.com/dream catcher/preregistered/home.html. A free program that allows you to create a visual collage of the images that capture your life goals.

134   *The resulting book of student essays*: Omaha Young Writers Program, *In My Shoes: Teen Reflections on Hope and the Future* (Omaha, NE: WriteLife, 2011).

134   *This exercise subtly reminds students*: This exercise is based on Appendix 1 from B. Kerr, S. Kurpius, and A. Harkins, *Handbook for Counseling Girls and Women: Ten Years of Gender Equity Research at Arizona State University* (Mesa, AZ: Neuva Science Press, 2005).

137   *Then you go beyond visiting*: P. W. Gollwitzer, "Implementation intention: Strong effects of simple plans," *American Psychologist* 54 (1999): 493–503.

139   *Comedian Jerry Seinfeld*: Personal archives, http://www.jerryseinfeld.com/ http://www.youtube.com/watch?v=W-Cz-LK16g4.

139   *Hal Hershfield, assistant professor*: Hershfield is an assistant professor of marketing at New York University's Stern School of Business and researches judgment, decision-making, and social psychology, with special emphasis on "how thinking about time can impact decision-making and emotional experience." http://www.stern.nyu.edu/faculty/bio/hal-hershfield.

140   *In one study, Hershfield*: H. E. Hershfield et al., "Increasing saving behavior through age-progressed renderings of the future self," *Journal of Marketing Research* 158 (2011): 23–37.

140   *A trip to the mobile app Aging Booth*: A mobile-phone-based software application that converts photographs of users into older versions of themselves, it allows a preview into the future and helps users imagine more vividly their future selves.

140   *The website futureme.org*: A free website that allows people to send their future selves a letter, to be delivered via email at a prespecified date.

140   *Hershfield says that if he'd thought long term*: http://money.usnews.com/ money/blogs/alpha-consumer/2012/02/13/how-to-meet-your-future-self-and-save.

140   *Do you have an older friend*: Ibid.

Chapter 10: Triggering Action: Putting Agency on Autopilot

143   *Jos Van Bedoff*: Robert Krulwich, "There's a Fly In My Urinal," NPR, http://www.economist.com/node/21554506#footnote1.

144   *Whether he knew it or not*: Ibid. A cottage industry has sprung up from this bit of insight about male bathroom habits.

146   *No harder than spreading the common cold*: For a survey of work on goal contagions, go to http://www.goallab.nl/index.php?page=about-the-goallab.

146   *Social psychologist Henk Aarts*: H. Aarts, P. M. Gollwitzer, and R. R. Hassin,

"Goal contagion: Perceiving is for pursuing," *Journal of Personality and Social Psychology* 87 (2004): 23–37.

146 *For example, he's shown*: R. R. Hassin, H. Aarts, and M. J. Ferguson, "Automatic goal inferences," *Journal of Experimental Social Psychology* 41 (2005): 129–40.

146 *Psychologist and blogger Art Markman*: http://www.psychologytoday.com/blog/ulterior-motives/200810/the-power-yard-signs-i-goal-contagion.

147 *Psychology professor Robert Cialdini*: www.psychologicalscience.org/ob server/getArticle.cfm?id1762. For a broad discussion of his work, see R. Cialdini, *Influence: The Psychology of Persuasion*, rev. ed. (New York: Harper-Business, 2006).

147 *The two-thousand-plus employees*: http://www.gallup.com/consulting/126908 /economics-wellbeing.aspx.

148 *One crisp winter afternoon I met Stanley Lombardo*: Stan and I met at the Community Mercantile in Lawrence, Kansas. This is the grocery store that Chuck started with his friends years before he opened the Free State Brewery.

148 *As a translator of Homer*: Homer, *Odyssey,* trans. Stanley Lombardo (Indianapolis, IN: Hackett, 2000).

149 *In particular, I wanted to talk to Stan about "Odysseus contracts"*: These contracts also are referred to "Ulysses Contracts" and "Ulysses Pacts." See the following for a brief description: http://www.ted.com/talks/daniel_gold stein_the_battle_between_your_present_and_future_self.html.

149 *Here, in Stan's translation*: This scene appears in Book 12 of Homer's *Odyssey.*

150 *Go online to contract for change*: StickK.com is a free website that allows people to design a "Commitment Contract" that supports their life goals, including appropriate cues and motivating incentives. Lose those last ten pounds or start saving more for your future today!

152 *Psychology professor Peter Gollwitzer*: When/where plans are built off what Peter Gollwitzer calls if-then plans. In some places in the text I use the term *when/where plans* as a direct substitute for *if-then plans,* as I believe the term is more straightforward. While I think that people need to understand the role of contingencies and intentions in their planning, it is most important that they understand that they need to set a time and place for action. For more explanation of those plans, see P. M. Gollwitzer, "Implementation Intention: Strong effects of simple plans," *American Psychologist* 54 (1999): 493–503.

152 *In Christmas Study #1*: P. M. Gollwitzer and V. Brandstatter, "Implementation intentions and effective goal pursuit," *Journal of Personality and Social Psychology* 73 (1997): 186–99.

152 *In Christmas Study #2*: Ibid.

153 *This simple tool*: www.futureme.org. A great way to automatically cue yourself to revisit goals or perhaps yank your own chain to regoal if you have gotten distracted. Or maybe it will remind you to take a moment to appreciate the results of your hard work and celebrate a success.

153 *A recent review of ninety-four studies*: P. M. Gollwitzer and P. Sheeran, "Implementation intentions and goal achievement: A meta-analysis of effects and processes," *Advances in Experimental Social Psychology* 38 (2006): 70–119.

153 *One of Gollwitzer's more recent studies*: M. A. Adriaanse et al., "When planning is not enough: Fighting unhealthy snacking habits by mental contrasting with implementation intentions (MCII)," *European Journal of Social Psychology* 40 (2010): 1277–93.

154 *If you were old enough*: This is an infamous and misunderstood contract rider for Van Halen concerts in the 1980s. The rider required that promoters provide a bowl of M&M's that contained "ABSOLUTELY NO BROWN ONES." It gained the band a reputation as spoiled prima donnas even among rock stars, but it actually was a covert and easy safety indicator. If there were brown M&M's in the bowl, the band knew that the local promoters hadn't read the contract and that their extensive technical equipment had probably been set up wrong. Then the band's crew knew to thoroughly double-check the entire production to protect the safety of both the band and the audience. David Lee Roth revealed the strategy in his biography, *Crazy from the Heat,* and the rider was also the subject of a feature on NPR's *This American Life.* http://articles.philly.com/2012-02-17/news/31071726_1_spectrum-richman-wells-fargo-center.

Chapter 11: Planning for Ifs: Discovering New Pathways

159 *Alisha McClung was a returning senior*: Elizabeth Redden, "One Student, and Thousands of Dollars, at a Time," *Inside Higher Ed,* Sept. 25, 2008, http://www.insidehighered.com/news/2008/09/25/spelman. One industrious college president took the future of her financially at-risk students in her hands by recruiting alumni to wipe out their tuition balances after the economy tanked.

160 *Tatum's answer was to establish*: Ibid.

161 *Consider a group of Kansas City high school*: For more details on the Hope Camera Project, see www.makinghopehappennow.com.

162 *Psychology professor Carla Berg*: C. J. Berg, C. R. Snyder, and N. Hamilton, "The effectiveness of a hope intervention in coping with cold pressor pain," *Journal of Health Psychology* 13 (2008): 804–809.

167 *Writer Dave Eggers*: http://www.ted.com/talks/dave_eggers_makes_his_ted_
     prize_wish_once_upon_a_school.html. Dave Eggers cracks up and inspires
     the audience with his stories about the founding of 826 Valencia, the first in a
     network of eight imaginative and innovative writing and mentoring centers
     across the country.

167 *826 Valencia is a tutoring center*: http://826valencia.org/about/history/.

171 Timebanks.org: A free website that builds "caring community economies"
     across the United States. Individuals exchange services across their commu-
     nities by trading them directly, one hour of labor at a time, without exchang-
     ing cash.

171 Crowdrise.com: A free website that uses a whimsical approach to raising
     money for charity, and blends online fund-raising, crowdsourcing, so-
     cial networking, contests, and other fun stuff. It also targets people with
     the motivation and resources to give something back with the funny and
     shameless tagline "If you don't give back no one will like you," which, when
     you think about it, is absolutely true. So perhaps it's also a warning not to
     be a selfish jerk, because if you are, that is pretty much exactly what will
     happen.

172 Challengepost.com: A free website that individuals and organizations can use
     to engage the public in solving problems around the collective goals of open
     government and software solutions. Promotes innovative competition. The
     process: post, submit/compete, vote. Winners receive prizes, recognition,
     and a reason to swagger. And who doesn't appreciate a nice swagger?

Chapter 12: Leading with Hope

177 *Gallup discovered*: T. Rath and B. Conchie, *Strengths-Based Leadership: Great
     Leaders, Teams, and Why People Follow* (New York: Gallup, 2009).

177 *Here, play along*: Ibid.

179 *Specifically, when Gallup asked followers*: Ibid.

180 *Shortly after an F5*: A town in the western plains of Kansas recovers from the
     F5 "monster tornado" that flattened it by responding with unprecedented
     innovation. Greensburg's civic leaders quickly develop a vision for build-
     ing a new and more sustainable kind of small-town America. In the words of
     then-governor Kathleen Sebelius, they are "putting the 'green' in Greensburg."
     http://www.youtube.com/watch?v=zxjn4i9PRhI; http://www.features.ku.edu/
     greensburg/.

181 *Within twelve hours of the storm*: Libby Pelham, "Tornado Turns Greens-

burg, Kansas Green," Families.com, http://green-living.families.com/blog/ tornado-turns-greensburg-kansas-green#.

181 *Upon her visit to Greensburg*: Steve Hewitt, personal communication, July 20, 2012.

181 *city administrator*: http://www.governing.com/poy/Steve-Hewitt.html?p =interview.

181 *Mayor Bob Dixson*: Frank Morris, "Tornado's Gifts: Greenburg Rebuilds, Revitalizes," NPR, May 4, 2008, http://www.npr.org/templates/story/story .php?storyId=90167618.

182 *a recent communication from Steve Rasmussen*: http://www.nationwide.com/ newsroom/stephen-rasmussen.jsp.

183 If you can't make followers excited: http://businessjournal.gallup.com/con tent/26380/Business-Case-Instilling-Hope.aspx; http://businessjournal.gallup .com/content/121211/Why-Hope-Matters.aspx; http://businessjournal.gallup .com/content/120791/leaders-next.aspx.

184 *With instrumental support*: C. A. Heaney and B. A. Israel, "Social networks and social support," in K. Glanz, B. K. Rimer, and K. Viswanath, eds., *Health Behavior and Health Education: Theory, Research, and Practice*, 4th ed. (San Francisco: Jossey-Bass, 2008); J. S. House, *Work Stress and Social Support* (Reading, MA: Addison-Wesley, 1981).

183 *John Fetterman has a clue*: http://www.youtube.com/watch?v=NhhQmr UKMsg. For a more critical analysis of Fetterman's leadership results, Sue Halpern, "Mayor of Rust," *New York Times Magazine,* Feb. 11, 2011, http://www.ny times.com/2011/02/13/magazine/13Fetterman-t.html?pagewanted=all.

185 *He believes that a leader*: "A Day in the Life: John Fetterman," http://new.hulu .com/watch/358111.

186 *I learned how great leaders face*: http://www.chop.edu/doctors/feudtner -chris.html.

187 *That was the case for Sandy Lewis*: Personal communication, Aug. 17, 2011; S. Lewis, "Positive psychology in the real world: Strengths, hope, and agency in a non-profit turnaround" (working paper, 2011).

Chapter 13: Teaching Hope to the Next Generation

190 *Since 2009*: www.gallupstudentpoll.com.

191 *No middle school student*: This sentence was inspired by Sir Ken Robinson, who said something similar and made many other poignant observations in his two TED talks: http://www.youtube.com/watch?v=iG9CE55wbtY; http:// www.ted.com/talks/sir_ken_robinson_bring_on_the_revolution.html.

192 *Fantastic Future Me*: http://www.ocm.org/exhibits/permanent/fantastic-future-me/.

193 *Mentoring for the future*: http://teammates.org/.

193 *New-style career days*: S. J. Lopez, "People who love their jobs," unpublished manuscript, Gallup, 2012; S. J. Lopez, "Kids Day 'Love my job' interview," Gallup, 2010.

194 *Project-based learning*: http://www.huffingtonpost.com/2011/10/11/west-philly-teens-build-g_n_1004723.html; http://www.youtube.com/watch?v=37jdpHXq6zU.

195 *Demystifying college costs*: http://www.whitehouse.gov/issues/education/scorecard.

195 *Bridging high school and college*: http://www2.ed.gov/programs/triotalent/index.html; http://www2.ed.gov/programs/trioupbound/index.html.

196 *According to a 2003 study*: http://www.oecd.org/education/preschooland school/programmeforinternationalstudentassessmentpisa/33918006.pdf.

196 *In 2009 the Gallup Student Poll*: S. J. Lopez and V. Calderon, "The Gallup Student Poll: Measuring and promoting what is right with students," in S. I. Donaldson, M. Csikszentmihalyi, and J. Nakamura, eds., *Applied Positive Psychology: Improving Everyday Life, Schools, Work, Health, and Society* (New York: Routledge, 2011), pp. 117–34.

197 *School counselor Jennifer Magnuson-Stessman*: Jonathan Braden, "Students See Hope in their Lives," *Omaha World-Herald*, April 30, 2011. This is a feature on the Hope Camera Project, a simple and easy-to-implement in-school project that engages students in understanding, documenting, and sharing the stories of what gives them hope in their lives. Educators and parents, if you want to do build a stronger hope culture in your school, this is a great place to start. http://www.omaha.com/article/20110430/NEWS01/704309832; http://intl.kappanmagazine.org/content/93/8/72.abstract.

199 *As principal of Liberty Elementary*: Leo Adam Biga's "Fast Times at Omaha's Liberty Elementary: The Evolution of a School" is the story of an inner-city elementary school transformed by a gutsy and innovative principal who attracted great educators to join her and create something great for kids and the surrounding community. In a culture of pundits blaming teachers without understanding their daily challenges, the Nancys of the world are too busy changing the world to stop and listen to them. It's a screenplay waiting to be written. Now on Leo Adam Biga's blog, a reposting from the indie publication *The Reader* in Omaha (it's unfortunately not online there anymore). http://leoadambiga.wordpress.com/2012/07/05/fast-times-at-omahas-liberty-elementary-the-evolution-of-a-school/.

Chapter 14: Networking Hope

203 *Charity Escobar*: http://www.seriesnow.com/mexican-telenovelas/vencon migo.html.

203 Ven Conmigo: "Lecture on Media and Fertility in Developing Countries," http://www.youtube.com/watch?v=Qg6Sg0UQHhM. Historical reference in Spanish: http://www.esmas.com/50anostelenovelas/historia/decada70/.

203 *Airing for thirty minutes a day*: http://www.apa.org/monitor/oct02/theory .aspx.

204 *Sabido wove his approach together*: S. Bansal, "Soap operas with a social message," *New York Times,* Jan. 26, 2012. One American company followed Sabido's lead by creating soap operas with purpose to be aired on television and radio around the world. Today, the Vermont-based nonprofit Population Media Center creates hope on most continents by building on Sabido's legacy. These serial dramas promote literacy, entrepreneurship, and reproductive health in countries from Mexico to Papua New Guinea to Ethiopia. In each of these soap operas, the heroes model growth in realistic achievable steps, showing the viewer the how of change.

204 *He also drew on the work of legendary Stanford psychologist Albert Bandura*: A. Bandura, "Self-efficacy mechanism in human agency," *American Psychologist* 37 (1982): 122–47; A. Bandura, *Self-Efficacy: The Exercise of Control* (New York: Freeman, 1997).

205 *As explained by network scientists:* N. Christakis and J. Fowler, *Connected: The Surprising Power of Our Social Networks and How They Shape Our Lives* (New York: Little, Brown, 2009).

207 *Classic epics like Homer's* Odyssey: Hero stories seem to contain many common elements, as described by J. Campbell, *The Hero with a Thousand Faces,* 3rd ed. (New York: New World Library, 2008).

208 *Social scientists call this instrumental support*: For a broad discussion of social support, including instrumental support, see S. E. Taylor, "Social support: A review," in M. S. Friedman, ed., *The Handbook of Health Psychology* (New York: Oxford University Press, 2011), pp. 189–214.

208 *At the depths of the Great Recession, Seth*: Seth Reams's story was first shared in A. Huffington, *Third World America: How Our Politicians Are Abandoning the Middle Class and Betraying the American Dream* (New York: Crown, 2008).

208 *McDonald's leveraged hope*: http://www.youtube.com/watch?v=Sao14ByruRI.

209 *My favorite example*: http://www.tide.com/en-US/loads-of-hope/about.jspx.

210 *Heifer International*: www.heifer.org.

210 *How do you give hope*: E. Duflo, E. (2012, May 3). "*Hope as a capability*," Tanner Lecture, Harvard University, May 3, 2012. This lecture is nicely summarized in "Hope Springs a Trap: An absence of optimism plays a large role in keeping people trapped in poverty," *Economist*, May 12, 2012, http://www.economist.com/node/21554506; A. Banerjee and E. Duflo, *Poor Economics: A Radical Rethinking of the Way to Fight Global Poverty* (New York: PublicAffairs, 2011), which provides meticulous research into how very poor people—the millions who exist on less than ninety-nine cents a day—make decisions about how to spend their energy and resources.

213 *Game designer Jane McGonigal*: J. McGonigal, *Reality Is Broken: Why Games Make Us Better and How They Can Change the World* (New York: Penguin Press, 2011). McGonigal argues that we improve real lives and fix what is wrong in the real world through cooperative games.

Epilogue: Ripples of Hope

216 "*Each time a man stands up*": Robert F. Kennedy, Day of Affirmation Address (news release text version), University of Capetown, Capetown, South Africa, June 6, 1966, John F. Kennedy Presidential Library and Museum, http://www.jfklibrary.org/Research/Ready-Reference/RFK-Speeches/Day-of-Affirmation-Address-news-release-text-version.aspx.

Appendix: Hope Scales Used in Research

218 *Scales*: C. R. Snyder et al., "The will and the ways: Development and validation of an individual-differences measure of hope," *Journal of Personality and Social Psychology* 60, no. 4 (1991): 570–85; C. R. Snyder et al., (1997). "The development and validation of the Children's Hope Scale," *Journal of Pediatric Psychology* 22 (1997): 399–421.

Acknowledgments

IT IS NOT HARD to find hopeful people. Each person in this book is part of my life in some small or big way, making today really good and the future even better. Some of these people I was fortunate enough to meet at school, work, or in my community. Many of them I sought out after I heard a story about how they were working to make their lives and the lives of others better. I thank them for their stories and for their hope.

C. R. Snyder taught me everything he knew about hope and how to spread it. Rick's investment in me made my life much more meaningful. I have done my very best to honor and continue his work in *Making Hope Happen*.

The fabulous Toni Burbank taught me more about writing in one year than I had learned in the previous twenty. When she wasn't making my thinking sharper, she was cleaning up my text. Her wisdom, grace, and style made her the perfect partner.

Neil Salkind (someone I want to be when I grow up) convinced Joy Harris that I could write a book that could spread hope. Joy then convinced Leslie Meredith and Dominick Anfuso of Free Press that readers needed such a book. Leslie, Dominick, and Suzanne Donahue then put together an amazing team of folks (Carisa Hays, Nicole Judge, Leah Johanson, Larry Hughes, Jackie Joy, Donna Loffredo) at Free Press and Atria who produced and promoted the book. This group made Lawrence, Kansas, seem like a short cab ride away from New York.

Acknowledgments

Connie Rath, Mary Reckmeyer, Jim Clifton, Tom Rath, and Geoff Brewer said "yes, whatever you need" every time I asked them for support on this project. Connie, in particular, has treated me like family.

My coach, Cheryl Beamer, convinced me that this book had to be at the top of my priority list. My Gallup friends Melissa Hinrichs, Valerie Calderon, Kristin Gregory, and Christine Sheehan never failed to ask, "How's the book?"

My writer friends, Douglas Crawford-Parker, Wendy Paris, and Haley Rushing, gave me instrumental support every time I reached out.

Hope researchers and practitioners including Jennifer Teramoto Pedrotti, Lisa Edwards, Jeana Magyar-Moe, Susana Marques, Matt Gallagher, Jen Cheavens, Kim Pulvers, Lorie Ritschel, Rich Gilman, Shannon Suldo, Becky Reichard, Kevin Rand, James Avey, Marin Dollwet, Christian Wandeler, and Emily Kroska change lives every day. We need more people like them.

The struggles and successes of my students, clients, and research participants taught me so much. I share their stories knowing that readers will be inspired.

Finally, I want to acknowledge the people who contribute the most to my hope for the future. As the editor of my first and last drafts, Alli Rose Lopez made sure that I kept the reader in mind at all times. More important, Alli shows me how exciting *now* and *then* can be. Had she not said yes when I asked her to dance in 1988, there would be no hope book. May I be blessed to grow old with her. And Parrish Lopez, the most hopeful kid in the world, gives me frequent lessons in how to turn *next* into a verb. I look forward to meeting his future self.

Index

Index

Index

Index

Index

About the Author

SHANE J. LOPEZ, Ph.D., a Gallup Senior Scientist, is the world's leading authority on the psychology of hope. He has published seven professional books, including *The Encyclopedia of Positive Psychology*. He lives in Lawrence, Kansas.